Learning Together

Learning Together

Children and Adults in a
School Community

Edited by

Barbara Rogoff
Carolyn Goodman Turkanis
Leslee Bartlett

OXFORD

2001

OXFORD
UNIVERSITY PRESS

Oxford   New York
Athens   Auckland   Bangkok   Bogotá   Buenos Aires   Calcutta
Cape Town   Chennai   Dar es Salaam   Delhi   Florence   Hong Kong   Istanbul
Karachi   Kuala Lumpur   Madrid   Melbourne   Mexico City   Mumbai
Nairobi   Paris   São Paulo   Shanghai   Singapore   Taipei   Tokyo   Toronto   Warsaw

and associated companies in
Berlin   Ibadan

Published by Oxford University Press, Inc.
198 Madison Avenue, New York, New York 10016

Oxford is a registered trademark of Oxford University Press.

Library of Congress Cataloging-in-Publication Data
Learning Together / edited by Barbara Rogoff, Carolyn Goodman Turkanis and
Leslee Bartlett.
p.   cm.
Includes bibliographical references and index.
ISBN 0-19-509753-X
1. Active learning.   2. Experiential learning.   3. Learning, Psychology of.
4. Group work in education.   5. Teacher-student relationships.
I. Rogoff, Barbara.   II. Turkanis, Carolyn Goodman.   III. Bartlett, Leslee.

LB1027.23 .C63 2001
370.15'23—dc21   00-064971

Photos © Barbara Rogoff, unless otherwise indicated.

1 3 5 7 9 8 6 4 2

Printed in the United States of America
on acid-free paper

Acknowledgments

We appreciate the participants in the OC throughout its history, and our predecessors and colleagues elsewhere who have also tried to build schools around children's learning in a community. We are grateful to each other—the OC parents, children, teachers, and former principal Dr. Carol Lubomudrov—and to our families who helped (and are still helping) us learn about how people learn in a community.

We thank principal Dr. Nancy McCormick for her support and help to the OC in setting long-range goals, along with the Salt Lake City School District. This innovative program began with the blessing of a supportive superintendent, Dr. Donald Thomas, who was committed to shared governance; he contributed inspiration for a parent co-op program. The OC has benefited over many years from the school district's commitment to those ideas. Few such programs exist in public schools; we believe that our school district has played an important role in the program's survival.

In addition, we appreciate the important suggestions on drafts of this book from Karrie André, Martha Dever, Sally Duensing, Luisa Magarian, Rebeca Mejía Arauz, Janine Remillard, Jim Rogoff, Martha Rutherford, Roland Tharp, Cindy White, and Joan Bossert and thoughtful anonymous reviewers from Oxford University Press. We thank the Spencer Foundation for its confidence and financial support of research referred to in the book; of course, the foundation and the others whose support we acknowledge should not be held responsible for the shortcomings in these ideas or their presentation.

Contents

Learning Together

Lessons about Learning
as a Community

Barbara Rogoff, *researcher*
Leslee Bartlett, *teacher*
Carolyn Goodman Turkanis, *teacher*

Throughout the past century, U.S. parents, scholars, and educators have debated how to help children learn in schools. This book contributes to the discussion by presenting ideas about how children can learn in a community organized to foster their learning. Our ideas stem from participation in an innovative public school that prioritizes *instruction that builds on children's interests in a collaborative way, where learning activities are planned by children as well as adults, and where parents and teachers not only foster children's learning but also learn from their involvement with the children.*

Despite some notable experiments to make changes in formal school instruction, the routines of U.S. schooling have remained quite stable across the past century, with the following characteristics:

- Being compulsory for all children
- Segregating children from the daily activities of the adults in their community
- Isolating several dozen children with a single adult charged with their instruction
- Grouping children according to their birthdates to provide large numbers of children with standard instruction in a step-by-step fashion
- Isolating skills from their integrated use in productive activities
- Attempting to motivate children by grading their performance

The familiarity of these aspects of schooling have led many adults to assume that these characteristics are necessary to learning in general. It is natural to take for granted the accustomed ways of doing things. As people continue to search for arrangements that communities can use to foster the next generation's development, efforts to try different arrangements to aid children's learning are very important, especially as times change.

The particular form taken by U.S. schools in the 1900s is only one configuration of possible solutions to the question of how to help children learn the skills that they will need as they mature. Formal, compulsory schooling is a brief experiment in the history of human learning. It was inaugurated in the late 1800s; not until the early 1900s were U.S. children almost universally in school.

For millennia, children have learned the lessons of their community by participating with their elders and with each other in activities of importance for their daily lives and those of their families. Around the world, for most of our ancestors, learning occurred as children figured out how to be a part of their family's ongoing activities—whether farming, weaving, fishing, bargaining over merchandise, understanding spiritual narratives, healing ills, or discussing moral principles. Children were in the same settings as their elders, their help was needed, they saw the importance of learning the skills needed for survival and respect in their community, and their elders sometimes facilitated their efforts to catch on.[1]

Children's learning was built on collaboration in ongoing activities, and the purpose of the daily activities and reasons for learning were obvious to the children. Rather than learning in step-by-step increments that did not require them to understand the purpose of the exercises, children contributed as they could in activities whose purpose was clear and had local importance. Their learning was not just in *preparation* for productive activities;[2] it occurred during their productive contributions. When children were not helping out, they often played together, emulating some of the community activities in which they were participating.

Some children and youth learned in classroom settings, but they were a minority, and their schooling differed in many ways from that of the 1900s. The gradations in European schools that began between the sixteenth and the nineteenth centuries were based on the students' progress in learning rather than on chronological time since birth. Age-grading began in the early nineteenth century—and even then, the usual age range within a class was six years.[3] Since then, schooling has become tightly age-graded, as educators and others sought ways to move large numbers of students through a bureaucratic system.

In the United States in recent years, scholars and parents have come to regard school learning as an essential part of growing up—so much so that it is difficult for many to imagine that children can learn without being taught, and to imagine instruction that is organized in ways other than what is common in schools. In 1948, Caroline Pratt, a renowned leader in innovative schooling early in the 1900s, reflected at age 80 on historical changes in U.S. children's learning settings:

> How utterly the life of a child in this country has changed during my lifetime I would scarcely believe if I had not seen it happen. Three-quarters of a century have spanned the change: my father was a Civil War veteran; I remember the day we all went down to the store to see my mother make

our first call on a telephone; I remember watching the explosive progress of the first automobile down our village street. . . .

Before 1867, the year I was born, only one out of every six people lived in cities of more than 8,000 inhabitants, and there were only 141 such cities; by 1900, one out of three people lived in such a city, and the number of those cities was 547. . . . Nearly half a century has passed since 1900, and the transition from rural and village life to a big-city industrial civilization is a half-century farther along.

When I grew up in Fayetteville, New York, school was not very important to children who could roam the real world freely for their learning. We did not merely stand by while the work of our simpler world was done; I drove the wagon in haying time, sitting on top of the swaying load, all the way to the barn. At ten, my great-aunt used to say, I could turn a team of horses and a wagon in less space than a grown man needed to do it.

No one had to tell us where milk came from, or how butter was made. We helped to harvest wheat, saw it ground into flour in the mill on our own stream; I baked bread for the family at thirteen. There was a paper mill, too, on our stream; we could learn the secrets of half a dozen other industries merely by walking through the open door of a neighbor's shop.

No wonder school was a relatively unimportant place—a place where we learned only the mechanical tools, the three R's, and a smattering about things far away and long ago. Our really important learning, the learning how to live in the world into which we were born and how to participate in its work, was right at hand, outside the schoolhouse walls.[4]

The ways that school instruction is organized reflect particular societal pressures, in addition to the need for children to learn mature skills. As compulsory schooling began, many U.S. parents were rapidly making a transition from working at home on the family farm to working for wages, away from the home, often in growing urban centers.[5] Children themselves often also entered the factory workforce, raising concerns not only for their own welfare but for the jobs they took that could be held by adults. In addition, great numbers of immigrant children were arriving with their families from Europe. Schools received the jobs of supervising children while their parents worked, efficiently socializing large numbers of children to U.S. ways that were often foreign to their parents, and sorting students into occupational tracks.

Modeling Schools after Factories

Early in the 1900s, school administrators responded to public pressures to run schools on the model of efficient factories[6] and instituted changes to manage the work of schools "scientifically." In those days, "scientific" management meant efficiency and mass production with the least wasted effort, using procedures designed by experts. Experts studied the most efficient ways to load bricks or mechanize other forms of manual labor and factory work. Housed in buildings that increasingly came to look like factories, schools were expected to efficiently process the raw material (the children) in standard ways prescribed by experts for the workers (the teachers) to carry out.

A great deal of the organization of formal schooling has stemmed from the effort to treat school instruction as an efficient factory. This legacy has led schooled people to think of learning as a result of adults' teaching—transmitting knowledge as if children were receptacles and knowledge were an object. In the factory model, teachers package knowledge by breaking tasks into small units and motivate students by applying incentives (or threatening punishment) for students to get through the teacher's tasks. The learner has little to do besides allowing themselves to be filled with the knowledge provided by teachers and texts.

However, it sometimes proves challenging to get children to think deeply in a factory model of instruction. They may get through their math pages or their science text, but they often do not understand the concepts.[7] Human learning requires being involved in exploring the ideas, engaged rather than simply receiving.[8] Some students are very good at doing math by formula, so their teacher may not even know that they do not understand. Their teachers often have so much "material" to cover (and a need to prepare children for tests that often involve only superficial knowledge) that their best intentions fall prey to the pressure to try to "fill the children up" with knowledge.[9]

Pendulum Swings from Adult Control of Learning to Children's Freedom to Discover

Throughout the 1900s, critiques of the factory model were raised, and reform efforts were made by parents, educators, and scholars who were concerned that efficient "processing" of children might not help children develop understanding and character. The innovations have taken a number of forms that often reflect a pendulum swing from adult control to child freedom. Some reforms reacted to the idea of adults controlling children's learning with an alternative in which adults are supposed to stay out of the way, to leave children free to discover the world. Many "free schools" of the 1960s and 1970s were apparently characterized by the attitude that children would learn best if adults merely stayed out of their way.[10]

Other alternatives also prioritized children's freedom but allowed adults the role of arranging children's learning environments, while staying clear of involvement in the children's activities. Early in this century, the leading educator John Dewey critiqued schooling in which adults avoided infringing on children's freedom: "I have heard of cases in which children are surrounded with objects and materials and then left entirely to themselves, the teacher being loath to suggest even what might be done with the materials lest freedom be infringed upon."[11]

Skills and ideas in such areas as reading, writing, mathematics, science, social studies, and interpersonal relations have developed over generations of invention and collaboration. Children are unlikely to "discover" them without being part of a historical community involving interaction with people who are already familiar with them.

Communities of Learners

This book is inspired by what we have learned by participating in a school in which parents and teachers engage collaboratively with children. Early in the history of this school, the pendulum swing between adult control and children's freedom was seen as a limiting option, and a third perspective developed that is not a compromise between models emphasizing adult control or children's freedom but, rather, relies on the active involvement of adults and children together.

In this perspective, which we call "a community of learners," both children and adults engage in learning activities in a collaborative way, with varying but coordinated responsibilities to foster children's learning. Adults are responsible for guiding the overall process and for supporting children's changing participation in their shared endeavors. Adults provide leadership and encourage children's leadership as well, and they learn from the activities in which they engage with the children. This perspective thus eliminates the dichotomy of adult-controlled learning versus children-controlled learning; it substitutes a quite different arrangement in which children and adults are partners rather than adversaries. The structure of the community is carried through the group's collaboration and can continue to function even in the short-term absence of any individual (including a teacher); people learn to fill in for others' complementary responsibilities.

Among researchers, there is growing interest in a community of learners philosophy,[12] inspired by work that appeared earlier in this century, especially the theories of John Dewey and Lev Vygotsky.[13] Dewey distinguished the teacher's role in a community of learners from the teacher's role in schools employing models based either on adult control or child freedom:

> It is possible of course [for a teacher] to abuse the office, and to force the activity of the young into channels which express the teacher's purpose rather than that of the pupils. But the way to avoid this danger is not for the adult to withdraw entirely. The way is, first, for the teacher to be intelligently aware of the capacities, needs, and past experiences of those under instruction, and, secondly, to allow the suggestion made to develop into a plan and project by means of the further suggestions contributed and organized into a whole by the members of the group. The plan, in other words, is a co-operative enterprise, not a dictation. The teacher's suggestion is not a mold for a cast-iron result but is a starting point to be developed into a plan through contributions from the experience of all engaged in the learning process.[14]

Communities of learners also have inspiration from the kinds of learning opportunities that are so successful for preschool children learning their family's language at home and from informal support of learning throughout childhood in some cultural settings (especially in Native North and Central American and Japanese communities).[15] Although schools organized as communities of learners are more explicitly focused on children's learning than are informal learning settings, in other ways the structure of such schools resembles the shared and interested participation in joint endeavors that has characterized young children's learning throughout human history.

The Ideas and Organization of This Book

Our aim in this book is to explore ideas about learning that we have developed through involvement in a public elementary school in which parents are committed to be involved in their children's classroom learning. Because the principles of learning that we discuss are illustrated by practices and events in the school, it will be helpful to have some orientation to the school itself, not as a model to copy but to provide concrete illustrations to clarify the principles of learning as a community.

The first section of this book discusses *how this community of learners developed, the principles-in-action of the learning community, and its structure.* The school originated more than 20 years ago, in Salt Lake City, Utah, and is called "the OC." (Since the early days, the meaning of the label "Open Classroom" has changed, so the full name sometimes confuses people regarding the school's philosophy. When people hear the full name, some of them assume that the school is a huge building where children run free through open, undivided space, rather than a community of learners with mutual responsibilities as well as choices, in separate classrooms.)

The school is a parent-teacher-child co-operative in which parents are required to contribute three hours per week to classroom instruction for each child enrolled. Families can choose this school instead of their neighborhood school if they are willing to fulfill the weekly three-hour requirement. Although parent involvement in instruction is central to this particular community of learners, we are not presenting this feature as a necessary characteristic of a community of learners. We do think that parents need to be involved in their children's school learning—this is hardly a controversial statement, given that educators across the nation are arguing for more parental involvement—but we believe that the form of parents' involvement needs to be adapted to the needs and circumstances of particular communities.

After giving an orientation to the origins, principles-in-action, and structure of our community of learners, we turn to a section on *how the school functions as a community.* The families and teachers who make up this community do not live day and night in the same small village or neighborhood, as one might imagine when hearing the term "community." So in what way is a community of learners a community? This is an especially important question because the phrase "community of learners" has become widely used in a shallow way just to mean a collection of people who are learning.

Parent volunteers helping children read in a third-grade OC classroom.
(Photo by John Schaefer ©)

In our sense, "community" involves relationships among people based on common endeavors—trying to accomplish some things together—with some stability of involvement and attention to the ways that members relate to each other. In other words, a community of learners develops "cultural" practices and traditions that transcend the particular individuals involved, such as expected ways of handling conflicts and interpersonal issues and crises, as well as traditions for celebrating turning points and successes. The relations among the members of the community are multifaceted. Although different members have different roles and responsibilities, their relations are not just focused on getting tasks done but also involve relating to each other as people and attempting to resolve inevitable conflicts in ways that maintain the relationships.

As members of the community, most OC children, parents, and teachers develop connections in the classroom and outside it. In this community as in others, members provide each other with support of many sorts and are familiar with each other's lives and families. At times we find ourselves caught up in disputes and intrigues, as in other communities where people's lives are connected and the future of the community is a matter of intense interest. Many students, parents, and teachers, after moving on from the OC, continue to regard their involvement in this community and their continuing relationships as central to their lives.

A true community develops a history across generations and has ways of handling the transitions between generations. To continue to function, a community also adapts as times change, experimenting with new ideas in ways that maintain core values while learning from changes that are desired or required. This means that developing a community of learners cannot simply involve applying a recipe of techniques to a new collection of people. It requires the participation of the people involved in inventing and adapting customs and traditions, who learn from their efforts to develop the principles and practices for themselves.

Following the parts of the book that focus on the development, principles-in-action, and structure of our community of learners and on the nature of "community," the book focuses on *how children's learning occurs in a community of learners.* This section discusses creating curriculum with children through flexible planning and respectful collaboration among children and adults. In addition, it describes how the children learn how to communicate their ideas with others and become able to manage the structure of classroom learning and their own time and plans.

We take the central purpose of a community of learners in an elementary school to be the children's learning—a topic that sometimes takes second place to issues of efficiency or of credentialing in some schools. This purpose organizes the daily activities of the school and helps members of the community make decisions about how time and resources are to be spent. Although teachers and parents are also learners in the community, the children's learning is the priority.

At the same time, one of the principles that emerges from our experience is that supporting the learning of adult participants is key to being able to foster the learning of the children. This is especially so because the principles of a community of learners are quite different from the ideas about learning that many

Fourth- and fifth-graders playing a geography game with a parent volunteer.

adults bring to their involvement in the classroom. Indeed, many scholars and researchers have for decades proposed some of the same principles of learning for improving children's schooling,[16] but the principles have rarely been adequately or coherently implemented. One reason that educators seem not to be able to transform learning environments for children is the unmet need to assist adults in learning about principles of learning. This is the focus of the next three sections of our book—the processes of *teachers' learning about teaching children in a community, parents' learning about children's learning in a community*, and *teachers' learning about parents' learning in a community*.

Most teachers and parents have been brought up in the learning formats of traditional public schools. Although they have chosen to be part of this community of learners because they question the traditional schools' emphasis on adult control of learning, they often struggle to understand the idea that the "control versus freedom" dichotomy can be abandoned and replaced with a collaborative approach in which both children and adults take initiative and responsibility, learning together.

One aspect of the OC that may have contributed to its survival for over two decades may be the parents' learning about principles of the school through their classroom involvement with the teachers and children. The average lifetime of innovative co-operative schools established in the late 1960s and 1970s was only 18 months,[17] due in part to a gap between the traditional schooling background of the majority of founding parents and teachers and their efforts to find an alternative to the approaches to teaching and learning that they themselves had experienced in school. Rather than attending to the needs of adults to learn about new ways of teaching and learning, many innovative efforts expected automatic change in all adult participants and the institution.

Adults' struggles to understand the collaborative approach of a community of learners are central to their learning, and their learning is crucial to their being able to contribute to the children's learning. Key adults in the community need to understand the principles of learning as a community and to assist others in their learning. It is not necessary for all the adults to understand the principles before they begin to contribute to the classroom—indeed, participating in the classroom is an essential part of coming to understand the principles. Newcomers make important contributions to the classroom while they are learning, benefitting from guidance and structure provided by the community's practices and traditions as well as by more seasoned members of the community.

After the sections focusing on the children's, teachers', and parents' learning, the book examines ways that *communities learn together*, focusing on the processes of creating learning communities in the OC and beyond. This section examines learning by the community as a whole, especially the processes of supporting adult learning and structures for community decision making about school policies and organization. This section also includes reflections on how the principles developed through participation in this particular school guide the efforts of some teachers who have been working on school restructuring efforts in other states.

We conclude the book by *summing up the principles of learning in a community and identifying pressing issues with which the community continues to struggle*. The pressing issues are at the forefront of this community's—and our nation's—learning, as interested people try to figure out how to handle challenges that have yet to be resolved. These include how to support the adult learning that is necessary to improve children's learning environments, how to balance the time and energy needed for collaborative learning and decision making with needs for efficiency, how to learn from conflicting views and change, and how to adapt the use of principles of learning as a community to changing needs (such as the changing cultural backgrounds of new generations of schoolchildren and their parents) by building on the differing approaches and circumstances of diverse individuals and communities.

Coherence in Principles of Learning as a Community

We hope to inspire readers to think about their own principles as they come to understand ours—we are not trying to convince readers to do things the way we do. But we do think that the principles we discuss apply, with adaptation, to many circumstances.

For most of the history of our school, we have swum upstream, developing and defending the learning principles of our school even when they were not understood by others. Currently, however, the principles of the program are associated with instructional methods that have become prominent in school districts and educational research throughout the nation—co-operative learning, multiage classrooms, integrated curriculum, authentic learning (in which the purposes of activities make sense and engage children), assessment in the context of instruction, and so on.

Now, with many educators recommending the approaches that we use, we feel it is especially important to consider the underlying principles that make the practices coherent. Adding new "techniques" to the classroom does not lead to the development of a coherent philosophy. For example, adding the technique of having children work in "co-operative learning" teams is quite different than a system in which collaboration is inherent to the structure. Co-operative learning sessions in U.S. schools are often brief and insulated from the overall structure of the classroom, where for much of the day, only the teacher is supposed to speak; if children speak, it is one at a time and only to the teacher. The exceptional times, when children tutor each other or work in co-operative groups, do not correspond to a community of learners which is itself coherently structured as a collaborative system. Piecemeal changes do not create an integrated and coherent new philosophy of learning.[18]

We find ourselves reexamining the principles of our educational philosophy again and again in order to orient newcomers, to explain within our school district why we do things differently, and to discuss whether a particular way of doing things fits with our philosophy. It is that philosophy—the underlying principles of our practices—that we are attempting to portray in this book.

For newcomers to understand the principles of learning at the OC usually requires becoming involved, not just being informed about them—consistent with our philosophy that learning occurs through interested participation. Many people who are used to a different way of thinking about learning and teaching find the philosophy (and practices) of the school difficult to understand until they

Students help each other throughout the day. (Photo courtesy Cindy White.)

have participated in the classrooms for a few years, observing and trying different approaches and discussing and struggling to make sense of the ideas. It would be convenient if adults could learn to parent, to reform school practices, or to do research (or if children could learn to read) just by listening to a lecture or by reading a manual. However, we have learned that to understand new ideas, people need to observe and participate in their use in an involved way.

It is ironic, then, that we are attempting to present principles of learning in a book for people who generally do not have the opportunity to pitch in and join us in everyday classroom and committee activities where the principles are enacted and discussed in the context of fostering children's learning. We try to bring the principles to life through sharing key everyday observations and experiences, hoping the principles make sense to parents and teachers elsewhere, as well as to researchers and scholars interested in how children learn.

This book, like the school, is a deeply collaborative project among people with very different roles—past and present teachers, parents, students, researchers, and administrators—who each offer their own perspectives in a coherent story. The book is more like a mosaic where the pieces fit together than like the usual multiple-authored book with chapters. As in any system in which the whole is greater than the sum of the parts, the contributions to the book build on each other, while each reflects some of the same story as all the others. The philosophy and traditions of the program are the source of our shared understanding.

An example of the coherence of the OC's principles is illustrated by the experience of one of the editors (Barbara Rogoff) when she met one of the original

Parents and teachers working on their contributions to this book.

teachers (Marilyn Johnston) at a national education meeting. Although Barbara and Marilyn had minimal overlap in the program (Marilyn had moved out of state about when Barbara's children entered the OC), they found that either of them could answer colleagues' questions about OC philosophy and practices, and the other would chime in with an example or extension, as though they had been working together for years. This coherence of principles across the several decades of this community of learners is what we hope to portray in this book.

The three of us who have taken the role of editors span the history of the OC and have each filled several different roles in the community, which aided us in helping authors to articulate the themes that they took on and to fit the mosaic of their contributions together. Leslee taught kindergarten to fifth grade in the school for almost as long as it has existed and has a child who has graduated from the school and one who is in the early grades. Carolyn has taught first through sixth grades in the school since its beginning and has two children who graduated from it. Barbara has been a parent of three children in the school for 10 years and, as a developmental psychologist interested in how people learn, has been carrying out research in the school for several additional years.

The initial motivation for this book was Barbara's conviction that there is much to be learned about processes of learning (and teaching) from the wisdom-in-practice in this school. Indeed, the book is an attempt to articulate the theory-in-action of the OC, as Barbara was convinced that it would contribute to ongoing theoretical discussions of how children learn in the context of their involvements with other people and their cultural communities.

We hope that our reflections provide inspiration for others to examine their own educational principles and practices and that through diverse efforts to understand learning in different settings, a collective understanding of learning and teaching can help shape the learning opportunities of the future.

The next contribution is an account of how the original teacher and parents experimented with ways of moving beyond traditional forms of instruction. Marilyn Johnston describes how the philosophy and practices of the OC evolved from Thoreau School, a private school initiated in 1971 by a small group of parents who hired her as the first teacher. In 1977, parents and teachers, together with the superintendent of the Salt Lake City School District, discussed the possibility of beginning a parent co-operative elementary school program as part of the public school system. Based on the six years of experimentation in the Thoreau School, the parents and teachers were interested in multiage classrooms, integrated curriculum generated by the needs and interests of students, site-based management, and using parents as coeducators in the classroom. The superintendent was supportive of these goals and recommended requiring parents to participate in the classroom three hours per week per child to provide an equal sense of community among all the families. Other stipulations were that class sizes and costs would be the same as in other schools throughout the school district.

When the OC began as a public school, a great deal of adjustment had to occur to align with the requirements of public education. Some people were afraid that making the OC into a public school would destroy what had been developed in the early private school years. But many of the challenges we faced as a public school actually helped us figure out what we really cared about as a matter of principle, and what we could let go. We had to keep on discussing our philosophy—a process that Marilyn Johnston, in the next pages, argues is at the heart of the vitality of the program.

Notes

1. B. Rogoff, *Apprenticeship in Thinking: Cognitive Development in Social Context* (New York: Oxford University Press, 1990).

2. J. Dewey, *The School and Society* (Chicago: University of Chicago Press, 1915); S. Scribner and M. Cole, "Cognitive Consequences of Formal and Informal Education," *Science* 182 (1973): 553–59.

3. R. Serpell, *The Significance of Schooling: Life-Journeys in an African Society* (Cambridge: Cambridge University Press, 1993).

4. Carolyn Pratt became a teacher in a one-room school near her town at the age of 16. C. Pratt, *I Learn from Children: An Adventure in Progressive Education* (New York: Simon & Schuster, 1948), xi–xii.

5. D. J. Hernandez, "Children's Changing Access to Resources: A Historical Perspective," *Society for Research in Child Development Social Policy Report* 8, no. 1 (Spring 1994).

6. R. E. Callahan, *Education and the Cult of Efficiency* (Chicago: University of Chicago Press, 1962).

7. A. L. Brown and J. C. Campione, "Communities of Learning and Thinking, or a Context by Any Other Name," in *Developmental Perspectives on Teaching and Learning Thinking Skills (Contributions in Human Development* 21), ed. D. Kuhn (Basel: Karger, 1990), 108–26; J. S. Brown, A. Collins, and P. Duguid, "Situated Cognition and the Culture of Learning," *Educational Researcher* 18 (1989): 32–42.

8. Committee on Developments in the Science of Learning, *How People Learn: A Report of the National Research Council of the National Academy of Science* (Washington: National Academy Press, 1999).

9. C. E. Silberman, *Crisis in the Classroom: The Remaking of American Education* (New York: Random House, 1970).

10. A. Graubard, *Free the Children* (New York: Pantheon Books, 1972).

11. J. Dewey, *Experience and Education* (New York: Macmillan, 1938), 84.

12. Brown and Campione, "Communities of Learning and Thinking"; D. Newman, P. Griffin, and M. Cole, *The Construction Zone: Working for Cognitive Change in School* (Cambridge: Cambridge University Press, 1989); B. Rogoff, "Developing an Understanding of the Idea of Communities of Learners," *Mind, Culture, and Activity* 1 (1994): 209-29; R. G. Tharp and R. Gallimore, *Rousing Minds to Life: Teaching, Learning, and Schooling in Social Context* (Cambridge: Cambridge University Press, 1988); G. Wells, G. L. M. Chang, and A. Maher, "Creating Classroom Communities of Literate Thinkers," in *Cooperative Learning: Theory and Research*, ed. S. Sharan (New York: Praeger, 1990), 95–121.

13. J. Dewey, *Democracy and Education* (New York: Macmillan, 1916); L. S. Vygotsky, *Mind in Society: The Development of Higher Psychological Processes* (Cambridge: Harvard University Press, 1978).

14. Dewey, *Experience and Education*, 85.

15. S. Ellis and M. Gauvain, "Social and Cultural Influences on Children's Collaborative Interactions," in *Children's Development within Social Context*, ed. L. T. Winegar and J. Valsiner (Hillsdale, N.J.: Erlbaum, 1992); J. Hendry, *Becoming Japanese: The World of the Pre-school Child* (Honolulu: University of Hawaii Press, 1986); L. Lamphere, *To Run After*

Them: Cultural and Social Bases of Cooperation in a Navajo Community (Tucson: University of Arizona Press, 1977); B. Rogoff, J. J. Mistry, A. Göncü, and C. Mosier, "Guided Participation in Cultural Activity by Toddlers and Caregivers," *Monographs of the Society for Research in Child Development* 58, no. 7 (1993).

16. These include scholars and researchers referred to in the other citations in this book.

17. W. A. Firestone, "The Balance of Control between Parents and Teachers in Co-op Free Schools," *School Review* 85 (1977): 264–86.

18. L. A. Cremin, *The Transformation of the School: Progressivism in American Education, 1876–1957* (New York: Knopf, 1962).

PART ONE

Origins, Principles, and Structure
of a Community of Learners

A group of former students were asked how they would characterize the most important aspects of the OC philosophy:

A fifth grader: "The kids help decide, along with the teacher. It's fun and educational at the same time."

Another fifth grader: "Parents working in the classroom look at the kids and go sort of freestyle, but still educational and not just conversation. And they do individual versions of the same stuff, so people work at their own pace."

An eighth grader: "One of the main things is choices, and another is helping each other, like the kids help each other, the parents help the kids, the teachers help the kids, the teachers help the parents, the parents help each other. So it's not just the kids learning; the parents and everyone are learning the OC way."

A parent volunteer helps children edit their creative writing.

Constructing Ourselves
The Beginning of an Evolving Philosophy

Marilyn Johnston, *teacher and researcher*

From the beginning of my experience as a teacher in the OC and its private school precursor, the Thoreau School, I was intrigued with the role that an evolving philosophy played in the development and sustenance of the program. The debating and refining of the philosophy stands in sharp contrast to my experience in educational settings before and after my involvement in this school. In other teaching contexts in which I have participated, both in elementary schools and at the university level, philosophies are seldom discussed or made explicit. Philosophical positions are sometimes imposed, other times taken for granted; seldom are they debated. Even less often are philosophical discussions used as the central activity for constructing the program.

In the beginning of the program, especially during the Thoreau School years (the private school endeavor that began in 1971 and led into the OC public school in 1977), our very survival depended on articulating a philosophy that would bind us together as a group and entice others to join us. Without a clear philosophy to guide us, we had no mission or purpose. As I worked with the program over 15 years, as both a teacher and parent, I was convinced that a continuing discussion of our philosophical roots and putting this philosophy into practice was our lifeline. I worry about the program over the long term if it loses this sense of debate and introspection. The process of clarifying the philosophy not only developed shared norms and practices and articulated these to others, it was also how we educated ourselves.

I was hired by the instigating group of parents to be the first teacher at Thoreau School. The first year I had 21 children from 14 families in a kindergarten-to-sixth-grade classroom, from age 5 to 12 years. The basic characteristics of this first school have survived past the Thoreau School years, over the more than 20 years of the OC program's existence as a public school. This was to be a parent co-operative program that encouraged children, parents, and teachers to collaboratively design the program and the curriculum.

I had taught elementary school for six years before taking this job. But nothing
in my experience or previous training, including a master's degree, had prepared
me for the type of education these parents wanted for their children. Most of
what they wanted was defined in opposition to what they experienced in the
public schools. None of us knew much about how to create something new. Of
course, we had all read John Holt's *Why Children Fail* and other free school and
protest literature. But these books told us mostly what was wrong, and little about
what to do to change it.

The parents who started the Thoreau School were by and large a highly educated and verbal group that included university faculty, classroom teachers, lawyers, artists, and businesspeople. While many of them were or had been educators
at one level or another, no one at this point could describe what our new classrooms would look like or how parents might participate in the program. My "job
interview" with the parents was more a lengthy discussion of what might be than
a formal interview. I was intrigued by the interview, so I took the job for $310 a
month. From my husband's perspective, I had decided to quit my professional
career and volunteer to work with a group of outcasts.

The several years that followed were grounded in a continuing discussion about
what we would become and how we would survive. We held school in Sunday
school rooms at the Unitarian Church (the minister was one of our parents).
Each weekend we had to clean and lock up everything; occasionally, things were
missing or broken when we returned on Monday. Equally bothersome, our stuff
was in the way for the Sunday school teachers. Space issues became more problematic as our numbers grew and we accumulated more furniture and materials
for the children to use. We then traveled from one location to another as buildings
we were renting were condemned, grew too small for our growing numbers, or
cost too much for our meager budget.

In 1977, when the program moved into the public school system as an optional
educational program—the OC—we gained regular teachers' salaries and adequate
space and supplies, along with a host of restrictions (district accountability, goals,
and testing) we had not previously had to deal with. We moved into the public
school system with a proposal to the district that stated our philosophy, curricular
approach, and commitment to parental involvement. The development of that
philosophy had evolved slowly during the six years the Thoreau School had existed, and it followed us into the public schools.

In that very first summer after I was hired to teach at Thoreau, the parents
and I spent many evenings sitting in someone's living room planning for the
coming school year. We read books and discussed them, debated the outlines of
a curriculum, scrounged furniture and supplies from attics and garage sales, and
went camping together. Many times there were children sitting around in these
meetings who asked questions and made suggestions as long as their attention
lasted, which was rarely as long as the meetings did. I often went home after
these long discussions and a couple of glasses of wine wondering what I had
gotten myself into. The discussions often ended without clear decisions. We were

learning a lot but did not yet have a clear direction or the skills to work together as a decision-making group.

In addition to group meetings, there were many discussions with individuals. Some parents approached me with individual concerns about their children or their disagreements with the decisions of the group. Some needed assurance that their children were going to be okay and that they would indeed be learning something. Even though they wanted something different for their children, it was hard to trust something with which they themselves had no experience. I often needed to sound more confident than I was and to argue for things even though I had never tried them out in a classroom. Sometimes I needed to provide leadership as things started to fall apart; other times decision making seemed to happen without me.

There were times when angry words were expressed and differences in temperament and levels of patience made things difficult. Group decision making is always a slow process, and constructing a shared sense of meaning never comes easily. In addition, most of us as parents feel very strongly about things that are going to directly affect our children. My own daughter was only three at the time, but I had a sense that I was creating something important for her future. This concern about our children fed a strong emotional commitment to our success. These feelings, however, sometimes led to divisiveness rather than consensus building.

While there were difficulties getting through this initial period, there was also a sense of excitement that we were doing something very different. It was risky and exhilarating at the same time. The 1960s and 1970s were times of national ferment in education—schools like ours were springing up around the country. Although our private status in the Thoreau School put us on the fringes locally, we felt connected to a larger national movement.

Early discussions about our development were always a mixture of abstract principles and practical realities. Sometimes the principles came first and then the practice. For example, we decided, "We are all learners in this program." We then tried to work out ways of putting the principles into practice. If we are all learners, then adults and children should be learning together, so we tried several approaches. We tried to put children in situations where they could teach us as adults. We worked with a child or group on a topic of their choice even if we were not experts in the area. We also did things as an adult group to educate ourselves—reading books and taking advantage of the expertise within the group.

We addressed some issues by making a policy and then developing the practical procedures. For example: How do we decide on whether an issue goes to the whole group? Should parents get their ideas approved by the teacher before using them in the classroom? Should the teacher check everything out with the parents (and kids) before setting it up in the classroom?

Other times practices came first, and then we had to evaluate them and construct theoretical arguments to support them. For example, a couple of children brought in math workbooks that their parents had purchased. Naturally, everyone else wanted them, and more children brought them in on their own. We had long discussions. Is using workbooks contrary to a child-centered curriculum? Is practicing skills in isolation antithetical to our commitment to a relevant and integrated curriculum?

The interplay of philosophy and practice was pervasive. Both were new and interdependent. They shaped each other as we tried to find ways to keep our philosophy and our practice consistent. Many times we made a decision and then, after watching the children, had to reevaluate that decision. We decided not to use workbooks because it felt too much like the kind of instruction that we were criticizing in traditional classrooms. But we found some children really wanted and liked workbooks, especially in math. Some needed practice on particular skills. So we compromised. We developed a sequenced set of ditto sheets, made from workbooks or handmade, that students, parents, and children could use to learn and teach a particular skill when needed. It made this part of math more individualized, but hardly more relevant or integrated.

We had few models of how to accomplish what we wanted and often had to rely on minor alterations of what we did know. Other times things just somehow developed within the social context. One of the fathers, a professor at the law school, had noticed that many of the kids were slow to add and subtract in their heads. He took it upon himself to find some things that would help them. He started playing Twenty-One with a few kids to see if this would help. Within a couple of days everyone was playing Twenty-One. There were 30 packs of cards, and students had figured out ingenious ways to wager this and that. I watched with amusement, thinking the kids were adding and subtracting for hours on end—what better way to learn to add and subtract in your head? Math was no longer boring or irrelevant to these students; they were using math in meaningful ways that connected with real-world experiences.

Within a short period, however, a couple of parents as well as a matron in the church got wind of the "gambling" and we called an emergency meeting to talk about it with the parents and kids and to respond to the church board. The wagering had to be stopped immediately and the card games eventually faded into oblivion, but not without much discussion with everyone involved. We learned a lot from incidents like these because they forced us to consider whether our practice was in line with our philosophy.

Some things we did were only mild alterations of traditional approaches; occasionally we took a bolder, more deliberate course. Our first bold initiative started with the decision to plan a big unit based on a topic that arose from the kids or parents. The first such unit involved a study of cultures from an archaeological point of view. A couple of parents were archaeologists, and others had training or interests that supported this. The children had begun to ask some interesting questions while doing some of the activities that the parents were planning as they were "co-oping" (working in the classroom). We held some planning meetings that included some of the older students to brainstorm ideas and divided up who would get particular materials ready. This project lasted for several weeks: We discussed the characteristics of a culture, studied some historical Native American and non-Western cultures, took field trips, and brought in resource people who knew about particular cultures or who had worked on archaeological digs. The students then got into small groups, with several parents helping each group, and designed their own culture—either a past, present, or future culture. Their culture was to have rituals, beliefs, and daily practices that made sense given their physical environment, time period, and type of people.

As a culminating experience, we made artifacts for our cultures and took them out to the Great Salt Lake shore and buried them, leaving archaeological clues of various sorts. Our archaeologist parents had shown us how to dig for artifacts and what kinds of clues we might leave. Then we switched groups and dug up some other group's cultural artifacts. Back at school, we developed our interpretations from the evidence and reported to the group whose artifacts we had excavated. At the end of experiences like this, we were typically exhausted but exhilarated. The children, participating at the level that they could from kindergarten to sixth grade, helped each other, generated ideas, and learned a great deal. As adults we learned a lot from each other, and often from the children as well. We could always think of things we should have done better and things that didn't go as well as planned, but it was these bold experiments that gave us courage to try more things that moved farther away from our own traditional school experiences.

There is no doubt that we romanticized what we constructed philosophically in the beginning. We wanted children to become good decision makers, so we avoided imposing decisions on them, but often went overboard. We gave children freedom, because we were reacting to overly structured classrooms. Often it was the children who told us or showed us where we had gone too far. About December of the first year, we were sitting around on the carpet in a circle trying to make a decision about something. Most of the kids couldn't have cared less about the issue, yet a decision needed to be made. It was after lunch, everyone seemed tired, and I was at a loss. Matthew, a freckle-faced six-year-old, was draped over my lap and looked up at me in frustration, saying, "Marilyn, can't *you* just make a decision once in a while?" "Sure, why not?" I replied, and I went home having learned an important lesson. Including kids in the decision making was more about including them in the decisions they cared about than including them in all decisions. Why force them into a process when they didn't care about the issue?

I slowly came to realize that there were some decisions that were not open, that the parents and I needed to make. I also came to realize that leading children to believe that they could be involved in all decisions was dishonest. It was unfair to ask them to be involved in a decision when the conclusion was already known or the decision needed to be made in a particular way for practical, political, or social reasons. Of course, I did not understand all of this immediately, but Matthew's comment was the pivotal point that led to a series of distinctions that became very important. I learned to be more honest with them about what decisions were open and which were "no-choice" items. I learned to better gauge their interest and to give them time to make decisions about things they did care about, some of which seemed unimportant to me.

The tendency to romanticize our original philosophical position was natural, given the reactive stance we were in. We knew more about what we were against (linear curricula, teacher-directed learning, standardized tests, and classroom structures that segregated children and restricted their learning or damaged their self-concept) than what we were for. In reaction to what we were against, the tendency was to move to the opposite extreme. Testing out the extreme positions taught us many things. I typically had to see these issues played out in practice before they made more general sense to me.

I eventually became convinced that extreme positions were problematic in important ways and should in general be avoided. For example, if I gave the children too much freedom, they might benefit from the freedom, but they missed developing the skills necessary to deal with more structured situations (with which they would inevitably come in contact). Limitless freedom also required that children often deal with more than they were prepared for. I came to believe that limitless freedom was insensitive to their developmental needs and abilities, as well as irresponsible on my part.

I came to a similar conclusion related to choice. I originally wanted them to choose what they would learn—again, a romanticized view that if the children were left to their own resources they would be eager learners. I still believe that children are basically inquisitive and know a lot about what is good for them, but they don't know everything. Many times they don't even know what choices are available unless they are nurtured and helped to see what is interesting or good about math, or history, or science. When we let Meagan (who did not like math) not do math for months on end, was she gaining confidence in herself or learning the wonders of mathematics or developing pride in her accomplishments? No—in fact, all of these positive things evaded her. She was more likely learning that she was a failure at math, that math was intimidating, and that she couldn't do it. It was true that Meagan finally got worried about going to junior high school and decided to have a stab at math again. A wonderful parent who loved math helped her to find excitement and accomplishment that maybe stuck with her longer because she decided to do it on her own. But I wonder whether the benefit of letting her go that long without math outweighed what she missed and how she felt about herself in the interim.

Choices about social behavior were also much discussed. In a parallel approach to dealing with academic choices, I initially tended to let children work these social problems out on their own rather than jumping in to help. I stepped in if there was physical aggression or disruption to other children's work, but otherwise I tended to watch rather than help. I eventually came to the conclusion that I was missing many opportunities for children's learning. If I gently became a part of their interactions, I could often facilitate a problem-solving orientation. I could ask questions, get them to talk about motives and feelings, and facilitate their coming up with alternatives. The same, I discovered, was true for group problems as well. If we brought issues to the group, I could facilitate discussions that led to group problem solving about social interactions. Over time we developed a set of procedures for talking and listening to each other as these issues were discussed. We debated heartily whether we should raise hands to speak or try to be sensitive to each other's need to speak. We took turns being facilitators. We talked about strategies for solving problems.

Over time some children became very skillful in using these strategies themselves. I remember vividly the first time this happened. Two boys came in from recess, their faces red and their hair mussed from a problem they'd had outside. In such cases, I often found a quiet place in the room or outside in the hall to sit down and talk. Instead of expecting me to help, they announced that they were going out in the hall where it was quiet so they could make a plan. They came back a few minutes later, arm in arm, reporting that they had made apologies and a plan for sharing the ball at the next recess.

We sometimes brought an individual child's problem to the group. For example, one of the students had a persistent habit of punching kids as he walked around. I had worked with him trying various things, but nothing seemed to work. The rest of the kids were fed up. One of the children suggested bringing it to a circle discussion. The group talked about their feelings about getting hit and made suggestions for ways they could help Tom, and he could help himself, stop hitting. Tom seemed impressed by the children's feelings as well as by their willingness to help him take care of this "problem." There were still times when he couldn't help touching others, but there was a group understanding of the problem, and he got consistent feedback and responses from children (and parents and me) that significantly moderated the choices he made.

Of course, none of these approaches worked the same for every child, and many aspects had to be considered as we decided what was the best thing to do in a particular instance. Children have different temperaments, interests, and abilities to handle choices, and parents have different goals for their children as well. Leaving a child to make choices about some things may be productive at one time or with one kind of choice, but not for another time at another task. And even when I had decided to let the child make his or her own choices, I had to watch closely and make ongoing decisions about whether to change my mind or let the process continue. Decisions like these I made within ongoing conversations with parents and with the children.

Over time we came to talk a lot about balance. This did not solve all our problems or help us with all decisions, but we found it productive to think about the benefits (and problems) involved in *balancing* rather than *choosing between* the extremes. "Finding the balance" became a watchword for discussions about many different topics as our philosophy evolved over the first several years. I initially thought of this as trying to grab the best of both extremes, the productive parts of freedom as well as of structure. This later came to seem naive, as I realized that different amounts of freedom and structure were productive in different measures for different children or situations. It was in the process of trying to decide what to do in particular cases, like with Meagan's math or Tom's hitting, that we had to both decide on practical strategies and discuss our philosophical commitments. The success of a particular student became the concern of the group, which often included other students.

We came to see ourselves all as teachers and learners, and we made decisions more often in conversation than in isolation. The fact that we talked about these kinds of decisions helped me as a teacher enormously. Having ideas from many people was richer than doing everything by myself.

Of course, this group processing of everything was intimidating as well. There was always someone watching me no matter what I was doing—planning, managing, teaching, evaluating. At first this bothered me a lot; eventually I came to depend on it for feedback that helped me to think better and work more effectively with the students. When I tried something with the students, there were others to talk with afterward. The same was true for parents. As they worked with a small group, they could ask me for feedback about their teaching or about the students' reactions. The students themselves gave us direct and indirect feedback on their learning. They often gave us direct comments about whether something was interesting or challenging. In circle times, we asked for their critique and ways to make things work better for their learning. Less directly, we watched them share and teach each other. From these observations, we learned what was important to them and how well they understood what they were sharing, teaching, and learning.

Working this intensely over a substantial period of time with a small group of people was not always easy. Even though we talked about our philosophy endlessly, it was not a finished product. After a while we were pretty solidly in agreement about the general principles, but often there were differences in opinions about how these principles should be applied in the classroom. Sometimes I got tired of having to justify everything I did; sometimes I was uncomfortable with what parents were doing with students and it was hard to talk about these differences.

It didn't take me long, however, to realize how enormously important it was to talk about what we were doing, especially to give reasons for why we thought something was better than something else. It was in discussing our positions that we developed shared meanings and goals. When we had some new children and parents join us the second year, we became aware of how much we had learned together and also how important it was that we talked with new parents to help them understand what was going on.

There were three major activities that evolved to support a continuing discussion about our philosophy. The first was a philosophy committee, the second was a yearly philosophy workshop, and the third was monthly classroom meetings. The philosophy committee focused on a number of projects over the years. At different times we tried to write down accounts of our philosophy for the express purpose of sharing it with the public, with new parents, or for writing a proposal (including the proposal to become a public school optional program). Whatever the purpose, the process was always an educative one, and the discussions often carried over from the smaller philosophy committee to the larger group.

About the time we reached four classrooms (about 60 to 70 students), we started having an annual all-day philosophy workshop. An ad hoc committee spent weeks deciding what we would do, what issues would be discussed, and how best to get everyone involved. Again, the process for developing the workshop was often as educative as the workshop itself. Deciding what issues and problems most needed our attention was a useful process that encouraged reflection and discussion. The philosophy workshops were always a mixture of large-group meetings to talk about the issues and small-group discussions to deal with teaching strategies and practical concerns. The goal was to get parents and teachers talking to each other about their concerns and to try to further develop shared purposes.

About the same time, we also began having monthly classroom meetings. There were many managerial things to talk about—schedules, curriculum units, and so on. My goal as a teacher in these meetings was twofold. First, I wanted to get parents to think about why we should do something one way rather than another. This directly related to building our philosophy. I tried to ask nonthreatening but provocative questions to get everyone thinking about the issues. For example, if we set up reading groups by skill level (as parents often wanted to do), would this support children of different ages and abilities learning from each other? And would this affect children's self-concept if they were not in the "high" group? If I felt very strongly about something, as I did about skill level groups, I tried to explain why and to suggest alternatives that might meet the parents' objectives in a way that was more consonant with our philosophy. Although debating these philosophical points sometimes made for heated meetings, it seemed critical that we educate ourselves and new families about our purposes.

My second goal for the classroom meetings was to find ways to avoid fragmentation. Parents were co-oping once a week, and many of them had particular things they wanted to do in the classroom. It became clear to me after a while that there was a problem with all these different activities. The activities themselves were often rich and wonderful. A biochemist father was doing a movement activity to teach about molecular reactions; another parent was setting up a pretend store to do some math and economics; a musician father was writing songs with small groups of children. But I watched students going from one activity to another unable to make connections between them, and I was unable to keep track of what they were learning from these diverse sets of activities.

At the parent meetings we discussed this problem and tried many things. We tried getting small groups of parents with similar interests to carry a project throughout a week. Each day the co-oping parent in that group would continue from what was done the day before. This took planning and coordination, but sometimes it worked beautifully. Parents also felt more connected and could follow the children's progress. Other times we planned larger units, like the cultures and archaeology project. At the monthly meetings, once the project was under way, we could discuss what was going on, what changes needed to be made, and how we were responding to new interests as they were emerging within the project.

As a teacher, I always went to these meetings with some fear and trepidation. I had an agenda, but I also encouraged parents to bring up their concerns. I often did not know ahead of time what would come up, and dealing with differences of opinion and strong feelings in this kind of setting was difficult. But again, it was through these discussions that we were learning. We were learning about each other, about our interests and talents, about our concerns for our individual children, and about how to share the challenge of helping children who were having difficulty. These meetings encouraged parents to take a larger view of the classroom than just their own child and helped them to become an integral part of what happened in their child's classroom.

A final context for discussing and building our philosophy was the Friday afternoon teacher meetings. When we grew to having three or four teachers, there was a need to coordinate and plan across classrooms. The teachers typically met once a week after school, often talking at a local health-food restaurant for several hours. The amount of coordination necessary to keep complicated classroom schedules and program activities in sync was sometimes overwhelming. We also talked about our frustrations, problems we were having with parents or children, and the differences in our approaches to managing our classrooms. We didn't always agree, but we needed each others' support as we tried to deal with the many roles a teacher played in this program.

I sometimes thought about the simplicity of a regular classroom job, of being the only adult in the room and having complete control over what happened in it. The simplicity was enticing, but the loneliness and sterility were also obvious. Other teachers helped me to see things I hadn't thought about; they challenged my thinking. I was always having to justify what I believed and why I wanted to do something. I came to relish these discussions and what I gained from them.

I have to admit that I went home from many days and various meetings in tears, feeling like I didn't have adequate professional knowledge or personal resources for this job. But these times diminished in frequency as I got clearer about my own beliefs and as I learned to use students, parents, and teachers as a means to continue my own learning. I lost my need to have all the answers and learned to enjoy new challenges. As I could do this for myself, I also got better at helping children and parents to be problem solvers rather than answer seekers and answer givers. I began to see the program as a true community of learners. What we had espoused early on, that we were all learners, was not easy to put into practice. It was hard to acknowledge that I didn't know something, because it felt risky. I was the teacher and felt that others expected me to be a knowledgeable professional. I wanted others to take risks that I found hard to take myself.

In the process of teaching in this community, I took time off to do a doctoral program. It gave me time to study the historical traditions from which our philosophy developed and the political ramifications of our private school status and to examine the taken-for-granted assumptions that had evolved. I went back to teach in the OC for two more years with renewed energy and new questions. These were our first two years in the public school system, and this move involved new issues and political aspects that I found interesting. The next year I took a faculty position at the university and continued as a co-oping parent for my son, who was in the OC program.

When I left Salt Lake City six years later for a university position in another state, I couldn't help thinking about the continuity and development in the program over the years. The Thoreau School parents feared that moving into the public school system would mean a loss of our central philosophical tenets. This proved to be wrong. There has been strong continuity in the approach toward

Kindergartners explaining their inventions to attentive fourth- and fifth-graders and a co-oping parent from another classroom. (Photo courtesy Cindy White.)

teaching and learning. Parent involvement and collaborative decision making continue in similar but more refined and experienced ways. Children still play a strong and collaborative role in determining the curriculum and learning experiences.

One issue that has been discussed many times is the consequence of our time as a private school—our first six years as the Thoreau School. Was it necessary for us to work outside the public school system to develop this philosophy and way of doing things? Could we have managed this level of reform within "the system"?

Like many parents of the 1960s and 1970s, the original Thoreau School parents decided to leave the public school system because it seemed recalcitrant and unresponsive to parental and student interests. A number of the original parents were or had been public school teachers themselves. Most participants were uncomfortable about working outside the public schools, yet they felt compelled to do so. As a consequence of our private school status, we had enormous freedom. We could try anything that we could convince each other was reasonable. We struggled together to create something new. We were accountable only to ourselves and bore the burden and rewards of learning from our mistakes and failures. I have rarely since been in institutional settings that allowed this kind of creative debate and risk taking. I have never participated in any other project where everyone was so committed to change and so stubbornly determined to make it work.

When we moved into the public school system, we had hours of debate and work behind us. This experience grounded everything we did, particularly the ways that we argued for what we wanted to do (as everyone outside the program seemed to want us to do things differently). The Thoreau School period was a laboratory for experimenting with the ideas and practices that grounded our move into the public schools. It created the umbrella that protected us from the shower of criticisms that became our constant companions as a fledgling public optional program.

While there has been strong continuity in philosophy and practices, there has also been change over the years. The continued growth in size, the requirements of school district programs and assessments, and the need of teachers to make the OC more efficient in order to have a life outside the classroom influenced aspects of the OC and, in general, diminished the time spent talking about issues. On the other hand, many of the changes produced growth and reflected the input of new participants. As always, the OC program was influenced by incoming teachers, parents, and children. It cannot remain static and still be true to a fundamental tenet of its philosophy—that it be responsive to participants' interests and needs. If the OC continues to be a community of learners, it will necessarily be influenced by the dialogue and learning within the group.

When teachers assembled for a 20-year reunion in the scenic canyons of southern Utah one summer, we talked nostalgically about the influence that this program has had on our subsequent professional lives. The power of this community of learners was evident as we collectively realized that each of us has continued to search for communities where collegial conversations push us to think hard and support our learning, as is still the case for teachers, parents, and students at the OC.

This program has lasted over two decades. I think a major reason for its survival has to do with its distinct philosophy, its defined way of putting these principles into practice, and the involvement of all participants. The philosophy that grounded these practices and parent involvement have evolved over many conversations and differences of opinion. Some of our struggles to reach consensus about philosophical positions and teaching practices were painful—it's hard to build shared meanings. But the struggles were also what created a sense of cohesiveness and purpose. We came to identify with a set of purposes that we helped to shape and that shaped our own thinking as well.

With success comes the possibility of complacency. With tradition comes the potential for uncritical continuation of counterproductive practices. It's easier for classroom meetings to deal with schedules and procedures than to struggle with principles and differences of opinion. Yet shared ownership and development depend on conversations that challenge business as usual. This kind of questioning takes time, and dealing with differences can produce conflict as easily as consensus. Yet both questioning and conversations about differences were essential to the program's development and are probably the key ingredients to its future growth and continued uniqueness.

An Orientation to
Principles-in-Action

Leslee Bartlett, *teacher*
Carolyn Goodman Turkanis, *teacher*
Barbara Rogoff, *researcher*

As mentioned at the beginning of this book, the key principle for learning as a school community is to *build instruction on children's interests in a collaborative way—learning activities are planned by children as well as adults, and adults learn from their own involvement as they foster children's learning.* Children are natural learners as long as they can be deeply involved in activities which they help to devise and for which they see a purpose—"minds-on" activities.

At the OC, children participate in setting their learning goals and deciding how to use their time and resources, with the aid of the adults. Discussion, conversation, and enjoyment are a valued part of the learning process. The children learn not only the academic subjects but also how to make responsible choices for their own learning and how to solve problems ranging from mathematics and writing to interpersonal frictions at recess. The children learn to lead others (including adults) in school activities and to build on their own interests at the same time that they contribute to the learning of others in the classroom.

Much of the day is planned flexibly, to build the curriculum around student contributions, staying open to the serendipitous "learning moments" that naturally emerge as interested people discuss ideas and issues and organize projects for children's learning. Small groups of children work at an activity with a parent volunteer (a "co-oper"), the classroom teacher, or a child who has organized an activity for the others. Most children stay with the same teacher for two years in blended grade-level classes, creating a supportive classroom environment in which people of differing skills and interests contribute to each others' learning and learn from teaching others. The children plan their day, choosing among some required activities and some optional ones. The whole class also meets several times each day for planning and for whole-group instruction connected with the learning activities.

The principles of learning as a community are not easy even for seasoned teachers and co-oping parents to summarize, since they are generally enacted in everyday situations rather than spoken. Usually, people who have been in the program for a while use the principles without having to think about them much. The principles guide our everyday practices in the classrooms, like having "sharing" (show-and-tell) all the way from kindergarten through sixth grade, holding planning and other meetings in "circle" (where everyone sits facing each other in a circle on the floor), and having parent-teacher-kid conferences several times a year. OC teachers refer to the shared principles and associated practices as "the common thread" that connects the practices across the different classrooms.

The principles are often articulated when we disagree about how something should be done and discuss the rationale for deciding how to proceed. For example, many adults are used to the idea of using candy, grades, or threats to get children to do schoolwork, clean up, or otherwise do what the adults want. Naturally, discussions arise surrounding the principle that children's motivation should derive from their interest or commitment to the activity itself. In the OC, children are supposed to develop the ideas that learning is interesting for its own sake and that being a member of a community involves responsibility to the group (for cleaning up after yourself, for example) along with the kinds of pleasures and support that the group can give each person. Through our discussions, we continue to learn about principles of learning as a community.

To help you visualize the scenario in which our principles are enacted, the next section gives an idea of what you would see and hear on one of our routine tours of the program for parents and others interested in this school. This orientation to everyday life at the OC provides background context for illustrations that clarify the principles throughout this book. Following the "tour" are sections describing what children are supposed to learn and how the children's interests and plans are coordinated with this curriculum, how the children's learning is evaluated, and the roles of the parents.

An Orientation Tour

As you cross the playground to enter the red brick public school for a tour of the OC, a spot of glowing color catches your eye, and a burst of laughter floats away to join the white clouds above. A small group of children and an adult huddle together stirring something; then, almost simultaneously, they turn toward the sky and wave a multitude of shining bubbles into the sun. Again, the laughter rises, following the bubbles, as the children race and twirl after them. The woman smiles at you, then turns to gather in her explorers for another round.

Just outside the door of the school you encounter another group, two young girls and a man, sitting in the small entryway. One girl is in tears, the other pouting, the man gently questioning each in turn. As you open the door, the crying girl sniffles and says to the other girl, "I didn't like it when you said I couldn't play. Why can't I play?" "You were being mean and not following the

Children and their co-opers experimenting with bubbles at the entrance of the OC.
(Photo OC archives)

rules," comes the reply. Although tempted to hear the problem-solving session reach its conclusion, you walk down the hall toward a classroom.

Before you reach it, however, a thin clipboard-carrying boy turns the corner and almost brushes into you. "Oh, hi," he says. "I'm taking a survey, do you have a minute?" "OK," you say, and he asks about your methods of recycling paper and plastic, whether or not you compost, and how often you open your refrigerator door. As his interview comes to an end, you hear fragments of conversation from five children seated in a circle on the hallway floor, discussing a book they have recently read. The carpeted hallway around them is strewn with their books and papers. One of the children glances up as you walk by; otherwise their work is uninterrupted.

You join others who have come for the tour. Before it begins, the parent who is serving as the tour guide gives a brief overview of the program using the *OC Mission Statement*, which emphasizes children becoming "responsible life-long learners" who are complex thinkers and problem solvers, effective communicators, cooperative group participants and leaders, contributors to the community, quality workers and producers, and self-directed learners. The guide encourages the group to look for these key features of the program during the tour.

You enter the fourth/fifth-grade classroom and see children working at tables with the parents who are there co-oping—working with children in the classroom.

Co-oper and first-, second-, and third-graders writing and drawing posters.

It is hard to tell who the teacher is because all four adults are actively engaged with the children. You notice that many children are sitting at tables, involved in skill groups with the co-opers.

But there is a wide variety of other activity going on in the room at the same time. Three or four children are reading books in the loft, and two are playing a spelling game. A couple of children are by the sink working at a snack center, reading a classmate's handwritten instructions for making their own mini-pizzas. At three or four "independent centers" set up around the classroom, children are working without adult help. Another child is gazing out the window. Three children stand at the chalkboard looking at the schedule for the day, talking about what they're planning to do next. Some children are at computers typing stories or practicing keyboarding skills. One of the visitors on the tour comments to another, "They have no desks!"

You go into another classroom where all the children are seated with four adults in a large circle on the floor. "They're having a sharing circle," whispers the tour guide, pointing to the little girl showing pictures from the favorite book she brought from home. One of the adults prompts the girl to call on people who are raising their hands to ask questions about her "sharing."

In the next classroom, children are all seated on the floor, looking up at the chalkboard. The teacher is leading a whole-class math journal lesson, guiding the discussion as children exchange math ideas with each other, write in their notebooks, and share their differing strategies by demonstrating them on the chalkboard.

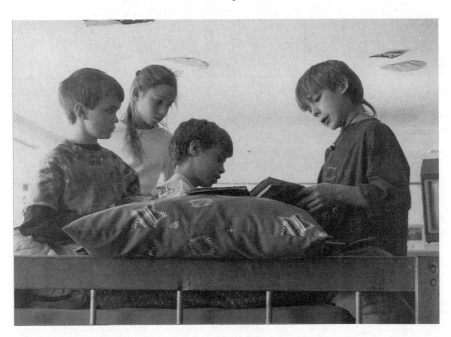

A group of third- and fourth-graders reading together in the loft.

Kids working at an independent center brought in by a classmate, creating geometric figures.

A young author calls on people with questions about his story. The teacher (Denise) is raising her hand with a question, at the right.

In the last classroom on the tour, the teacher seems easy to identify, too. One adult is leading a whole-class discussion in circle about the stories the children have been writing, requesting that several children read their stories aloud and then ask others for "questions and comments." The other adults present raise their hands along with the children to say, "I liked it a lot, and what gave you the idea for that story?" or "What did you mean when you had the fox say . . . ?" But then the tour guide says that the woman leading the discussion is a co-oper who has had children in the program for six years, and the teacher is the one who still has her hand up waiting to be called on.

When the tour ends, the tour guide explains a few features of the program that visitors usually want to know: What is the overall plan for what the children are supposed to learn, and how are children's interests and plans coordinated with this curriculum? How is the children's learning evaluated? What sorts of parents can participate in such an intense way, and how are they qualified to help with instruction?

What Are Children Supposed to Learn—What Is the Curriculum?

The teachers shape the curriculum around the children's interests, using children's curiosity and events in their lives to spark units of study, being alert to opportunities for learning as they occur. Indeed, a basic aim of the curriculum is to foster children's enjoyment of inquiry and curiosity as a source of understanding, to support lifelong learning. Although the teachers use the Utah State Core Curriculum as a general guide for highlighting the concepts from which activities and projects develop, the curriculum goes beyond those guidelines as the teachers make reasoned choices about directions for classroom activities.

The teachers' decision making about daily and long-term curriculum in the classroom focuses on guiding the children toward understanding several "Big Ideas." These are not just collections of facts, which may soon be forgotten if not connected with conceptual understanding; the Big Ideas involve understanding key patterns in the world and ways of learning about them. These Big Ideas connect across the curriculum:

- Learning involves *problem solving*, whether the problems are interpersonal or academic.
- Language, mathematics, and science are ways of *communicating* ideas.
- Complex *systems of relationships* connect natural and human phenomena.

For example, in learning to write, a Big Idea is that writing is communication and that people write differently for different kinds of audiences, for different purposes. When children are immersed in a variety of kinds of writing (such as stories, poetry, research papers, a class newspaper), they can also learn the important technical things (such as punctuation, spelling, and proper format of paragraphs) that make sense once one understands that writing is communication for differing purposes and audiences.

The Big Ideas help teachers prioritize the children's development of a deep understanding of each subject area, so that the facts and technical aspects make sense as they fit with central concepts. For example, in mathematics, until children have an understanding of the number system as a way of communicating quantitative information, they are not ready to learn about place value. Once Leslee asked the children in her first/second-grade class, "What's math?" and a student said, "Math is the language of numbers; it's communicating with numbers." His answer shows understanding of a Big Idea in math. Some other children, even in second grade, do not understand that a number is a symbol for measuring quantity—they might argue vehemently that zero is not a number, not aware that it makes just as much sense to need to say "I have no apples" as "I have 55 apples." Before children add and subtract and work on number facts, they need to have a sense of number and how numbers work together within our place value system, as a system for communicating quantities and solving problems.

For literacy and math, the Utah State Core Curriculum is consistent with the Big Ideas and well articulated; it is helpful in finding the sequence for what to do with students, in what order. In science, though, the state core curriculum has been less helpful—the grade-level units seem more arbitrary. It is difficult to see why one would need to know about rocks, for instance, before studying

Leslee works on a Big Idea in multiplication with a group of students. On the chalk-board behind her are written multiplication examples. On the floor are groupings of little toy bears, which the children are using to examine the relation of multiplication to addition.

insects. Children should study rocks when they are interested in rocks, instead of conforming to specifications that a student should be able to identify particular kinds of rocks at a specific grade level.

The Big Ideas in science have to do with relationships—the ecology—of rocks and insects and landscapes and people. We are all so interrelated that no matter what we do, from taking a step in the desert to flying in a rocket ship in space, our actions affect the world around us. If we keep that in mind, with whatever we're studying and how it relates to the other things around it, it doesn't really matter whether we are studying rocks or insects first. Science is a process of problem solving and communicating a new understanding of the world. It involves exploring the world, testing ideas to make statements that are backed up with evidence from observations that someone can check, discussing the observations and reading what other people have thought, and trying to put it all together to come up with an understanding that goes beyond what was understood before.

The Big Ideas in literacy and math and science connect with each other, and the children's learning of them occurs in an integrated way. For example, children learn about number concepts and literacy in recording observations in a science activity. That way, they learn about the Big Ideas in each subject as well as how the Big Ideas span different subjects. By integrating across subjects, the children can see the general importance of strategies of problem solving, ways of communicating, and the concept that phenomena connect with each other in systems.

Classrooms that blend grade levels help people learn about the Big Ideas, since they facilitate thinking about ideas in a variety of ways. Of course, even in single-grade classrooms the range of understanding is great, but the temptation is to try to teach all the children the same way or to find fault with the children if they're not all at the same place at the same time.

With a focus on the Big Ideas, students at different levels can be learning from the same sort of activities as long as the activities engage their interests and support their understanding. A myriad of activities are provided for children's learning, and children participate in ways that support their own learning needs. An example is the publication of a fourth/fifth/sixth-grade classroom newspaper for which all children contribute articles. There is no need for separate newspapers for the fourth, fifth, and sixth graders; children at all grade levels simply contribute at their own level, learning as they stretch their skills. The children learn from each other's different perspectives, which are a resource for the children who have a deeper understanding as well as for those who are just getting into an area.

The Big Ideas also extend beyond the traditional school subjects of reading, writing, and arithmetic to encompass several nontraditional areas that are of key importance in the OC curriculum. They include learning to solve interpersonal problems and to make responsible choices regarding one's time and actions. These curriculum areas also emphasize the Big Ideas of problem solving, communication, and thinking in terms of systems of relationships.

Indeed, OC teachers emphasize that learning about problem solving, communication, and systems of relationships through dealing with interpersonal problems and issues of personal choice and responsibility are very helpful for children learning these Big Ideas in academic subjects such as math, science, literacy, and social studies. The problems that inevitably crop up in group situations provide numerous opportunities for learning the skills of problem solving across the curriculum. As problems arise, the class takes the time to allow children to develop solutions and reflect on the problem-solving process itself.

The same key ideas are involved in problem solving in interpersonal and academic areas: Try to figure out what the problem is, and be open to revising what you consider it to be. Consider other perspectives on the problem; weigh the possibility that there may be various solutions and that plans may need revision. Take risks in trying new ideas and learn from the ones that don't work. Reflect and evaluate what has been learned in preparation for the next time such a problem is at hand, recognizing the learning in failures as well as successes. Learning to solve problems, communicate, and think in terms of systems of relationships—in interpersonal as well as academic areas—are essential life lessons.

How Are Students' Interests and Planning Coordinated in the Curriculum?

Students' interests and plans are a part of curriculum planning on a moment-to-moment basis, as flexibly designed activities develop through the collaboration of students and adults in the classroom. Students' interests also guide planning in larger units of weeks. Teachers and co-opers develop curriculum areas that interest the children and integrate the subjects they are learning. Some themes involve the whole school, such as when we studied Inventors and Inventions and built up to an Invention Convention at the end of six weeks. Some are classroom themes for a month, such as when the children choose to study dinosaurs or the rain forest, and the parents, teachers, and children work on developing reading, writing, math, science, and social studies activities that connect with the theme of the month.

The children's interest and responsible planning are also central to their daily choices of which activities to engage in, and when. Children are involved in planning their time during the day and the week, and they learn to be responsible for their decisions. Many activities are required, but children can choose when during the week they do them (they are offered several times); other activities are optional, and children can choose among them or other available activities. To guide the children's (and adults') planning, each classroom has a schedule written on the chalkboard, indicating the activities, projects, and skill groups available.

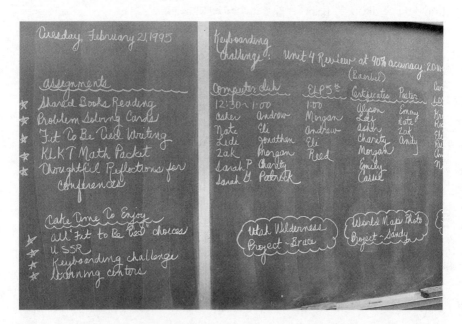

The afternoon's activities on the chalkboard in the fifth/sixth-grade classroom.

The teachers (and co-opers) help children evaluate the impact of their choices on their own activities and those of others. Generally, when children are actively involved in their own learning, they see disruptive behavior as a waste of their time, and classmates tell each other to stop because it bothers them. If a child is having difficulty with completing work, an adult may discuss the issue with the child.

For example, a teacher might initiate discussion with a fifth-grader by saying, "I don't have your article for the class newspaper, and today was the deadline—what's up?" When the student responds, "Oh, I haven't had time to finish it, I've just been really busy," the teacher asks what the student means by "busy." The student elaborates, "Well . . . I spent a lot of time playing math games on the computer, and I worked at the independent center all week . . ." The teacher guides the student in planning for improvement in this area: "Hmm. As I see it, we need to have a conversation about two issues. First, how can you take responsibility for getting your article finished? Second, let's evaluate the choices you made this week and reflect on what you might want to do differently next time."

The emphasis on children's interest and planning means that children are encouraged to find their own paths to learning. Their own interests come into their choices of what to do and how to do it, and their interests expand as they become fascinated by the adults' and other children's interests. For example, parents are encouraged to participate in parts of the curriculum that they enjoy, and this provides children with opportunities to share the adults' enthusiasm, which is contagious. Doug Bodkin, a co-oper whose two children graduated from the OC, put it this way:

> The question naturally arises how to instill enthusiasm and curiosity in children in the education process. I believe the OC facilitates the incorporation of these qualities . . . as modeled by the co-opers and teachers. It is impossible to find a teacher who has a high level of enthusiasm for all possible . . . areas of curriculum. But it is more possible to draw from the co-oper pool of parents a broad base of experience, talent, and even passion that can be modeled to the kids—and it just may strike a responsive chord in the student. When the students see co-opers really interested in the topics they are teaching, they may think to themselves, "Hey, this really must be neat if _____ is so enthusiastic about it." I've seen this occur in many different areas, from Ukrainian eggs to Shakespeare, from tie-dyeing to principles of color vision, from baking to algebra. This, I think, is the key to the success of the OC—the ability that the co-oping process has to instill the love of learning in our kids, by translating that joy of learning from their parents and their friends' parents to our kids and their friends.

For most children, the structure supports building a strong foundation around their interests and those of the other children and the adults in the classroom. A student, Sonja Knaphus, writing a few years after graduating from the OC, recalled the support she received in the OC for following her interests and making her own plans:

In the OC individuality is recognized and praised, and people learn according to their personal strengths and weaknesses. When I started the OC, in fifth grade, I was interested in math. I worked in the fifth-grade book for one week and got frustrated, it was too easy. So every day I took a chapter test, and in practically no time I had finished the sixth-grade book. I was unbearably excited and proud. I went on to do powers with [a cooper] and then algebra.

Another student, a very capable fifth-grader working on pre-algebra, wanted to develop her own math agenda. While most students checked in with the teacher once a week to evaluate progress, diagnose needs, ask questions, and correct work, Ruth explained that she needed to check in on a more flexible basis. The teacher asked, "How often will I see you about your math?" "Oh, sometimes I may need to see you every day if I need help. Sometimes I may go for a week or more before I need to check in with you. Don't worry about me. I'll see you when I need you." Some weeks the teacher saw Ruth almost daily, other weeks not at all. Ruth recorded her progress in a math notebook that she shared with the teacher every time they met. They developed a mutual trust in Ruth's educational plan, and Ruth progressed at her own pace and excelled in her math skill development.

When children have difficulty managing their time responsibly or getting involved in some areas of the curriculum, they and their teachers and parents work together to develop ways that the children can master this part of their learning. Children's consideration of how they use their time is an important part of the regular parent-teacher-kid conferences, where children reflect on how they are doing and set goals and make plans for themselves with the help of their teacher and parents. This part of the curriculum could not be taught if teachers took all the responsibility for managing the students' time.

For a few children, however, the OC learning environment can be distracting—there is so much movement, so many choices; classrooms are busy with the sounds of learning. If a child is having difficulty, a variety of educational strategies are used to help the child understand how to participate in the classroom—conversations, conferences, and contracts to help the child make progress in the areas of concern. If the child continues to struggle, the teachers help parents search for a more successful learning setting, and the child moves from the OC to another school. The few children who have such trouble seem to be those who still do not seem to discern the structure of the classroom.

On the other hand, many students who would have difficulty with the traditional structure of school thrive in this environment, along with those who breeze through academic material. Merritt Stites describes her son's response to the OC environment:

Jack was a bit different. From early on we knew he had learning problems. . . . It was absolutely necessary to find a flexible, caring way for him to learn. . . . [In the OC,] he was allowed to set goals he could achieve without embarrassment or shame. He was also given plenty of opportunities to share with other kids things he could do well, like plan a minicourse, share his athletic knowledge, tell stories, and solve classroom dilemmas. He was great with words and ideas. Just not written ones. Because he was allowed to develop at his own pace, he could feel good about his choices as he went along. . . . It gave him time to get to know himself and created a way for him to interact with other kids in a confident and responsible way. He now chooses 11th-grade Honors English, Intermediate Algebra, and a pilot's license course. . . . He just goes ahead and keeps tackling life and its hassles with good cheer.

The collaborative nature of developing learning activities and the emphasis on helping students find their "way in" is facilitated by the multifaceted structure of the classroom. Activities with multiple entry points that are open to varying interests and backgrounds—and that are worth revisiting or exploring from various angles—facilitate children's finding their own "way in" and learning from others' interests and knowledge.

How Is the Children's Learning Progress Evaluated?

Evaluation of children's progress occurs in the process of assisting their learning, so assessment is an aid to learning. The children's learning is mostly evaluated as teachers (and co-opers) work with them in collaborative activities.

For example, in the process of providing instructional support when children write reports, an assisting adult is able to observe the extent to which the children need help formulating ideas, using resources to search for information, putting ideas in their own words, or understanding the mechanics of spelling and punctuation. In addition, collaborative involvement provides key information on the extent to which the child is motivated to enter into, and sustain involvement in, the specific activity and to seek help effectively.

The OC has standardized tests (as does the rest of the school district) and occasional classroom tests (especially in spelling), but most assessment is done by teacher and co-oper observations and children's self-evaluations. Parents involved in the classroom on a regular basis can see the learning in ongoing activities rather than thinking of tests or completion of worksheets as the main sign of learning.

To see the learning in ongoing shared activities, we constantly reflect on what children are learning from their experiences. The children evaluate the process and the products of their activities in everyday classroom conversations as well as in parent-teacher-kid conferences.

Some of these conversations occur around the record-keeping charts that are kept for many of the classroom activities (designed to communicate across the many people involved in the classroom), as co-opers and teachers enter their observations of children's progress or difficulties. (In the upper grades, the students also contribute to record-keeping, such as when they keep track of their classmates' progress on drafts and revision of articles for the class newspaper when it is their turn to be its editor.)

In conferences, teachers assist students in reflecting, with their parents, on which aspects of school are easy and which areas they feel they should focus on to try to improve in over the next few months. (They receive report cards, required by the district, but these receive little attention relative to the conference itself.) Most students become skilled in self-evaluation with teachers' assistance, and their written goals for the coming months are kept handy in the classroom to serve as a resource in the students' decision making in the classroom and in the adults' support of the children's activities. Some students develop a more specific "contract" with the teacher and their parents to help them learn to manage their daily decision making.

Although OC students have little practice taking tests, they usually perform at about the level of students in other schools on the mandated standardized tests. When they reach junior high and high school, their grades and their standardized test results are higher than those of students from neighborhood schools with similar family backgrounds.

The reputation of OC graduates among junior high school teachers is that they are especially well prepared in conceptual aspects of mathematics and writing, oral expression, science, and social science compared to graduates of the more traditional neighborhood schools. They stand out in their management of their own learning, effective use of teachers as resources, social maturity, and group and community leadership. Interviews with recent graduates and their parents are consistent in reporting that OC students are especially well prepared in academic skills, managing their time and resources, motivation to learn, and leadership.

Of course, when the sixth-graders make the transition to junior high (along with other sixth-graders throughout the school district), they have an initial adjustment to make, which is challenging in the first few weeks or months. The biggest changes that OC children experience are: homework assigned by teachers without input from students, little or no involvement in planning and evaluating their own learning, and taking tests for letter grades. What our children take with them, in addition to the usual academic skills, stems from the principles that distinguish our philosophy: responsibility for their own learning, ability to make decisions and plan their time, and skills in seeking meaning, reflecting, evaluating their own learning, and solving problems.

Many OC graduates continue to seek learning situations that resemble those in which they participated at the OC, but they also learn how to participate in situations that are structured differently. When they participate in other schools, they learn how to perform in competitive situations on tasks that are not of personal interest; however, they sometimes transform them into situations that they can approach collaboratively and with interest. OC graduates often report that they get along well in varying educational settings, and with different teachers, due to their experience with many OC co-opers with varying approaches. After their close relationships with teachers and parents developed over the years in a learning community, OC graduates take with them an expectation and eagerness to engage with adults in learning.

What Sorts of Parents Participate, and What Are Their Roles in the Classroom?

The main criterion for inclusion in the program is that the family must be able to meet the co-oping commitment. Strong motivation is required for parents to be interested and able to spend three hours a week in the classroom, for each child they have in the program—in addition to curriculum meetings, monthly class meetings, and workshops. Families who choose this optional public school program, instead of neighborhood or private schools, are interested in being part of their children's education (in addition to valuing the excitement about learning, the enrichment provided by other parents in the classroom, the respect for diversity, and the community atmosphere of the school).

The program involves children and families representative of the district as a whole, including some with special needs and special skills. OC families have a wide variety of backgrounds. Parent education varies from high school degrees to Ph.D.'s. Although most are European American (which reflects the population of Salt Lake Valley), there is a wide range of economic status. Most of the parents work outside their homes in a wide range of working class or middle class occupations, such as postal worker, high school French teacher, hospital cook, artist, mathematician, firefighter, geologist, homemaker, lawyer, carpenter, construction worker, and painter; a few parents receive public assistance. The typical family structures reflect those of our region, mainly including two-parent, single-parent, and blended families. The diversity of religions represented in our families is wider than that in the valley as a whole.

The commitment of the families to their children's schooling appears in creative solutions to finding the three hours per week per child to contribute to the classrooms. In two-parent families with several children, the parents may split the co-oping responsibilities. In some families, a grandmother or adult sibling is the co-oper for a child. Some families arrange alternative co-oping responsibilities outside of ordinary school hours for part of their time commitment, such as finding materials for the teacher or arranging field trips. One mother made an arrangement with her employer to skip her lunch hour three days a week in exchange for a three-hour block of time to do her co-oping. Other parents split the three hours into two sessions to fit their time constraints. Whatever the arrangement, it is a big responsibility.

Everyone has something to offer. As their children's first teachers from birth until kindergarten, parents have been teaching day in and day out. There are many things parents do in the classroom that contribute to the children's learning environment that build on this everyday teaching role and do not require a degree in elementary education: helping children put on their smocks to paint; sitting with a small group of children and playing multiplication war or practicing times tables with a deck of cards; walking a few children to the library for books for some research; reading a Shel Silverstein poetry book with several children curled up on pillows; helping a child practice spelling words or work on editing a story.

A co-oper teaches fifth- and sixth-graders to play chess (under the loft). In the background, a group is working on watercolor techniques.

Some help children learn math, others teach Spanish or sports, with the teacher's guidance. Some bring in music or teach the children to play chess. Others are most comfortable helping the teacher with an activity the teacher has prepared. Some have particular expertise in being understanding and helpful when a child is having trouble getting going on a project. The different backgrounds and interests of the parents and their varying relationships with the children are an important resource in the classrooms.

The teachers' goals for parents' first year is to build on what they already know how to do with their children, to become comfortable with their co-oping role, and to use their intuition about children to support their own child as well as the other children in the class. With the teacher's assistance, they develop ideas about using their interests and skills to help the students learn. Other resources include the more experienced co-opers, workshops, and curriculum planning meetings. However, the main qualifications for co-oping are a commitment to participate and an interest in continuing to learn.

In the next contribution, one of the teachers, Leslee Bartlett, discusses the process of co-opers learning to be part of the structure of the community of learners, as they develop from newcomers to people who enact the principles of learning as a community.

Seeing the Big Picture

Leslee Bartlett, *teacher*

When someone walks into our community of learners for the first time, his or her initial impression is often one of chaos. How can you tell what anyone is doing? Why are those children under the table? Who is watching the ones in the hall? The range of activity may include a lone reader curled high in a loft, an animated group involved in a dice game, or several students in elaborate costume refining the dialogue of their latest play.

A visitor may also be hard put to identify the teacher among the four or five adults scattered throughout the room. That suited gentleman on his knees by the computers? The guy in jeans and T-shirt at a table, laughing with five children over a storybook? The woman in a flowing skirt sitting cross-legged on the floor, surrounded by young mathematicians intently measuring their row of brightly colored cubes? All look equally engaged with the students—no one is sitting at the desk in the corner!

If the visitor pauses more than a moment or two, however, at least one of the adults (and, most likely, several children) will excuse him- or herself from the group and approach the newcomer: While from the outside it may seem impossible to detect much of anything, once you're in the know—on the inside—the slightest variation in activity is immediately apparent.

All well-run classrooms, regardless of educational philosophy, have a highly developed internal structure that is invisible to the uninitiated, consisting of the philosophy and practices that help participants determine expectations for themselves and others. These are the "cultural" guidelines—surrounding subject matter, group discussions, playtime, and so on—that allow students to settle into a familiar pattern and free them to explore their learning. This internal structure determines how children learn with their teacher, each other, the parents, and the materials they use in the classroom. It's the structure that sets up boundaries for communication, outlining when and how students relate to one another during the day. Is this a *silent* reading time? Is it a small-group lesson in which students work independently or with a classmate? When are the times that no collaboration is required or allowed?

In most classrooms, both within the OC and in schools in general, these structural tenets are developed by the teacher, with varying degrees of help from the students. Not having been part of this important process, a chance observer would find it difficult to identify the patterns underlying the activity they see taking place. Detecting this structure becomes especially difficult when the learning environment differs greatly from what we are used to, from what we *expect* to see.

For most of us, the idea of a classroom invokes images of children sitting quietly at desks, working from textbooks or listening to a teacher impart information—a setting that conjures up memories of our own school experience, perhaps, or fits in with the popularized view we get of classrooms from TV and movies. When this image is shattered by groups of conversing students working together or moving around a classroom cluttered with a loft, a couch, independent centers, games, and blocks, it can be difficult for a newcomer to identify the learning taking place, let alone the structure that makes it possible.

First- and second-graders reading, all over the place (but not at desks). The teacher consults with some of them. (Photo OC archives)

In studying similar school programs in England in 1970, a scholar describes such an initial impression:

> Understandably, in view of all the sound and motion, the first impression may be one of chaos. In most schools, it is a false impression. "You always have to assess the nature of the noise," the headmistress of the first school the writer visited helpfully explained. "Is it just aimless chatter, or does it reflect purposeful activity?" And as the visitor becomes acclimated, it becomes clear that the activity usually is purposeful. . . . As the strangeness wears off, one becomes aware of many things. One becomes aware, for example, of the teacher's presence: in contrast to the first moments of wondering where she is, or whether she is even there at all, the visitor begins to see that the teacher is very much there and very much in charge. She seems always to be in motion, and always to be in contact with the children—talking, listening, watching, comforting, chiding, suggesting, encouraging. . . . One becomes aware, too, of the sense of structure.[1]

If you've ever explored one of those computer-generated Magic Eye pictures where at first glance all you see is a million dots, squares, or flowers—but people tell you there is a deeper image too—you may have an idea of the challenge involved in deciphering the deeper structure of the kind of learning environment I'm describing. Initially the picture looks flat and two-dimensional. Other people, often children, ooh and aah and start talking about something that, as far as you can see, just isn't there.

Someone may even begin to instruct you on how to look at the picture: "Let your eyes unfocus" or "Pretend you're looking farther away than the picture." Still you see dots, squares, flowers. But then, gradually, over in the corner, a glimmer of depth, a hint of shape, and suddenly there it is, a three-dimensional scene plain as day—the Starship Enterprise floating past Saturn, the Statue of Liberty raising her torch into the clouds, or (as in the figure on the next page), a three-dimensional image of the globe!

You've got it! You may find, however, that even once you've discovered the trick of seeing the hidden picture, you can still lose it. A shift of light or focus can make it vanish, and you need to go through the entry process again to bring it all back. The entry usually happens much more quickly, however, once you know what you're looking for—once you really believe that picture is there. This process is similar to the one that new participants in a learning community go through as they find the structure, and the learning, in their classroom.

Most children seem to quickly get beyond the seemingly chaotic nature of a learning community to be able to work within its structure. They become so directly involved with the process that they are, in a very real sense, part of the picture. Their presence, through the sharing of interests, talents, and needs, helps create the structure within which they learn.

Most parents reach a comfortable stage at which they have enough working knowledge to be highly effective in their dealings within the classroom commu-

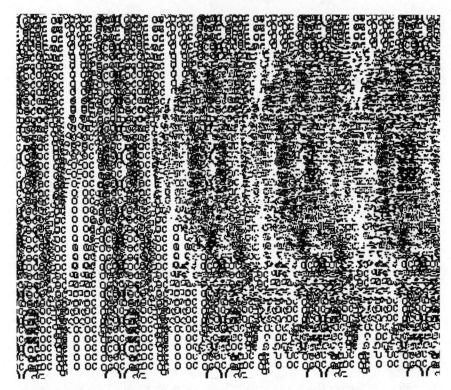

"Seeing" the big picture in the classroom requires looking deeper than the surface, as in this stereogram. If you can diverge your eyes to the right extent, you will be able to reconfigure what seems to be just a chaotic jumble of "OCs" and see a three-dimensional globe on a stand. (Stereogram created by David Magarian, an OC graduate.)

nity. Some of them become attuned to many aspects not readily visible to most and play an important part in the ongoing maintenance and growth of the program.

This structural learning process happens for adult participants in somewhat similar stages, although at widely different rates. The first stage is usually the "What's going on here?" feeling, and the reaction people have to this feeling—whether it makes them curious or horrified—often determines whether or not they look further.

Assuming that they stay—that somewhere in the chaos something sparkles at them, some giggling child or soft-spoken parent—the next step happens rather quickly. Elements of the structure begin to make themselves known. The daily routine that determines the rhythm of the room—planning circle, sharing, read-aloud, recess, or activity time—follows predictable patterns apparent to most who experience them more than once.

For parents who are successful in identifying this basic structure, the next phase involves familiarization with their personal co-oping responsibilities. Do they explore science each week with the children, or movement, or language? As an understanding of the daily workings of the room falls into place, the co-opers' energy can focus on the activity and the children who are their immediate responsibility. Who are these students that gather around the microscope or are engaged in a writing assignment? Personalities emerge, and the co-opers develop relationships with their child's classmates. Eventually, often after many struggles, they become confident of their ability to manage a group of students, to provide worthwhile activities, and to learn along with the kids. At this stage they are an integral piece of the picture, part of what makes it make sense, and many remain quite happily at this level.

Some parents pass beyond this stage and, while staying involved with their own activity, are able to glance around the room and evaluate the rest of the picture. These co-opers would be able to articulate what all 28 or so students were doing and why or why not they had made appropriate choices.

Parents at this level are very close to the next level and usually venture on, often with the help and encouragement of their teacher. They begin to take ownership of the structure and to not only recognize the strong and the weak points but also work toward improving and strengthening the learning environment. They reflect on the room as a whole and make suggestions for its smooth running. They see beyond the needs of *their* child or *their* activity group to the welfare of the community, and they feel able and willing to contribute their skills toward the community's success. They truly become learning partners with the children and the teachers.

The sense of being a *learner* within the community is a key aspect of the OC and distinguishes it from many traditional views of education in which adults are seen as givers of knowledge and children as receivers. In a learning community, participants share the learning and teaching roles; as parents become comfortable with this, they enjoy the excitement and fulfillment of learning along with others.

When parents reach this stage—or even before, as a way to help them reach it—they are sometimes asked to take on more and more of the "teacher" role. The teacher may need to leave the room for a few minutes while students are occupied with activities and may ask a co-oper to "keep an eye on things" while she is gone. Or the teacher may ask a co-oper to take over with reading the read-aloud book so that he can discuss a problem with two students in the hall. Even more responsibility may be placed on parents when they are asked to facilitate a sharing or planning circle or to listen and mediate as a group of children hash out a problem between themselves.

Through these experiences, although they may seem daunting at first, parents become increasingly comfortable working with the class as a whole. An even more challenging time comes if they are asked to officially substitute for the teacher during a morning, afternoon, or entire school day. For a few, this ultimate experience has awakened or enhanced such a feeling of confidence and love of the classroom that they have gone back to school to obtain teaching degrees! About half of our faculty members began their teaching careers as parent co-opers.

As a parent, Trudy Ross has been part of this learning community for several years and has passed through these stages to become an experienced co-oper and a trusted and sought-after substitute teacher. She remembers with some astonishment how the process began for her:

When I started I had two kids in the program—a second-grader and a kindergartner. In my second-grader's class I was doing one-on-one reading in the hall, so I didn't get to see the workings of the classroom except at circle times. I know that there were lots of fun things that kids did that year, but I only saw the end result.

In my kindergartner's class, I didn't have any preparation to do normally because for the most part co-opers facilitated the teacher's activities, which was easier for a new parent. However, when we were assigned to do minicourses, I was really terrified. I don't know why you should be scared of little kids, but I was. I didn't know all the kids, because minicourses are offered to all the classes, and I was fearful because I was doing the actual planning. I chose something I knew and had done before—holiday crafts. I had about eight kids in the group, and it worked out okay even though I was scared at first. The second minicourse went much smoother; I did science experiments, and most of the kids were from my child's class, so I knew them. We did salt crystals and sugar crystals and something to do with ink—they were fun activities and it was something I knew how to do, so I felt comfortable doing it.

The next year, my co-oping involved reading/writing activities and I was asked to do more planning on my own. I called my sister-in-law, who had wonderful plans for this stuff, and I used hers. I learned a lot from that stressful year—I learned how to adjust to a situation that wasn't cut-and-dried. I couldn't just sit back and expect somebody else to step in and fix things for me. I learned what to do with the group when I had extra time, or when we ran out of time, I learned how to finish things and not leave kids dangling and lose closure. I also learned to rely on other parents in the program. We got together and made plans so that we could coordinate our activities.

The next year was the year it came together for me. Once, the teacher asked me if I would take over in the classroom while she went to a meeting. I said I would do it, but I nearly died. I didn't think I could do it—not only would I have all those kids in the room, but I'd have parents there watching me too. I had to do circle and attendance and all that kind of stuff. I'd seen it done a million times, but to sit there and do it like I'd seen it done, with all these eyes on me, was hard. I was so flustered that it was hard to remember if I was getting everything done. I remember sitting on the floor and all those kids were looking at me and I just wanted the floor to swallow me up. But I did it and I lived through it. I found that kids know when you're feeling stressed and they'll help you. They'll remind you if you left something out, in a nice way; they'll help you out if you're feeling uncomfortable. That year was a good year in that it gave me a perspective on how the teacher sees the classroom. I began substitute teaching, and two years later I substituted for two months during a teacher's maternity leave; then I could really see the classroom from the teacher's point of view.

In the beginning I was an observer at all the meetings I went to, which helped me to learn and to see what other people felt and what they could offer. As time went on, I felt free to offer opinions or to ask questions. In the beginning I didn't have any confidence in creating curriculum, but I was able to ask teachers who would give me help and ideas. Now I feel like I can develop curriculum outside of the room and it will be successful and kids will like it. I think parents grow in this program just as much as kids do. . . . I have grown leaps and bounds from the time I walked in to now.

Trudy's story illustrates the process parents go through as they become more and more "a part of the picture." In the beginning, many pieces were unclear, and she relied on a belief and trust that "there were lots of fun things that kids did that year," although she didn't actually see them happen. She focused on her own activities and worked at becoming more confident with small groups of children. Through further experiences, some of them stressful and frightening at first, she began to take on responsibility and ownership for her own curriculum and of the class as a whole.

Trudy's experience also portrays a learning journey. Her fear of working with children she didn't know, her frustration in managing time constraints, and her struggles with planning were all ultimately viewed as *learning* experiences. This perception of herself as a learner and her willingness to take risks have enabled her to become a successful and valued member of the learning community.

The teachers, if they are to be effective members of this learning community, know their classrooms inside out. This sometimes requires a learning process for new teachers. For seasoned teachers, the jumble of bodies and materials instantly focuses into clear, sharp scenes of productive (or, sometimes, inappropriate) activities, which can then be dealt with. A large part of the teacher's job is to guide the other learners through the "seeing" process. This happens through discussion as questions about the structure and learning are raised, through modeling, and most of all by providing experiences for the students and parents to take responsibility for the structure and for their learning within it.

For example, teachers help students "see" and contribute to the structure in discussions about noise level; in these discussions, the students offer their opinions and examples of what would constitute an appropriate amount of talking during activity time. As a group they decide on guidelines for behavior during this time and then are expected to follow them. If someone becomes too unruly, the other students very likely call his or her attention to the noise level set. They realize that someone is out of bounds and take responsibility for helping that other child—since the students have helped construct and thus come to understand the structure. This process is repeated many times in all aspects of the classroom, from brainstorming topics for study to negotiating for extra recess.

Parents also are helped to see and become part of the picture through their increasing responsibility in the classroom. In addition, the parents' needs and interests help create and mold the learning environment. The structure of each morning and afternoon is often dramatically influenced by the co-opers and by the learning experiences they provide. For example, on Monday afternoons one year, all four parents engaged in various math activities, and all of the time between lunch and recess was spent working on math in one way or another. Tuesday afternoons were very different—the kids were involved in many varied projects: One parent worked on fitness throughout the year, and he often had almost half the class involved in an outside game, while the rest of us worked with a talented artist, solved word problems, or learned about Utah history.

Because of the attention given to children's and parents' changing interests and needs, the structure of a learning community itself is constantly subject to change. Part of the teacher's role is to determine which changes can be accommodated within the overall theme of the classroom without losing the integrity of the bigger picture. This calls for a great deal of fluidity as well as a strong grounding in what the overall picture needs to be. For, on top of the deeper "big picture," there are countless scheduling variations that can make the learning harder to see. These are the "dots" that make the classroom seem chaotic to newcomers and that require teachers to make innumerable on-the-spot decisions throughout the day.

For example, what happens when four co-opers have brought activities for small groups and most of the children want to work at the independent science exploration center? Or when one child shares in morning circle about the praying mantis she found and everyone's hand goes up with a valuable discovery story of their own? Or half the class marches in from recess steaming about the conflicts encountered during a kickball game, providing a great opportunity for learning to solve problems?

A teacher who views teaching in terms of being a learning partner will recognize the value in allowing students to follow a topic of high interest, share personal experiences, and spend classroom time working through a problem-solving situation. The teacher will also realize the need to balance these valuable experiences with parents' expectations and other needs of the classroom as a whole. Adapting the schedule to incorporate the immediate and long-range needs of children, parents, and teachers is a constant challenge.

For some, no matter how long or how intently they gaze into the dots, the bigger three-dimensional picture never emerges, or it comes but stays so fleetingly that its true meaning cannot be grasped. Some children find the amount of activity or the responsibility of choices too confusing and get lost among the changing patterns. Some struggle with the process, finding it difficult to relate to the other parts of the picture or to find meaningful learning for themselves.

The same is true for some of the adults, who find the learning community too different from their perception of what schooling should be or find the amount of time required to discern the structure and become a part of it too great. These students and their families are then helped to explore other educational settings in which the child's or the parents' needs can be better met. Although for many of us involved in this learning community, it seems the best possible environment for our needs, the OC approach may not be appropriate for everyone.

When people become part of a learning community, they begin a journey that, if successful, will enhance and enlarge their world for the rest of their lives. It is not always an easy journey, but as they develop the persistence to look closely at the "dots" and then beyond, into the deeper picture, they often find a greater vision not only in their classroom but within themselves as well. The joys and frustrations of viewing *life* as a learning environment open up a string of vistas beyond imagining.

Note

1. C. E. Silberman, *Crisis in the Classroom: The Remaking of American Education* (New York: Random House, 1970), 225–26.

PART TWO

How Is This a Community?

When we first started in the OC, we didn't know anyone. Now we know most of the families and are quite close to some. We have developed a commitment to the program and the people. Like marriage and family, committed relationships have taught us a lot about where to put our energies, whom to trust, and where our best feelings come from. Last fall, when our baby Isaac was born with serious handicaps, . . . there were so many meals brought in by OC families that we didn't have to cook for three weeks. All this attention was provided not just by close friends at the OC, but also by families that we really didn't know very well . . .

Someone may wonder what all this has to do with teaching children to read and write. I think what has happened with the OC is that it has developed into a community . . . one that cares for its members in difficult times, accepts their differences, and shares the skills of its members. Because of this, my children are taught not only by dedicated teachers, but also by parents, many of whom have helped and been helped by [each other's] families and have come to care about each others' welfare. I greatly value this kind of education—a community passing on both the education basics and also skills for living.

—Ann Larsen, an OC parent, writing in Al Fresco
(an OC Philosophy/Education Committee booklet, 1988–89)

A co-oper, a teacher, and classmates enjoy each child's year-end award.

A Home and School Community

Ann Chalmers Pendell, *parent and co-chair of the Steering Committee, the central decision-making and coordinating committee*

What about OC you ask?

It's a family, a friendly community, a structure that is continually changing its structure to insure the process of learning is always fresh.

It's a learning space that draws kids in, a user-friendly environment that is more like a best friend's bedroom than a classroom.

It's taking advantage of the energy and uniqueness of parents and sharing it with kids.

When it works there is joy in learning and creative minds are developed.

When it does not, we figure out ways to make it work . . .

OC is what it teaches; school, life, learning are not separable.

Our children are in good hands;

Your hands.

David Pendell, Al Fresco: An OC Family Portrait

I put my first child in the OC because I wanted to be part of her school life. When my husband and I chose to adopt her, it was because we wanted the experience of raising her. We didn't want to shuttle her off to a day care or school for someone else to raise. When Alysha was old enough to attend preschool, I found a parent co-op, and when she was old enough to attend elementary school, I heard about the OC and was glad to be able to continue participating in her education.

The OC community became important not only as a support in educating our children but also as a community of families with similar goals—helping our children to get the best education we can provide. Other committed parents provide activities for our kids that the teacher and my husband and I cannot. David and I are both artists and can provide techniques and insights for their creative efforts, but we also want them to be able to work with adults who are dedicated to and enthusiastic about math, science, history, ecology, and other aspects of today's world.

A Community Caring for the Children

The community extends beyond educating our children at school. For 10 years, our family has gone on OC class camping trips sponsored and planned by parents, exploring places we might have never seen on our own. With our children's classmates and their families we have hiked, shared food, and shared good experiences and bad, warm and cold, the joy of discovery and of watching our children grow.

We have learned about children and how they learn and about how to work with other adults. We have developed deep friendships with other families in our children's classes and have memories and photo albums full of good family experiences that include our OC community. The children's learning is enhanced

OC families and teachers gather for the winter holiday celebration, with warm greetings and a song that the oldtimers annually teach everyone else, followed by a family brunch in the classrooms. (Photo OC archives)

by the caring evident in the OC community. For example, the community supports its members in times of family crisis by providing emotional support and practical support—bringing meals, providing child care, and helping with carpools and other responsibilities.

When we are co-oping with other parents, we can exchange concerns and advice regarding our children's development. The classroom community is also supported by parents sharing information about each child at the monthly parent-teacher meetings. This helps the teacher and the whole parent group be aware of a child's hidden talents or particular issues or family circumstances that help explain a child's behavior.

Often, other parents are able to point out characteristics of the children that the parents may have overlooked. As parents we often focus on behavior that is bothering us, and in our concern we may overlook the good points or progress in our child. It is helpful to have another parent comment on how successful our child was in their classroom activity or how supportive our child was when another child had a problem. At one class meeting, a parent was concerned that her child was not making friends and asked the parents to encourage him to play with different classmates. Other parents responded that they had observed the child making friends at school and were able to assure the parent that her child was making progress in expanding his circle of friends.

Co-oping helps parents understand their children. We see them in a different setting, yet we're a part of it. So when they come home and say, "Brian hit John and had to problem solve with a co-oper today," we know who Brian and John are and probably the dynamics of their relationship. One co-oper commented that the OC influenced how she and her child relate to each other: "When you see your child in relation to the rest of the children in the class, you are much more accepting, easing many frictions. That also works in reverse, as they see they don't have the only 'strange' parents."

Because we know what our children are working on at school, we can also support their learning at home. If they comment on a visual pattern, math problem, or news event that relates to their school experience, we understand and are able to develop the concept further.

As part of the OC community, parents also have the support of the teacher's example for their parenting and their co-oping. Every time I am in the classroom I am learning from the teacher. Just observing how the teacher manages the class or a particular child is a lesson on how I could manage a kid or group of kids. These lessons also come home with me, sometimes in desperation when I am trying to resolve a conflict and the method I am using is not working. I stop and think, "How would my teacher do this?" I reach for help in my memory bank, and the OC philosophy is there, helping me see that I don't have to take charge to find a solution, but can instead listen to the child.

A parent supporting her child's learning at school.

Coming to See Children as a Key Part of the Community

Parents who are a part of their children's classroom come to understand the respect for children's input in the OC community. In classroom circle meetings, the children, parents, and teacher express themselves in a safe environment and listen and support others. In activity groups with one adult and several kids, the children often gain "authority" as a group, and the parent learns that valuing their input makes the activity a more effective learning experience. As another parent, Andy Hayes, wrote, "Our kids learn that people are valuable resources and fellow discoverers. A place of learning like the OC can be wonderfully spontaneous, where there isn't [a] hierarchy that is difficult or intimidating to kids and parents." In "kid co-oping," in which children develop activities for their classmates, they learn how to listen to and lead their peers—and these experiences help them contribute to the community, with greater understanding of adults' roles and the challenges involved in leading a group.

Parents often have to learn to be flexible enough to include the children's input. I learned about flexibility when I was on a field trip to the zoo with my daughter's class. One of the first exhibits my group of five girls came to was the gorilla enclosure. The girls were really interested and seemed in no hurry to move on. My normal method of visiting the zoo is to hurry around the whole zoo in order to see everything, so I became concerned that we would run out of time unless we moved on. We had two hours to see the zoo before rejoining the rest of the class for the carpool back to school. My suggestions that we continue on our way were wasted, as the girls seemed quite content watching the gorillas' actions and interactions. I tried to be patient for a while. Then, as I stood there on that beautiful sunny day, observing, I realized that there was no reason to rush. Observing the gorillas really was interesting, so I decided to follow the girls rather than lead them. It turned out to be one of the best trips to the zoo that I have had. We didn't see everything, but we really *saw* the animals we did visit.

In leading activity groups, co-opers learn to be open to changing their plans in accord with children's inspiration. Generally when I lead an art activity in the classroom, I encourage the kids to be creative and develop their own ideas within a framework. In my son's kindergarten class, a boy who was having difficulty working within the classroom structure had trouble choosing an activity and preferred to do his "own thing" rather than follow directions. My project was to make birds out of cardboard tubes and paper, but this boy wanted to know if he could make "jet airplanes." I said there certainly were similarities between planes and birds, so go ahead. This boy—who generally avoided activities—had a wonderful time and made very creative jet airplanes. He learned as much about manipulating the materials and being creative as he would have if he had made birds.

Another parent told me about the unforeseen benefits of being flexible to children's input in a spelling group she was leading. In the process of discussing how to spell certain words, the group started to discuss what words were. They talked about how words were symbols and what other symbols there were. Then the group began exploring pantomime, charades, and rebus puzzles, following the kids' interests around words. The changed activity went far beyond what the parent had planned.

Shared Decision Making and Trust as Children Move beyond the Community

OC kids are involved in a lot of decision making in the classroom, and this process carries over to home and out-of-school activities and later schooling. A friend of our family thought that I was being far too lenient with my kids by including them in decision making. Now that my kids are older, though, I find that they are especially honest with us. Because they know we value their input, we develop mutual respect and trust.

OC kids trust the adults around them and are comfortable asking for help when they need it. My son's violin teacher commented to me that she admired the fact that the OC kids she knew could express their feelings honestly. When she asks them to do something they don't want to do, they tell her, and then she can negotiate a compromise with them, whereas some other children agree to do things they never intend to follow through on.

Parents whose older children have made the transition from the OC to junior high school say that their kids did well in junior high because they were comfortable asking the teachers for more information or other help they needed to accomplish their assignments, and the teachers appreciated having students who were interested enough to ask questions. OC kids have confidence that adults are part of their community and that adults will assist them in learning or in solving other problems.

Part of what parents learn at the OC is when to help and when to step back. When my daughter graduated from the OC and began attending a neighborhood junior high school, she and I both had concerns about the transition. Her concerns were about leaving the familiar, having to make new friends, remembering her locker combination, and being able to find her way from class to class. I was concerned about her entering a school that seemed to be bound by a bureaucratic system whose main goals were discipline and "crowd control." In addition, I was suddenly not part of the system. It was now solely Alysha's job to keep track of assignments and deadlines and to let me know when she needed help.

Fortunately, OC kids are prepared to be responsible for completion of their work, and they are accustomed to asking for help when they need it. In the beginning of seventh grade, Alysha asked for help on almost all of her homework. I wanted to help her rather than have her feel so overwhelmed that she would give up in frustration, but I didn't want to spend the rest of her school years helping her complete her assignments. In the beginning I would type a report she dictated to me; later I had her type or write the report, and I would help her edit it and get the final copy ready. As the school year progressed, I reduced my input, and Alysha took more responsibility. Our experience at the OC prepared both of us for this process of asking for and giving the necessary support on the way to greater responsibility.

The OC experience has been much more than I expected it to be. I expected to participate in my children's education, but in addition to participating in their education, I became educated myself. Our family is more closely bonded because of our participation with our children in their education. We are richer for the friendships we have made through the OC, and we have learned many lessons, social as well as academic, which also apply to our lives outside the OC community.

Coming Home to School

Carolyn Goodman Turkanis, *teacher*
Leslee Bartlett, *teacher*

The continuing involvement of parents and of children from before they enter school to after graduation contributes to the commitment and comfort of this learning community. In the younger grades, there are a lot of little siblings that visit. These preschoolers will later be OC students—and they already feel that they belong and don't want to leave when their parents need to go. Leslee remembers an enchanting two-year-old who would come in with her older brother. Soon she was a student in Leslee's classroom—and recently she was interviewed as an OC graduate for a BBC film about the OC. One four-year-old whose big sister was in Leslee's class just couldn't wait to have Leslee as his teacher, so his mother hired Leslee to take him to a museum one summer day so he would be satisfied to have Leslee as his teacher *now*.

Three-year-olds join in their older sisters' and brothers' classroom celebrations; they dance around on the playground, holding hands with kids that are two years older—the little ones are part of the community already. By the time their first day of kindergarten arrives, they and the teachers begin the school year feeling that they are in the company of friends and thinking of school as a place that is known, comfortable, and loved.

For OC students, school is not a place that you *have* to go, but a place that you *want* to go. Recently, two little boys came into school after a weekend, and Leslee said, "Hi, how was your weekend?" and one said "Too long! I wish the weekend was just so quick, so I could get back to school." John Hayes, as a parent, reflected on the importance of enjoyment of learning in this school community:

> I am a product of traditional education in Utah which served me well and prepared me to be competitive in higher education. When I compare the reluctance with which my three grade-schoolers view the ending of school,

however, to the ultimate jubilation associated with the last day of school that I experienced as a child, I understand clearly why I opt for this educational alternative for my children. Coincident to this writing, this very day, in fact, my nine-year-old daughter asked me if I ever cried on the last day of school. Incredulous, I confessed to the negative.[1]

Carolyn is always amazed at the number of fifth- and sixth-grade moms and dads who come with their children to share the first day of school, to enjoy the sense of learning and adventure. Instead of dropping their children off, many parents join in this new beginning. It is common to have not only the usual three or four morning co-opers participating in the classroom but also an extra seven or eight parents who have come "just for the fun of it." They join in the renewal of old friendships and the initiation of new ones, sitting in circle for summer stories and planning the very first morning together. As the morning progresses and the class engages in projects and activities, the "extra parents" quietly say good-bye to their children and go off to the other parts of their lives, knowing that soon they will return to the classroom in their official role as co-oper.

OC graduates also come in to visit. In fact, having graduates visit seems to be one of our rites of passage. Upper-grade students watch junior high and high school students return to visit throughout each school year, knowing that in time they will be the graduates returning to visit, sharing their current experiences and reflecting on their OC learning.

Several years ago, right before the end of the school year, when Carolyn's aging but all-too-sharp father asked her the usual, "So how was school today?" she replied that she was absolutely exhausted with end-of-the-year activities. He wondered how she could be exhausted: "It's the end of the year. Things ought to be winding down."

"Well, actually, things are winding up. I'm getting ready to graduate the sixth-graders."

"You're not graduating them! They're graduating themselves, aren't they?"

"Well, actually, we're all graduating them. The whole OC is graduating them."

"Don't make such a fuss over it! Just say good-bye and shut the door!"

During the sixth-grade graduation ceremony a week later, Carolyn reported her father's advice to the assembled students and families and added, "This may be the beginning of good-bye, but the door is always open."

Recently, as Carolyn sat down to begin the morning in circle with her fifth- and sixth-graders, she glanced up to see two former students, grinning. They eagerly announced, "Today is parent-teacher conference day at our junior high. We've come to spend the morning with you!" The kids already seated in circle applauded the seventh-grade visitors and scooted over on the carpet to make room. No sooner had they adjusted their seating arrangement than three more smiling kids appeared in the classroom doorway. More applause! More scooting! Within minutes this same scenario was repeated over and over again until the kids had wholeheartedly welcomed back 18 junior high school kids. What a sight! Thirty-three current OC kids and 18 former OC kids crowded together in circle, laughing, visiting, reconnecting.

A sixth-grader reads a message to younger students at graduation; three prior graduates help Carolyn, at left, with the ceremony.

Co-opers and prior graduates enjoy hearing Carolyn read excerpts from letters in each student's graduation book.

After circle and planning, the kids quickly became involved in classroom learning activities. It would have been difficult to distinguish the fifth- and sixth-graders from the seventh- and eighth-graders (except, perhaps, by height). They became, fairly quickly, 51 kids learning together in an expanded community of learners.

By midmorning, three high school kids, formerly in the OC, arrived to join in. An assembly had canceled their fourth-period class. "We could have gone to the assembly, but we thought this would be much more fun!" What might other kids this age do on a day off from school? Sleep late, or go to a mall, or watch TV? OC kids return to school. They know the door is always open. These 21 kids knew they didn't have to call and get permission—they knew they belonged here, and they knew we would welcome them back, and this is where they chose to go on their day off.

The attraction of connection with the classroom has recently included the return of several OC graduates as adults. One is now a teacher in the OC; another is co-oping for her younger sister.

Another graduate is a volunteer who is co-oping just for the fun of it. Ollie Knudsen, now a college student, periodically popped in while he was in high

OC teacher Ruth (Kottler) Hansen in the lower right corner, when she was an OC student. Marilyn Johnston, the program's first teacher, is at the left. (Photo OC archives)

school for a hug and a chat or a thoughtful meander through the classrooms. When he was 20, Ollie continued his spontaneous visits, always pausing to watch kids involved in activities, to look at artwork on bulletin boards, and to reminisce about his own days spent learning in the OC. On one visit, he lounged comfortably in the pillow-filled bathtub, remarking quietly, "I spent a lot of time in this tub as a sixth-grader, thinking deep thoughts. It's nice to be back!"

Ollie visited again recently for the usual hug and chat, then volunteered, "I think I'd like to co-op this year! Could I teach creative writing? What day could I come in each week?" Carolyn connected him immediately to the already-started annual book publishing project, one that he too had experienced as an OC kid. On his first day as an official OC co-oper, Ollie arrived with such a look of excitement and anticipation! He chatted briefly with Carolyn about his co-oping plans, then he joined kids and parents in morning circle. After introductions and planning, he was ready to meet with kids, browsing through books published by previous classes and chatting with kids about possibilities for this year's project. After just a few minutes, Ollie said, "Carolyn, I'm going to need a clipboard, pencil, and paper. I'll need to take some notes as I talk with kids about their ideas." A short while later, he observed, "Carolyn, I'm going to need a classroom record-keeping slip. I need to keep track of the kids I work with today so I'll know who to work with next week when I co-op." As Ollie finished his first morning as a co-oper, he requested, "Carolyn, next week I'd like my name added to the schedule on the chalkboard with all the kids who will be working with me."

The door is always open.

Note

1. In *Al Fresco: An OC Family Portrait* (an OC Philosophy/Education Committee booklet, 1988–89).

Setting the Scene
Coordinating a Classroom Community

Donene Polson, *teacher*

Throughout my years at the OC, first as a parent and then also as a teacher, I have given a lot of thought to the structure and coordination of the classroom, which supports parents, children, and teachers in creating a community of learners. I had enrolled my children in the OC because I liked the idea of students, teachers, and parents all working together as a community to help children learn. After spending a great deal of time as a co-oper, I returned to the university to earn a degree in elementary education and then added the role of teacher to my established parent role in the OC.

In a community of learners, a tremendous amount of work is done behind the scenes—extensive coordination, planning, and structure allow the daily learning and activities to flow smoothly. It is like a ballet, where the performers move so gracefully, flowing to their positions and cooperating with such beauty that it looks deceptively simple. Yet we know it is preparation, planning, refining, and cooperation that allow the production to run so smoothly. In the OC, the coordination is based on backstage efforts among the adults of each classroom, teamwork among children and adults, and daily and weekly routines around which children's, co-opers', and teachers' activities are organized. Although the teacher plays a unique role, coordination and planning are shared among all participants and extend beyond individual classrooms to the OC program as a whole.

Backstage Coordinating among Adults in the Classroom

A key support for coordinating the classroom community is the collaboration among adults. Before the school year begins, parents and the teacher hold a meeting at a family's home to prepare for the upcoming year, getting acquainted and establishing weekly co-oper schedules and curriculum areas for the parents' contributions to the classroom teaching. As teacher, I figure out how to coordinate the co-opers' schedules, interests, and talents from their work, hobbies, and outside activities to create a balanced weekly structure that becomes the framework for the children's activities.

Many events throughout the year support co-opers in learning OC philosophy and educational practices, as well as fostering relationships among the adults and families. In addition to monthly classroom parent meetings, such events include a New Families Orientation, a philosophy workshop, curriculum area meetings, a winter holiday dinner, a classroom camping trip (sponsored by parents) for the whole family, and all-program family picnics.

At the monthly parent meetings, co-opers and the teacher plan curriculum and discuss what can be done to help in the classroom. Often I take a topic to the co-opers that the children have decided they would like to study, and we develop curriculum together around the topic. The co-opers brainstorm the resources that we have in the community and consider the skills and resources they and the teacher can bring to the project.

We also share information about the children at parent meetings in order to help co-opers better understand each child's learning style and life events that connect with what happens in the classroom. I remember coming to the OC with only the needs of my own children as my priority. However, by the second year, I broadened my attention as a co-oper to wanting to help all the children in the class.

Co-opers who teach the same subject sometimes develop projects together. For example, Las Vegas Day was planned by five math co-opers who worked together to teach math in a way that was interesting (shown in the photo on the next page). They covered probability and games of chance (recommended as math studies by the state core curriculum guidelines). Activities included bingo—to study probability—and Twenty-One. We played a dice game in which children added, subtracted, multiplied, and so on, to try to run their points down to zero without going below it; when they lost a game, they lost a poker chip. Soon many children had lost the chips with which they started, so they came up with the idea of earning chips by completing math drill sheets. The team of co-opers had planned an activity that the children built on.

Becoming a Classroom Community:
Team Building with Children

In support of building a community in the classroom, as well as fostering children's interpersonal skills, the first weeks of each school year are spent in cooperative games and projects. We take an all-day hike in the mountains to share the beauties of nature and learn more about each other. There are always fantastic finds and conversations about the trees, rocks, and wildlife as new friendships are formed.

A co-oper playing a game of chance with a group studying probability. (Photo courtesy Donene Polson.)

Children interview each other for newspaper articles so that we can get to know each other better. The co-opers help children learn to ask interesting questions, such as "What is your favorite story about a sport at which you excel?" and "Do you have a pet who recently died? What happened?" (There was a pet obituary section in our newspaper.)

As a new co-oper, I felt that the time at the beginning of the year should have been spent directly on academic subjects. I was looking for the same textbook learning that I had when I attended school, not recognizing that academic learning was involved in observing wildlife, writing questions, and interviewing. Then another parent told me that one of her children went to a district program for gifted and talented children where the teacher began the first day of school with testing and homework; her child was frightened and ill by the end of the day. We both now value the time the OC takes to set up a warm, safe environment where there is trust among the child, classmates, and the teacher.[1]

We build classroom unity over the year through the OC tradition of sharing circle. On Monday mornings in my class, students have an opportunity to tell the group about their weekend and what is going on in their lives—a lost tooth, a new pet, a brother in the hospital, or a letter from someone special—and I also share my experiences with the children. Everyone sits on the floor, including the teacher and the parent co-opers, and we can all see each others' faces, so each person has an equal and involved position.

The sharing topics often relate to the curriculum or allow us to discuss current events. For example, during one circle, two students told us about their visit to the public library in which a man with a gun came in and took hostages. The man was eventually killed by the police, which made national news. The children "sharing" this dramatic event brought us to a class discussion of social problems and how we support each other in times of crisis.

It took a while for me to see the significance of the sharing circle, especially when some children frequently shared plastic action figures, troll dolls, or comic books. I now realize that this process gives children a chance to develop speaking skills and respectful listening in a relaxed environment.

Sometimes I select themes for a week's sharing in an effort to expand our knowledge about each other. We get to know about each other's families and friends, interests, hobbies, hopes, and dreams. It facilitates our relationships as well as the opportunities to learn from and support each other.

Planning and Coordinating the Days and Weeks

As teacher, I coordinate how everything fits together in my classroom over the year, incorporating the co-opers' areas of interest while making sure that the activities are relevant and interesting to the children. The weekly schedule devel-

A child shows his "sharing" around the circle after describing it.

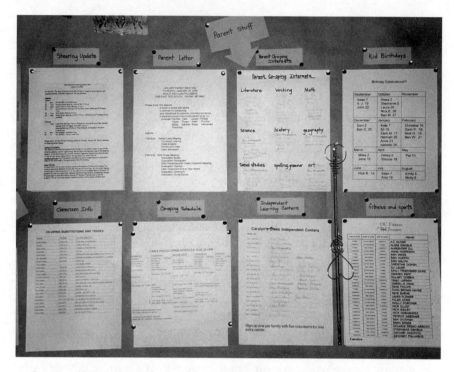

A classroom bulletin board for parents, with parent letters, Steering Committee "Update," co-opers' schedules, and plans. (Photo OC archives)

oped by the teacher and co-opers establishes a routine so that the students can anticipate who the co-opers will be and which curriculum areas will be addressed when. This is communicated in regular parent letters outlining the upcoming activities at school, as well as through the morning and afternoon schedule of activities written on the chalkboard as a resource for children to make initial and ongoing choices and plan their day.

We coordinate our activities several times each day in circle. The day's first circle unites us as a group and allows us to share, conduct classroom business, and plan the morning activities. A typical morning in my fourth/fifth-grade class might look like this (the afternoon planning circle involves a similar schedule):

8:30   *Morning circle* (sharing, business, planning)
9:00   *Reading-writing workshop*
       Literature study group with a co-oper
       Grammar skills games with a co-oper
       Independent computer group
       Writing response group with teacher
       Independent learning centers
       Snack center

10:20	Recess
10:35	*Activity time*
	Music with a co-oper
	Cooking group with a co-oper
	Writing group with teacher
	Newspaper group with a co-oper
	Computer group
11:20	Clean up and co-opers leave
11:30	*Read-aloud circle* (the teacher reads aloud to the children)
11:50	Lunch

During the planning circle, the teacher and co-opers give brief descriptions or demonstrations of each activity that is offered and discuss the options for independent activities. After discussion and clarification, the children choose from among the required and optional activities and make their plans for the morning. If more children are interested in particular groups than there is space during that session, more sessions may be added, or a random method (such as picking a stick with children's names on them from a can) may be used to determine which students join the activity during that time. Sometimes teachers or co-opers choose members of a group if the co-opers haven't had a chance to work with certain children yet, or to ensure that group members can work well together for a specific project, or to provide short lessons to children who need to focus on specific skills (such as a math concept or grammar skill).

Throughout the day, as they work in the small groups led by the co-opers and teacher, children of different ability levels, grades, and genders work together. If a child were constantly in the same group, the diversity that we all have to offer would be lost. Mixing of groups often occurs on the basis of children's interests, as they choose new projects. For example, when we prepare to read fairy tales, the books are displayed on a table with a sign-up sheet, and the students join together on the basis of wanting to read the same book. As long as the interest is there, differences and diversity complement the activity. Although some parents worry that a child with advanced skills in some area isn't challenged in a group with varied skills, a child who excels at something benefits from opportunities to clarify and share this knowledge with classmates.

Children Sharing in Planning and Coordination

Many aspects of the OC involve shared responsibilities throughout the community; planning and leadership are not just the teacher's domain. Taking the position of facilitator in the classroom allows me to build respectful relationships with children and co-opers, and to learn from the students and the co-opers as they learn from me.

For the most part, space and resources are shared. There are no desks—the room contains many small tables for small groups to work together, a carpeted area where the class can sit in a circle, a snack center and learning centers, a loft,

Children of different ages and skills benefit from reading together. These two read comfortably in the classroom loft. (Photo courtesy Donene Polson.)

and computer stations. The only exclusively private spaces are the children's mailboxes, coat hooks, and "cubbies" where notebooks, papers, and notes for home are stored. Paint, markers, and paper are set out on a supply table, and students remind others to take equal shares and to use supplies responsibly—"If you use up all these supplies, there won't be any when we need them. Take what you need, but just leave some for the rest of us." Sharing community supplies helps the students become aware of mutual needs in community living.

During the first days of school, we create our own Classroom Constitution. We brainstorm as a whole class about what makes a safe and productive learning environment. We then break into small groups of children, with a co-oper or the teacher acting as recorder, to generate guidelines that are made into positive action statements. Each group brings its easel paper filled with ideas back to circle, where the ideas are discussed and debated. Once the group has achieved consensus, we all sign our names at the bottom of the constitution as you can see in the photo. The process takes time, but it is very important in helping students take ownership of and contribute to a physically and emotionally safe learning environment.

At times, children take important leadership roles, coordinating with each other and with adults. Chief among these are times that children plan whole

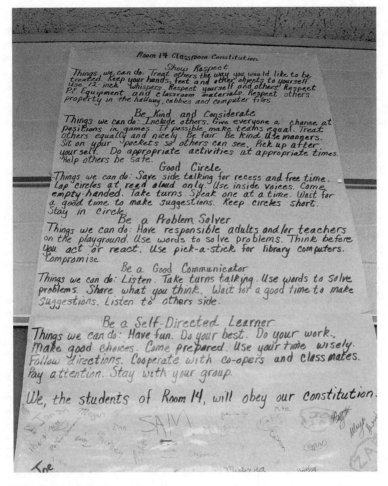

One classroom's constitution.

activities, with teacher support. On Thursday afternoons, when there are no adult co-opers in my class, we have "kid co-oping." Children who volunteer for the role of kid co-oper come prepared to help classmates learn from their expertise in the activity they design (which might be cooking, paper airplane making, chess, math games, story writing, art, computer games, crafts, and so on). Kid co-opers announce the theme of their activity in circle, and other children sign up for their activities, just as with adult co-oping.

Kid co-oping gives children experience in communicating, taking responsibility, leading and cooperating in a group, and motivating themselves and others. It helps them understand the structure of their learning environment, as another teacher, Leslee Bartlett, pointed out:

When children take the role that the co-opers usually have, organizing activities and needing to coordinate participants' ideas and involvement, they have a chance to learn the adults' roles in planning and coordinating. This facilitates their development of an understanding (parallel to that of the co-opers) of how the classroom functions as a whole as they take on the responsibility of organizing their co-oping activity. Kid co-oping makes the backstage aspects of the classroom something that the children have the opportunity to learn about by making it part of the children's performance.

This experience makes the children more empathetic to the challenges of co-oping and provides numerous opportunities for learning about problem solving.

One of the favorite kid co-oping activities—planning and performing a play—always involves problem solving. The children struggle to coordinate ideas for the play and to meet the challenges of planning together. Although the kid co-oper has the responsibility of organizing the play, other children are also invested in decisions. The children are expected to solve problems (such as who gets which part) as they arise; however, the teacher is always available for help and support when needed. My daughter Breanne, an OC graduate, reflected as a 14-year-old about her own development through OC plays: "My skills were improved by participating in drama. . . . Leadership and self-esteem came from performing and instructing. Rather than just learning from one teacher, I learned from all my classmates and co-opers. Students were so involved that they rarely wanted to create a discipline problem."

One year, my class was enthused about extending the Egg Baby City activity that they had started during kid co-oping afternoons the year before, in Leslee Bartlett's class. Leslee describes how Egg Baby City developed through the children's initiative and planning in her classroom:

A group of third-, fourth-, and fifth-graders had had experience with egg babies in a prior class—they had drawn little faces on eggs, given them names and personalities, made clothes and little houses for them, and taken care of them. One day, two fourth-grade girls wrote me a note: "Leslee, we need to talk to you about something really important, and please, please, please, let us do this, and when can we talk privately?" signed Morgan and Moey. I found a time to talk to them as soon as I could—I was very intrigued. They had an idea for an egg baby city. They wanted to present it to the class to see if their classmates would like to do it on Thursday afternoons, when we traditionally have kid-co-oping.

I said "Sure," and at the next circle time they presented their idea to the class. What they envisioned was a whole city, and they had thought up all the different jobs you would have in a city—a day care, a school, a bakery, a drive-in, a bank, a doctor's office, a dentist, a dead person. At this point I raised my hand and said, "Excuse me, what does the dead person do?" They said, "That's the person who takes care of the dead people when they die." "Oh, you mean the mortician." "Yes." So they had that as well.

All the kids loved the idea, and during that afternoon they signed up for the job they would like to have in the city, and the next week we started. The two girls who had thought up the idea called themselves the Congress. They asked to use the classroom play money, and from that they paid a salary to everyone who had a shop or a job to get things going. And then the kids took it from there.

They made signs and advertisements for their businesses. They began to have sales if business was slow. Some new businesses sprang up—at one point, one of the fifth-grade boys got out cards and set up a casino, playing Twenty-One. He immediately became one of the wealthiest citizens of Egg Baby City.

The "dead person" was a girl who made a wonderful little cemetery and office building for herself. One day I overheard her talking to a friend— "You know, people are taking really good care of their egg babies and no one is dying, so I think I'm going to start a retirement home." And she branched out into a new business.

About two weeks into the city, which took place Thursday afternoons, the Congresswomen told me they had a problem and needed to have a whole-group discussion. They announced to the kids that they needed to start collecting taxes because they were running out of money and had no other way to get it back. So they told the kids that for every $30 they had, the kids would need to pay back $1 so there would be enough money to continue paying everybody—otherwise the economy would break down.

Most kids were amenable to this, but the "casino kid" and his partner didn't think this was fair, because they'd end up having to pay much more than anyone else, since they had, over the last week or so, collected almost all of the money. One of the casino kids asked, "What happens if we don't pay?" And the Congresswoman said, "Then you'll have to go to court, and I'm the judge." So he ended up paying his taxes, and the city continued.

Egg Baby City lasted about four weeks in my classroom. It was an unusual kind of kid co-oping, going beyond the usual five or six separate activities to coordinate the whole classroom in a common theme, since all groups directly related to the management of the city. Each of the children's businesses served as an activity in which the kids participated, with the owners taking the co-oper role. In addition to generating valuable academic curriculum, the city provided many opportunities to learn and use organizational, management, and leadership skills.

In my classroom the next year, the children extended Egg Baby City in ways that often involved the academic curriculum, especially in math, reading, and social studies. We scaled the egg babies' houses to the size of egg babies. Some of the children chose to "buy" lots on the classroom loft and bring in their dollhouses, inherited from the egg babies' "parents," so we talked about probate tax and inheritance tax, and they looked up assessments on tax tables. A carpet company and wallpaper company started up for the dollhouses—and we calculated square feet and square inches. One child started her own version of H&R Block and charged other children to do their taxes for them. But some children didn't want to pay her, so they checked out the booklets to take home and read so that they could do their own taxes.

Two girls suggested having elections for an Egg Baby City Council to decide what happens in the city and make rules. This was around the time of local elections, so we looked at real ballots and read the newspaper for election news. Those who ran for office gave an election speech to the class, and everyone had the opportunity to vote on election day.

When the children began discussing how to increase their incomes, they de-

Egg babies, with their "parents" and a house. (Photo courtesy Donene Polson.)

cided to borrow money from the Egg Baby City Bank to start small businesses. The businesses started out selling soda and cookies, but soon they had the idea to start a real business and make real money. They organized a fund-raiser and started an environmentally beneficial project, printing inexpensive labels that could be pasted over previously used envelopes to allow the envelope to be recycled. We designed the label for the envelopes, brainstormed on how to raise capital, looked for donations from parents and companies, and investigated the cost of printing the labels.

We often reflect on the learning in our activities. I ask the children to explain how an activity contributes to learning. When we decided to start a casino, we discussed gambling, lotteries, and probability. When the principal happened to drop in during Egg Baby City time and asked, "What are you kids doing?" they replied, "We're running our casino." The principal inquired, "What are you learning?" and the children responded, "We're looking at probability and chance, which is in the state core curriculum." The children's contributions to planning and structuring the curriculum are enormous, and part of their learning comes from this involvement.

Coordinating beyond the Classroom in the OC

Organization that occurs beyond the six individual classrooms unites the children in a cohesive school community. Various all-program experiences allow children of differing ages, including siblings, to learn together. Co-opers offer minicourses to children across classrooms several times a year, on topics such as ceramics, first aid, chess, and model building. In glee club, many kindergarten-through-sixth-graders sing together and perform for holiday and graduation programs, and in the weekly sports afternoon, children join together across grades to participate in sports and fitness activities. The whole OC works together on all-program study themes, such as inventions, space, and the human body. For the inventions theme, the programwide curriculum committee made a packet of resources and ideas for everyone to use and sponsored an Invention Convention in which every class visited other classrooms to look at their inventions.

Children are supported in learning to solve problems across classrooms. One year, there were conflicts during recess because the children had varying ideas about how an ongoing game of kickball should be played. Doug, a co-oper from another room, brought the players together to brainstorm and design a kickball constitution to help establish the rules and guidelines for the game: What makes the games fun for you? What makes you feel sad or hurts your feelings? Doug was a kickball expert and had credibility with the children. Together Doug and the children clarified the rules of the game and coordinated a set of rules that everybody could live with, and the children learned about goal setting and positive ways of competing and solving problems.

A key aspect of coordination and planning of everyday practices within our community of learners is the coherent interconnections of the practices. Over the years, some practices that we use in our program have been introduced in other schools: conflict resolution, multigraded classrooms, co-operative learning,

Children and co-opers from another class view the inventions by Donene's class during the Invention Convention. (Photo courtesy Cindy White.)

student-teacher-parent conferences, performance-based report cards, and parent involvement, among others. While each new technique may find relative success on its own, the difference between simply implementing techniques and building a community of learners is very dramatic. Collaboration and a sense of respect are key to building community and to helping the children as well as the adults become lifelong learners.

The contribution of time and energy that the OC requires of its members is repaid in the spirit of community that is built as children, parents, and teachers contribute to the structure and planning of education. Older graduates often consider the OC more central to their student identity and their educational background than their high school experience. Many students report that their involvement in this community of learners prepared them in important ways for their later roles. One graduate, Luisa Magarian, reflected on how her experience as a contributing member of the OC community helped her in coordinating and planning with others in high school:

From having responsibility in groups, kids learn how to deal with problems and to listen to each other to try to understand different points of view. They learn how to help a group work together smoothly and how to keep people interested in what they are doing. Now, as a high school senior, I am aware that my experiences in the OC have helped prepare me for leadership roles. As coeditor of the student news magazine at my high school and codirector of the school musical, I have to balance my eagerness to get things done with patience to work with other students and thoughtfulness in attempting to get the entire group of students to work well together. My job is to lead the other students—not to do the work myself or just drag everyone along behind me, but to make it possible for the group to progress.

At the OC, I learned how to communicate with people in a way that helps to avert problems. If people seem to be feeling dissatisfied, I try to talk with them before things blow up and help them see that they're doing something that matters and is important. Of course, I learned problem-solving skills at the OC, and I use them—but it's always hard once something has already become a problem. My OC experience helped me gain perspective about what it takes to help people work together.

In a learning community in which children and adults coordinate to provide direction to the curriculum and the classroom structure, students prepare for other settings in which they will later participate, especially as contributors to learning communities.

Note

1. I hear from parents over and over, "My child loves the OC and is excited about going to school." One time my own daughter had the stomach flu and was very ill. She crawled to the door that morning and said she wanted to go to school. I told her she was too sick to go; she replied, "I'll feel better when I get there."

The Classroom Community
"in Control"

Leslee Bartlett, *teacher*
Carolyn Goodman Turkanis, *teacher*

M any people think a well-functioning classroom needs a teacher to be in control. In the OC, the structure of the classroom is not based on a teacher or other adult controlling the children. A key aim of the OC is for children and adults to collaborate, with responsibility to the group, so that the *classroom community* is in control, not the teacher. If adults controlled the children, it would impede the children's opportunities to learn how to become responsible for their own learning and their collaboration with the group. Building the skills and expectations for responsible participation in a group is an important part of the curriculum from kindergarten through sixth grade.

On a daily basis in Leslee's kindergarten classroom, time is spent helping children take responsibility for their own behavior. Five- and six-year-olds are capable of discussing, following, and reflecting on classroom guidelines that allow productive and co-operative learning to occur. The guidelines come from the class constitution that children help develop at the beginning of the year, which sets up expectations for behavior.

A daily opportunity for the kindergarten classroom to learn to manage itself occurs during a challenging transition time between snack and story circle. Although this transition may last for only five minutes, it is easy for these young children to forget appropriate behavior—when children finish their snack, they can either choose a book to read or visit quietly in circle while waiting for the rest of the class to join them. The challenge of this transition often provides a learning experience through a conversation that takes place once the whole group is assembled in circle. With guidance from Leslee, the children evaluate their own behavior and that of the classroom as a whole. The goal is a classroom in control, not a teacher in control.

To evaluate how the group is progressing in learning to manage the classroom structure, Leslee purposely leaves the classroom at times and asks a co-oper to keep an eye on things in case there are any issues. When Leslee returns, she is easily able to see whether the classroom was able to manage itself in her temporary absence. She can see if the children are engaged in activities or just fooling around. How well a class does on days when there is a substitute teacher also indicates the extent to which the classroom is managing to run itself.

An example of children's developing skills in managing their fourth/fifth-grade classroom occurred while the teacher was attending a short meeting. The co-oper who had stayed in the classroom was helping two students solve a problem while the rest of the class was quietly reading. Several children, who heard stomachs growling and glanced at the clock, realized it was time for lunch. They informed their classmates, who proceeded to put their books away, get their lunches, and line up at the classroom door. Realizing that the co-oper was still involved in problem solving, the children quietly walked themselves to the cafeteria for lunch.

Usually, the teacher and co-opers assist the children and each other in the flow of activities in the classroom. For example, adults keep an eye on children's choice of activities and evaluate whether a child needs help to "get on track" or avoid disrupting other activities. For some children, awareness and skill in coordinating with the group is more of a challenge than for other children; in such cases, this becomes a central part of the learning goals that they construct with their teacher and parents.

At times, children may need help figuring out how their actions affect others. For example, a child taking a survey for a classroom newspaper may unthinkingly interrupt a book group to talk to a classmate to collect data for the newspaper article. The teacher may suggest, "Look around the room, and describe to me what kinds of activities are happening. Which kids can you talk to, which kids are in skill groups and can't be interrupted?"

In her fifth/sixth-grade classroom, Carolyn focuses on how children's actions can better support a learning community. For example, if a group of children are noisy, instead of simply saying "Please be quiet," she asks, "What kind of learning is happening here? How might this group be affecting other groups in the class-room?" Often instead of having a conversation with a child or a small group at the time of a problem, Carolyn makes a mental note and brings up the issue in circle, saying, "I saw some really odd things in the groups this morning, you guys. I saw a kid thumping a pencil on the table, and in another group I saw somebody upside down, and then I saw other kids come over and interrupt a group." She suggests, "Let's talk about what makes a really good skill group," or "How do you know when it's okay to go have a conversation with a student in another group?"

Co-opers often feel responsible to the teacher to keep their small group "in control," and they feel guilty if the teacher comes over to the group when several children are being loud or silly. The teachers try to reassure co-opers that the issue isn't about the co-oper's control, it's about the children knowing what the expectations are. Carolyn asks the children, "What kind of learning is happening here? How do you become a participant in what you're learning? How do you support the group and the co-oper?" This helps the children learn how to manage their own involvement and also helps the co-oper understand that the aim is for the children to manage themselves, not for the co-oper to be in control.

Adults are not responsible for the children's behavior. Adults are responsible for providing learning opportunities and learning along with the children. The children are responsible for their own behavior, and the goal is to help them develop responsibility to themselves and to the group. Carolyn sometimes hears co-opers telling children, "You guys be quiet, because Carolyn's coming over." Carolyn responds, "No, don't be quiet for me, this is *your* learning. It's not about me or for me." Leslee adds, "The children shouldn't be 'behaving' to make me happy, or to make the co-oper happy. It's so that learning happens. I tell them that I expect certain kinds of behavior, and I do, but the reason is so that learning can happen."

The children are expected to be attentive, working on their activity, and responsible. If they are not following expectations, adults shouldn't just push ahead with the plans for their activity but instead should help the children learn how to learn and be responsible to each other, by asking, "Why isn't it appropriate for you to be poking this guy with a pencil? What's happening to his learning? What's happening to your learning?" The children need to learn to foster their own learning and to make learning possible for everybody.

Ultimately, for small periods of time, it shouldn't matter whether the teacher is in the classroom or not, because children should be motivated and self-directed enough that there doesn't need to be an adult imposing order in the classroom. Creating a well-running classroom is not for the sake of the teacher or other adults—it's for the sake of the children and the learning community. A classroom community in control.

PART THREE

Children Learning in a Community

In my daughter's first/second grade class, every Monday morning for the whole year was devoted to building a city. From a casual look the kids were having a great time, choosing what part of the city they wanted to develop and building store fronts. Sure, they were learning to cut cardboard and paint it, but what about math, reading, and writing?

With a closer look it truly was a comprehensive learning experience. The kids developed their own jobs and a government, named their town by popular election, printed money, and published a newspaper. At the close of each day the business counted their cash, prepared a deposit, and took it to the town bank where figures were verified and credit given to the businesses' accounts. The newspaper accepted advertisements developed by the business and reported on city residents and activities. When a problem arose they would have a "town meeting" and find a solution. . . . By the end of the year they had a well-running town with all needed services and they invited other classes to come patronize their town.

The children of that class brought their life experiences and interests into the classroom and took home a better understanding of the interrelationships of a business community, as well as the use of math, reading, and writing, and skills in problem solving.

—Ann Chalmers Pendell, OC parent and former Steering co-chair

Children choosing activities in Marcy's class. (Photo by John Schaefer ©)

Creating Curriculum
with Children

Carolyn Goodman Turkanis, *teacher*

Children are natural learners, curious and inquisitive, wondering why and who and how. They thrive in an environment that allows curriculum to emerge naturally, with support from other children, co-oping parents, and teachers, around their needs and interests. They are quick to express opinions, offer suggestions, and invent projects. They are an incredible natural resource, and in a community of learners, they contribute to meaningful, exciting curriculum.

In a community of learners, everyone has a part to play in supporting the learning process. Children help plan and develop curriculum and are expected to be active participants and responsible learners. Parents support projects and activities with ideas and guest speakers; they teach and present curriculum. The teacher supports both children and parents in their planning, organizes and facilitates all the learning involved, and is ultimately accountable for curriculum development and content. Each role is valuable and part of the whole—more than the sum of the parts.

Curriculum can be built by the community together, making use of children's interests and experience as a key impetus. Such curriculum builds on individual and collective interests to weave together instructional interactions that support and inspire learning by:

- Seizing the moment to build on interesting ideas that emerge in classroom discussion
- Recognizing that children have their own learning agendas that can provide motivation and the "way in" to learning about all kinds of other curriculum areas
- Supporting units of study that often emerge as a group process, as people

become interested in each others' interests and build on each others' expertise
- Using resources of all kinds (with little reliance on textbooks)

After exploring these points, I will discuss how the classroom structure and the teacher help create such an emerging curriculum, and the question of what the children learn.

Seize the Moment

Curriculum is all around us, just waiting to happen. This is frequently referred to as "teaching to the moment," or "seizing the moment." Dozens of these ideal moments occur daily in the classroom. Recognizing them allows a wide variety of learning to happen on the spot. In my fifth/sixth-grade classroom this spontaneous curriculum constantly develops from sharing circles, conversations, remarks, and, of course, questions.

In an emergent science discussion about avalanches, our fifth- and sixth-graders were all snuggled together on the carpet in circle, some sitting up, some lying on pillows, others comfortably curled around each other, ready to enjoy our read-aloud book, *Nightmare Mountain*. We were well into the drama. The main character was on a snowy mountain, in fear for her life because of a llama-stealing villain, when an avalanche began to roll toward her. Glancing up to look at the kids to see how they were reacting, I noticed several raised hands. Should I stop to answer questions? Would it interrupt the flow of the story? A glance at the clock on the wall. Was there time? Were there other pressing things we must attend to? A glance back at the kids. Lots of hands now.

That was a clear directive that kids had things to say and needed to be heard. Everything else could wait. Questions and comments erupted as fast as the avalanche on the mountain. What causes an avalanche? How can you predict an avalanche? Can you survive an avalanche? There was an avalanche yesterday. . . . A man was killed. . . . Two men survived. . . . I read about . . . We stopped to look up "avalanche" in the dictionary and discussed the various definitions. Then a quiet voice suggested we return to the book, and we did. Time had passed, and our afternoon had changed. We had learned a great deal from the emergent curriculum and had some new common knowledge that we carried back into the read-aloud book. The story became more real for us than it was before.

Another science "teaching moment" emerged from an earthquake drill. We prepared at the beginning of the morning, reviewing all the procedures and expectations. Questions filled the air. There were fears and stories of earthquake shock and horror, death and destruction. Before we could even begin to thoughtfully address any of these issues, the intercom began to play a tape recording of a real earthquake—our signal to begin the earthquake drill. After finishing the drill outdoors, we assembled again in circle to evaluate our experience. Once again, when I thought something would be short and sweet and routine, the kids let me know that they needed time, care, thought, and discussion. Our schedule for the day had changed almost before it had even begun.

We developed vocabulary together (tectonics, Richter scale, seismologist, and so on), listed questions and concerns, and decided we needed help getting answers. We made arrangements for a guest speaker that very week; the speaker brought maps for us to study, expertise we were lacking, and answers to our dozens of questions. If someone had asked me earlier in the week whether I would be planning any earthquake follow-up activities or a guest speaker, I probably would have said no. The experience extended to home projects, with kids getting emergency kits ready and figuring out possible escape routes from their homes. One earthquake drill developed into geological study, problem solving, current events, and local history.

Once when a student was heading off on a trip to Europe, her travels became geography curriculum. Caroline's dad was an airline pilot and had just invited her to travel to Europe with him; she began to share her itinerary with her classmates. A friend replied, "This time next Thursday we can all wave to you at the Eiffel Tower in Paris!" In a moment or two, after this all sank in and we fully realized that Caroline would be halfway around the world, another kid remarked, "You know, you guys, there are different time zones around the world. When we wave in Salt Lake City, it will be a different time in Paris. How will we know when to wave, and how will we know where she is at different times when we're here?" Another child informed us that we could locate time zones in atlases, on some maps, in encyclopedias, and even in the telephone book. A few interested kids formed an informal committee and met later on in the day, using Caroline's itinerary and some reference books. After a lengthy work session, they had successfully coordinated the time zones so that at any time during Caroline's European jaunt, we would be able to know exactly where she was and what she was doing. During her worldly adventure, several times each day, someone would share with the class Caroline's current activity. It kept us in touch with her and, in the process, provided meaningful geography curriculum.

One current events discussion in circle enlarged into service learning, with participation in local current events. Spring rains, heavier than usual, overloaded mountain streams, and the runoff caused severe flooding in the valley. There were constant news bulletins on radio and television, and the floods became the big current events topic of sharing and discussion circle. We were about to set out to a local park for an afternoon of games and friendship when one quiet voice in the crowd said, "I feel bad about going to the park to play when so many people are being flooded out of their homes and apartments." Another voice echoed the same concern. Ideas flooded the room as fast as the flood that filled our city. Kids suggested we change our plans and figure out how to volunteer our time and energy to the city. It took a few phone calls to find the necessary information, but then we were able to generate a list of possible class projects. A discussion and vote produced a unanimous decision to drive to the city emergency sandlot, where we filled sandbags for the afternoon. On our return to school, we drove to several local flooded areas to get a firsthand view of the flood's destruction. We became involved in our community's problem and became part of a solution, generated by one quiet voice. That one voice, when heard in an open, flexible learning environment, changed an afternoon for our community of learners.

Individual Kids Have Their Own Learning Agendas

Teachers have learning agendas for children, as do school principals, local school boards, and national boards. But we also need to remember that children often come to school with their own learning agendas. Allowing them to pursue these agendas optimizes their learning by using their own interest and motivation. A child may be fascinated with butterflies, intrigued with tools, interested in foreign countries, or excited by poetry. Why not give that child time to explore these topics further in the classroom? This fosters a connection between home and school and validates the child as a learner who embraces curriculum "in mind" and "in heart."

An example of one child's learning agenda was Ali's fascination with haiku. The classroom had just finished a poetry unit that explored numerous forms of verse. Ali gleefully announced that she would author 100 haiku over the next few days and would let us know when her task was accomplished. All she needed was time and support and permission to get on with her own agenda. Every day Ali worked in short and not-so-short blocks of time when she was not involved in required classroom activities. When her 100 haiku were completed, she bound her poems into a book to be given to her parents as a gift and shared her finished poems with the class a few at a time, day after day, until we had enjoyed them all! The classroom's flexibility and Ali's motivation were key factors in her success.

Travel fever sparked Emily's announcement that she was going to plan an end-of-the-year trip for graduating sixth-graders; it yielded an exercise in planning and decision making. I was concerned about expenses, parental supervision, the itinerary, and all the work Emily's idea might entail, but I gave her time and support. She gathered together a small committee with kids who were eager to help her plan this trip. Over the next few weeks, they pored over atlases and mileage charts, planning an itinerary to take them across the United States and back again. Figuring time, mileage, expenses, parent help and numbers of vehicles and coordinating family schedules became exhausting, and the committee unanimously decided that the trip was too cumbersome to orchestrate. Emily, now satisfied, had provided herself and the committee with a curriculum rich in geography, math, reading, writing, and logic, not to mention skills in planning, organizing, compiling information, and decision making. She was driven by her own interest and desire. Giving her time to pursue her idea was a very simple thing, thanks to a flexible classroom schedule and attitude.

After a local artist had completed a two-week session supporting kids as they painted a mural on the classroom wall, a few kids decided they wanted to continue the art project and paint some classroom furniture. They chose their pieces of furniture and completed their projects, but one student, Lindsey, wanted more. I was getting tired of paint and brushes and tarps and mess. I must have looked a bit downtrodden when Lindsey approached me with her thoughtful agenda. "I will be really responsible, Carolyn. I want to paint the long table that's by the sink. I'll put it out in the hall, with a tarp underneath. I'll wear a smock and be careful with all the paints. I will wash all the brushes I use, and I will clean up after myself every day. You can trust me." How could I possibly say no? The table was painted. Lindsey did exactly what she said she would do. Lindsey took responsibility for the rest of her classroom work as well. She planned her schedule, evaluated available time for extended painting, and used sophisticated decision-making skills as she pursued her project.

Planning a dance curriculum for which she could be responsible lit a fire under another child. During an informal visit, as I inquired about Jasmin's dance lessons and baby-sitting, she commented, "I sure wish I could teach dance to some little kids. I'm really good at dance." The perfect opening. "How could we make that happen for you?" I asked. "Well, I could go talk to the first- and second-grade teachers and see if they have some kids who would like to learn some dance. Then I could come tell you and we could pick a good day and time." This was the beginning of a year-long relationship between Jasmin and dozens of younger children. She taught eight-week dance lessons, and her students gave a costumed performance for parents at the end of each session. Jasmin was ultimately involved in planning and organization, selecting music, orchestrating dance steps, teaching dance skills, problem solving and group discussions, coordinating with three classroom teachers and her young dancers' parents, and decision making throughout the experience.

Units of Study Emerging as a Group Process

When people work together as a community to develop curriculum, fascinating units of study emerge as individuals make suggestions for topics, objectives, sequence, learning activities, and culmination. Multiply this by 30 children and 30 co-oping parents, and there is a wealth of energy and support for the joint-effort curriculum. Planning together validates the study and gives pride of ownership to the curriculum creators.

In Leslee Bartlett's first/second-grade classroom, curriculum units were often based on class decisions; parents and teacher together developed the chosen theme into an integrated curriculum. Leslee recalls the challenges and success of one unit—with the theme of Pizza!

One strategy we've used for developing curriculum that is of high interest to children is to have them brainstorm a list of things they'd like to study and then choose one as a focus for a month or so. We then build as much of the curriculum as possible around this central idea, incorporating language, science, math, social studies, art, and so on, so that a strong connection was made for the students.

One year when I was teaching first- and second-graders we used this process to determine our focus for the cold, bleak months after winter break. The kids suggested a wide variety of subjects, from spiders to submarines, trees to tigers. Suddenly one child said, "How about pizza?" and a muted roar of approval swept across the upturned faces of 28 six- and seven-year-olds. Even though it was a foregone conclusion, we continued the process and voted for our two favorite subjects—tigers and, what else? *Pizza*. Before our final vote, we listed several things that we could learn about each subject, and, I admit, I did my best to steer them toward the animal kingdom. However, my best efforts fell far short and we unanimously voted on our next focus—*pizza*!

"Okay," I thought, "this will be a real challenge to build meaningful curriculum around dinner." But at the monthly parent meeting I presented the idea to the parent group and together we thought up one of the most successful units of study I've ever seen. For the next month we read about pizza to check ads for comparative prices and specials; we wrote about pizza as we designed menus and advertisements for our own in-class restaurant; we engaged in mathematical learning as we divided up pizza pies, compared prices, measured and counted ingredients for the pizzas we cooked at school. We learned about nutrition and how a well-thought-out pizza can meet several nutritional requirements at once. We also traced several traditional pizza ingredients back to their sources and learned how tomato sauce and cheese are made, how meats are processed, and where mushrooms, peppers, and olives are grown. We developed a social studies unit around Italy and looked at how the original "pie" had become Americanized. We ended with a trip to a local pizza parlor, where we had a firsthand look at how a restaurant is run. "How do you order ingredients, how do you know how much to order, how do you decide what to charge?"—these were just a few of the questions kids posed and discussed. By March we all had learned a lot about and from pizza!

In my fifth/sixth-grade classroom, a whole unit of study will often emerge from group discussion. For example, one day in a sharing circle, Colin told us about his upcoming surgery. Because he was pigeon-toed, both his tibias would be broken and reset, straightening his legs. Kids were fascinated. Colin explained that he would have both legs in casts for six weeks and need to be in a wheelchair in the classroom during that time. The conversation blossomed into dozens of issues. How will Colin get to school? How will he get into the building? What about getting to the bathroom, the lunchroom, the library? Given that our classroom contains not desks in tidy rows, but a variety of tables, a loft, a bathtub with pillows, two sofas, and lawn furniture, how will he move around in our space? We set out on a small unit of study, driven by our concern for a classmate and by our motivation to seek answers and solutions to potential problems. We launched into examining Colin's X rays, visiting with Colin's mother to discuss the details of the surgery, exploring the school grounds for Colin's access to the building, inviting a representative from the Handicapped Bus Service to talk to us, moving and rearranging classroom furniture for accessibility, and borrowing six wheelchairs so all kids could experience what life was like for a classmate in a wheelchair. Many of these experiences were designed and created by kids; others needed support and guidance from parents. It was the combination of support and a flexible classroom that allowed this unit to emerge successfully.

Another unit of study emerged from current events discussions. It was time for local elections, and television was full of debates. Someone began to discuss the debate process, and kids began to offer their own knowledge about debates. Someone asked me a question, and I confessed that I knew very little about debating and the rules involved. "You should know all about this, Carolyn, you went to college!" I explored with the kids the idea of learning more about debating, and they seemed very intrigued. With parent help, we contacted the debate teacher at West High School, who offered several of his students as teachers. The high school students met with us, and together we planned a debate curriculum that was centered around the kids' needs and lack of knowledge about debating. Together the high school students and my fifth- and sixth-graders brainstormed, answered questions, and developed a sequence of debate experiences. This curriculum effort was successful because kids were interested and motivated to learn and were involved in the planning.

On another occasion, we developed a social studies unit that brought the children together with nursing home residents. I had been hearing children talk at length about their relationships with grandparents and realized there was great interest in pursuing some sort of involvement with older citizens. We could create a partnership that would serve everyone well: grandparents for children whose grandparents were no longer alive or lived so far away that the children rarely saw them, and grandchildren for older citizens who did not have family nearby or were rarely visited by family. Our year-long relationship with 30 residents of a nursing home near our school began when a parent contacted the home. Soon each child was partnered with a special friend for the year, going back and forth in small visiting groups each week.

As kids began sharing their conversations, worries, and delightful times, it became clear that we needed to learn more about the people with whom we were spending so much time. We brainstormed to collect our questions. With parental help, guest speakers from the gerontology department of the local medical school and from the College of Nursing presented lessons on aging and facilitated informal discussions. The nursing home also offered several speakers from among those who provided services to the patients, including physical therapists, recreation specialists, psychologists, and social workers.

During the year, kids became very involved with their older friends and planned activities for their weekly visits. Some played cards or chess. Some read aloud or offered to write letters. Some painted fingernails and brushed or braided hair. Kids began to see the bigger picture—the needs of a large group of older people living together—and wanted to provide for some of those group needs. They commented that their older friends needed more time to be together, sharing music, enjoying programs and guest speakers, participating in activities and projects—opportunities to share ideas and learn about and from each other. We planned a party for every major holiday, made refreshments at school for the home, and organized skits and songs for entertainment.

Parents reported that many children asked to see their older friends on week-ends or during school vacations, so they took their children for an extra visit. During the year, a few of the older friends passed away. Children experienced the death of a friend and were supported by classmates, the nursing home staff, and often the older friend's family. The child, in turn, was able to offer support to others. If anyone had asked me earlier in the school year if I would be involved in putting together a unit of study about the elderly, community service, and values education, I probably would have said no. Kids' interests and motivation were the driving force behind this emergent curriculum.

Using a Variety of Resources to Design Curriculum with Children

As the foregoing examples show, we use many different resources to inform us in our emergent curriculum. Curriculum developed with and by kids, using whatever resources we can find, feels alive and invigorating. In contrast, learning solely from textbooks to me feels stale, limiting, lifeless. Of course, curriculum developed with kids includes good books—children's literature in shared reading groups, nonfiction references, encyclopedias, dictionaries—used in ways that the children help devise. Books, but not textbooks, have a central place at the OC.

I had to think twice about the resources to use to help the kids develop some dictionary skills. I had watched kids struggle to locate words they wanted to use in their writing, and quickly developed some dictionary-skills worksheets that I thought would give kids practice looking up words. They located each word in the dictionary and wrote down the page number and the definition, proving that indeed they were able to locate each word. Boring. Tedious. I had goofed some-how. I brought my concern to the group, sharing with them that I perceived they needed some dictionary work but clearly I had designed tasks that were dull. They agreed, so we launched into a discussion about how to develop dictionary skills in a way that they could really "get into."

Their ideas were quite amazing. The children invented dictionary games to use a variety of dictionary skills, including alphabetical ordering, diacritical mark-ings, pronunciation, multimeaning words, guide words, main entries, syllabica-tion, parts-of-speech labels, etymologies, and correct usage of words in sentences. They each designed personal dictionaries for organizing their own spelling words or interesting words they wanted to use in their writing. They offered to make small, individual dictionaries for first- and second-graders, to help them record vocabulary. They looked up the most unusual, or funny, or polysyllabic words and shared them regularly with the class. To end our study, they invented words of their own, gave each word a definition, and challenged us to incorporate these new words into our daily conversations. We accomplished the goal of working on dictionary skills and enjoyed ourselves immensely as we did so, because the kids were motivated by their own ideas.

Every year when I plunge into Utah history (which is mandated by the state core curriculum), it becomes a brand-new experience for me, since the resources are developed by a different group of kids and co-oping parents. Although the basic facts of Utah history have not changed, we change, and our approaches change. We usually brainstorm as a class and come up with a list of questions about the topic, ways that we would like to find the answers, and possible resources—guest speakers, field trips, projects, and activities. This is far different than reading chapters in a history textbook, studying its vocabulary section, and discussing the chapter's content and answering the textbook questions, with perhaps a few guest speakers or field trips on the side.

One group of kids approached this study through their intense interest in food, cooking, and eating! We researched the various groups of people who played a part in the history of our state and set out to learn about their food and recipes, eating our way through the year. Another group approached Utah history through their interest in local areas, so field trips to places such as the Bingham Copper Mine and the Daughters of the Pioneers Museum became our learning vehicle. One class was fascinated with the peoples of Utah, and our interest took us into the lives of early Indians in the Salt Lake Valley, the trappers, the mountain men, and the pioneers' trek across the plains. Another class focused on their own family histories. Each child made an individual family tree, interviewed grandparents and great-grandparents, and wrote letters to relatives living outside Utah to collect family history. Learning about our roots helped us understand our personal place in the history of our state. Another year, the class was eager to learn about individual people who impacted the state: We began with research on local personalities, past and present, and then studied events that occurred in their lifetimes. Every year this experience has been rich and distinct, designed and generated by kids, parents, and teachers, using a variety of resources appropriate to the theme.

How Does All This Happen?

What aspects of the classroom structure and the teacher's role help in creating curriculum with children? How is a classroom organized to allow kids to pursue their own agendas, stopping classroom schedules for seize-the-moment curriculum and giving children the opportunity to plan and organize their own curriculum? I focus on classroom climate, time, and keeping our philosophy in mind.

Classroom climate is key. We all have been in classrooms that feel tight and tense. Imagine trying to learn while worrying about pressures, limits, disapproval, and criticism. We establish our classroom climate together as a community of learners, at the beginning of the year, as the children, parents, and I describe what we believe in and how we want to treat each other and be treated, as we create our class constitution. We all value safety, both emotional and physical, in order to foster a classroom where children feel comfortable to be themselves, to ask questions, and to make mistakes and learn from them. We all value trust and want to be in a learning environment where children trust parents and teachers and where both parents and teachers trust not only the children but also each other. We all value mutual respect, which develops as the community recognizes each person as a unique and worthwhile individual. We all value honesty, caring, thoughtfulness, and responsible behavior that fosters learning and friendships. As we discuss what matters to us, our constitution emerges, and because it is ours, it is easy to support and honor throughout the year. It becomes the way we are in our classroom, the way we treat each other, and the way we learn.

Time is an important element. Does the classroom provide time for kids to relax and enjoy? To be kids? To ask questions and explore their own interests? To learn at their own pace? To be with each other in learning and in friendship? Time to create? For emergent curriculum to actually emerge and be explored in depth? Time to change directions, to reflect, to resolve? Giving a classroom time to learn is the basis for creating curriculum with children.

Keeping our philosophy in mind guides myriad decisions that are required in creating curriculum with children. I always think about whether and how what we are doing is "learning-centered."

Opportunities for building emerging curriculum occur at almost every moment, sometimes several at a time. There is no shortage of ideas. Decision making focuses on which idea to follow, and for how long, not on how to get something to happen in the first place. The classroom is an intellectually lively place.

I constantly reflect on how the possibilities that we could pursue at any moment would enhance the learning in the classroom, focusing on what the possible directions would provide in the way of opportunities for us to learn about the world and ourselves. Should we stop to talk about an avalanche? Should we go play in the park or volunteer to help our city? Should we figure out what time Caroline will be in Rome? Sometimes the decision is clear, sometimes not.

It is difficult to put into words how these decisions are made, because so many facets of the classroom structure are a part of my ongoing decisions. But clearly, I play an energetic role by anticipating and shaping the direction of classroom activities, helping build the emerging curriculum with the kids. I ask myself a lot of questions as I'm making split-second decisions:

- How interested and invested are the students?
- Is the endeavor educationally sound?
- What new skills might we learn?
- What areas of the curriculum can I incorporate?
- What are the implications of the learning?
- How does this learning relate to real life?
- How much time do I anticipate we might need?
- How will this change affect the rest of the morning or afternoon?
- How long have we been sitting in circle already? How much longer can the kids sit still?
- Is there going to be learning lost in what we *didn't* do? Is that okay? Or can we retrieve the postponed learning? What would that entail?

Sometimes I'm the one who gets the honor and pleasure of making the deci-sions, and sometimes I give them to the kids. Does it always work? No. Is there always time? No. Is everyone always happy? No. Does it get complicated? Yes. Are there lots of decisions to make? Yes. Is it exhausting? Sometimes. There is no formula for success—but with experience, patience, and commitment, a reward-ing curriculum emerges.

Are the Children Learning?

The flexibility required in creating curriculum with children yields a different classroom structure than in schools in which the structure and curriculum are determined by the teacher and texts and packaged curriculum, without the chil-dren's involvement in what and how they are learning. People unfamiliar with the flexible structure sometimes ask what the children are learning. The Big Ideas mentioned early in this book guide the emerging curriculum, along with the skills that are required by the state, albeit in a more flexible fashion than laid out in the state core curriculum. As Marcy Clokey-Till, an eight-year veteran teacher of the OC, observed:

> How does the teacher assure that the "basic skills" are incorporated into child-generated curriculum? Ultimately the teacher is responsible for assur-ing that state requirements (the core curriculum specified for each grade level) are "covered" in the classroom curriculum. Teachers know the basic curricular framework for the grade levels they are working with, what con-tent areas should be covered in the course of a year, and what skills need to be addressed within the context of a particular content area, as well as individual needs.
>
> These considerations are in the background of daily, monthly, and even yearly planning, balanced equally with current needs, desires, and interests of the students, the parents, and the teacher. Sometimes the suggested topics for particular content areas are not covered in a given year, but because students are in multigraded classrooms that cover a variety of topics in many years, the chances that each student actually engages with all required curriculum are very high. It just may not occur on the schedule prescribed by the school district or the state.
>
> "Basic skills" can be taught within the context of *any* content, and in-structional opportunities carry more weight when the student has a vested interest in the topic and making sense of their world. Students who have a need to convey their learning for a real purpose are much more likely to remember the skills and tools they need to do so.

How do we know kids are learning in the classroom? I usually reflect that the learning is "in your face"! For example, from the very first minute that my fifth-and sixth-graders began painting a mural on a bare wall of our classroom to the washing of the last paintbrush at the end of the week, the kids were immersed in learning. Friends who usually worked together and kids who only sometimes work together eagerly collaborated, willingly teaching and learning from each other. Kids were involved in brainstorming, decision making, planning, discussing, questioning, voting, analyzing, organizing, and problem solving. They learned with members of their own small committee and challenged their learning as each individual committee needed to work with other committees.

We made decisions about the mural's theme (getting 32 kids to come to consensus involved a *lot* of learning for us). We studied a wide variety of art concepts—perspective, how to make colors, color scheme, how the mural would relate to other murals in the classroom. We planned the preparation of the space as well as when each committee would paint and how cleanup would occur.

Kids did research to support the part of the project they were working on. In the middle of painting a palm tree, one girl said, "No wonder I can't paint this! I can't remember what a palm tree looks like." Her classmate replied, "Well, how about getting a picture of a palm tree?" Later, after extensive reading in the encyclopedia, the girl announced, "No wonder I couldn't paint this. But now I have a picture in front of me and I know more about palm trees." She had learned from her reading about growth, climate, the shape of fronds, and the pattern of the bark. She brought her new learning to the mural and translated it into art.

Children learned as they participated. They learned information and skills that had meaning and value to them, in the midst of an authentic and purposeful project. They learned alone and together, and for each child the learning was probably different. The learning became part of the child. The palm tree artist may not remember the details of the mural when she's in high school, but her learning since then will have been built upon that learning experience. The children's learning was obvious to me as we worked together. It was "in my face."

In later life, children who have had years of experience designing and creating curriculum feel adept in decision making, problem solving, and creative thinking. They have learned to "own" their learning. With this understanding and self-confidence, they can enhance and embellish assignments, discuss requirements and expectations, seek new depths and experiences, and search for meaning and value in projects and classroom studies. An example is provided by an OC graduate who, in eighth grade in a new school, said to her mother, "Mom, I've figured out that it's my fault if school is boring. Just because the teachers give boring assignments, it doesn't mean that I have to be limited to that. I could find *something* interesting in a textbook, some little thing, and go to the library to expand on it, and make it my own project, like we did at the OC. And would you help me with editing what I write?" Her mother smiled, grateful that her eighth-grader remembered such an important lesson that she had learned in the OC.

Kids who design curriculum and have a say in how it is presented are much more likely to participate willingly and with open hearts and minds. Attitude on the part of the learner is critical. How does that saying go—"You can lead a horse to water, but you can't make it drink!" With the aim of really understanding what is learned, and being prepared for lifelong learning, there is no substitute for being involved in creating an emerging curriculum.

Caring Conversations

Theresa Cryns, Marcy Clokey-Till, Carolyn
Goodman Turkanis, and Marilyn Osborne,
current and former OC teachers

One thing that characterizes the OC is the respectful way OC teachers talk with kids. When two former OC teachers who had moved and now teach in different schools viewed a videotape of one of them teaching, the other was struck with how, after many years apart from each other, they still talk to kids the same way. Respectful conversations happen in the OC and in other schools where many exceptional teachers reach out and make connections with students. An OC teacher recounted an event that illustrates the contrast with other ways of interaction:

> When a junior high school counselor came to register the kids in my room for junior high the next year, there was not an available table where she could sit with a small group. So I said, "Just a minute, I'll get you a space." I asked a few kids who were working together at a table if we could use it for a while and then they could have it back. We teased each other a little and then the kids packed up their supplies and moved to work on the floor. The counselor said, "Is that how you talk to kids usually?" I said yes.
>
> She told me that in her school adults didn't treat kids like that at all— "There's hardly anyone who would have fun with kids, or even ask them for the table." I was so stunned, I asked her what she would have done in that situation. She said she would have told them to just "move out, I need the table." So there would have been no conversation. I asked her if that was the way the whole school interacted with children, and she said there was one person who talked just like me, and it turned out to be a former OC co-oper who now teaches there.

If the classroom structure allows conversations, people can learn to converse with respect. Children themselves can play a role in helping adults communicate

A co-oper and students conversing with respect.

with them. One teacher remembered a child in her first year of teaching who would bounce off the walls if the teacher didn't stop and say "Hi, how are you?" and make a personal connection with him before he went flying into the classroom. When she did this, he seemed more connected to his classroom and his learning. "That has been one of the most valuable communication lessons of my 16 years of teaching. Making a personal connection with kids. And the kids taught that to me."

Another OC teacher reminisced about how she learned to take up the kids' topics, as a way of connecting respectfully with the kids.

> I had my best conversations with students when we were standing in line, or hanging out waiting for something, when they were just sort of chatting among themselves. When I was supposed to be keeping them quiet, but I didn't care about keeping them quiet. Someone would say, "I had a really lousy weekend," to no one in particular. Then they'd say it again. . . . And finally it would dawn on me, and I'd say, "Why was your weekend so lousy?" And then I'd have this conversation. Kids invite you into those conversations all the time, I discovered, by those words to no one in particular. I learned to go for that story—when they drop a little nugget, explore that nugget a little.

A former OC teacher was surprised when she moved to a different school and found that some fifth- or sixth-graders who weren't used to respectful conversation didn't know how to participate in it. They didn't have the trust level or the skills built up in their previous classrooms to engage in respectful conversation in the classroom. If a few new kids join the fifth/sixth-grade classroom in the OC, they learn fairly easily how to engage with other people with respect, since the rest of the class is doing it. But when a whole classroom is not used to that kind of interaction, the teacher has to work hard to build the norms with the group, since they haven't been learning it for years already.

The attention given across the grades in the OC to building a classroom community and to supporting children's "sharing circles" with structures for learning from each other shows in the children's respectful classroom conversations. As pointed out in the next contribution, by an OC student, the way that OC teachers talk to kids helps the kids learn to be respectful with adults and with each other.

Respect from Respect

Valerie Magarian, *OC student,*
after sixth grade

Because the adults and kids respected each other, I was excited about learning and felt appreciated in the OC. Teachers treat kids with respect, and parents learn to respect kids' ideas by observing the kids and teachers in the classroom. Lots of people might wonder why co-opers need to learn, since it's the kid who's going to school. If the parent has never been in the classroom and the kid says, "We're doing kid co-oping, and we're making marshmallow houses," a parent might say, "What does that have to do with school? Are you learning anything from making marshmallow houses?" The parent might not notice that their kid is learning about angles, architecture, how to make a structure that stands, and being creative. But when they see what their kid and other kids do around the classroom, they get more confident, and they respect the kid more and learn to respect the kids' ways of learning.

Adults learn to respect kids' ideas even if they don't agree with them. They can respect a kid's idea and express their opinion and what most people think about it and why—rather than saying, "You're wrong." An outsider who comes into the classroom and sees kids discussing history might think, "There's only one right answer, and that's the teacher's, so don't debate about it because it wastes time."

It's important for kids to be allowed to express their ideas and opinions, because that makes them really think about the topic and makes them more comfortable taking a different stance on something. They can learn about subjects by listening to other people's opinions, too. In the OC, the teachers trust people to help each other. They know you can learn a lot from each other and from teaching others.

The kids learn to understand and respect the adults who help them by leading activities in kid co-oping. Kid co-oping teaches them what it's like to be in the co-oper's place and how hard it is to organize a group and keep people interested.

Then the kids treat the adults better because they have learned what the adults go through. So when a co-oper comes in to do an activity, the kids respect the co-oper and appreciate the co-oper's help.

OC teachers can take charge but still respect kids. Sometimes they might correct kids, but they just tell them in a helpful way, in a way that they'll learn from, not in a way that will make them ashamed. Like if a kid did a math paper and got a lot of it wrong, the teacher wouldn't get mad, but would be concerned and help with it. I think the teachers know they are an important part of children's lives and can help them by supporting them and having patience.

Teachers can respect kids and have a relationship with kids, too. They don't act like kids, but they don't look down on the kids either—they treat kids as *people*. In a kindergarten classroom, the teacher might play Lincoln Logs with a little kid, because maybe the kid is scared about being in a new classroom. They build a relationship with the kids so the kids can feel comfortable.

OC teachers respect kids' work and don't just interrupt kids all the time. For example, when it's time for everyone to come to circle, they don't just tell everyone to stop immediately and come right away, they walk around the room and kind of whisper, "Come to circle," or they'll tell the group that circle time is in five minutes, or they'll just tell a few of the kids and it will spread around and everybody will know it's about time for circle so they should finish what they're working on.

I learned to respect myself and other people from how my teachers respected me. I learned that even if you have a different idea from other people, you can still respect them. My teachers taught me how to respect people, by being good role models.

"What about Sharing?"

Pamela Bradshaw, *teacher*

I looked down at six-year-old Patrick, who stood at my elbow, while I scanned the crowd near the exit gate of Salt Lake's Hogle Zoo. "What about sharing?" he asked.

It was a bright May morning; hundreds of children with name tags streamed by our kindergarten group as we gathered on a small patch of lawn. As the teacher in charge of this group, I was to meet the co-opers at this spot with their smaller groups so that we could count noses before heading back to school. With only four mornings a week for kindergarten, time was always tight, and using one morning for a zoo trip was like trying to make a shoebox into a garage for an elephant. Patrick wanted to share?—surely he could see that there was no way. He just had to be kidding.

I shaded my eyes to better see through the crowd for the missing zoo-explorers. Patrick asked again; his eyebrows pinched a crease on his forehead as I began to realize how serious he was. He waited patiently, tenaciously as only a six-year-old could, for my reply.

If time was normally limited, and tremendously limited for a trip to the zoo, on this particular day it was impossibly limited. Already Mary's dad held out a Tupperware container that held precious birthday cupcakes Mary had waited all day—all year—to present. I called Mary to me, positioning her before the handful of gathered children for her Happy Birthday song. If the children were ready to sing, we might still have just enough time to buckle seat belts and drive across the valley. We would pull up to the curb at school just in time for the children to meet their rides home, but certainly not with enough time to regroup in the classroom for what we knew as a sharing circle.

Sharing circle was a much anticipated time every day when four or five children would present something they chose to show us. At this show-and-tell time, their classmates could admire and ask questions about the object of choice. Sharing circle became so important that in spite of any interruption, whether it was a fire drill, an assembly, or a guest speaker who took most of our time with live exotic animals, my kindergartners would never let me forget to provide them with a chance to share objects sometimes as ordinary (to my way of thinking) as a clothes hanger from their brother's closet or a rock from Grandpa's driveway.

I was dumbfounded, however, that Patrick insisted on sharing at the zoo. Under the pressure of watching the time and gathering the group, I had held off his question. Now I had to explain the simple facts to him.

"Patrick," I began as I kneeled to be at eye level with him, "there won't be time for sharing today. Could you maybe bring your sharing back on Monday instead?"

Patrick's face answered what he didn't verbalize. His anxious expression was transformed to one of total dismay before I could convince him with reasons. Patrick was usually so happy-go-lucky, so willing to go with the flow, that I had to wonder what could make this sharing so important to him. Only then did I remember that his family needed to leave about a week before school ended to begin their summer jobs in Wyoming. This was, in fact, his last day at school, his last chance to share, his last opportunity to be a member of this bonded group.

"Oh Patrick, I forgot!"

He looked up at me hopefully, as if I could manufacture more time. I considered our situation. If we actually allowed time for Patrick to share after Mary's birthday song, I doubted that the children would even be able to hear him above the noise of the people around us. And I worried about anxious drivers waiting at school for late kindergartners. But one more glance at his face made the decision for me.

"You can share after we sing to Mary," I told him.

And he did, producing a plastic "frilled lizard" from his backpack, explaining its origins, then calling for the ritual questions or comments from his classmates.

Even with the jostling and shouting crowd surrounding them, the children raised their hands. Patrick called on kids whose faces were smeared with chocolate cupcake icing; Patrick's frilled lizard, for the most part, was the focus of their attention. I checked my watch again, and just as I was hopeful that we could still make it through the exit turnstile and back to school in time, I was surprised to hear Patrick shout, "Next sharer!"

According to custom, it was indeed Patrick's privilege to choose the next child for sharing time, but I smiled, knowing that only a child such as Patrick, aware that this was his last day, would remember to bring an item to the zoo for sharing. The other children who routinely took their turns on Thursdays wouldn't want to lug something around for three hours.

There on the bright patch of lawn, four kindergartners tossed aside half-eaten cupcakes as their hands shot up, each competing for Patrick's attention while trying to unzip backpacks with the other hand. My jaw must have dropped as I watched them push aside their water bottles and crumpled lunch bags for the item they had indeed lugged around the zoo for three hours.

While I caught up with my own astonishment, Patrick quickly chose Will. Before I could move, Will stood to tell the group about his "Nintendo guy" with a clear voice.

As any OC teacher will tell you, there are times when eye contact with other adults feels like a gift from heaven. The children didn't see me as I looked again at my watch, then at the co-oping parents who, one by one, settled back with amused faces. Patrick's dad just shrugged his shoulders and smiled. Will's mom slightly shook her head, and we all silently understood we would be late.

Only eight months before, many of these kindergartners had hidden behind their parents on the first day of school. September sharing circles were painful stabs at overcoming shyness, and sometimes the sharers were completely unable to say a word.

But now, in spite of the noise, the commotion, and their own weariness at the zoo, my kindergartners conducted and participated in their own independent sharing circle. I stood in awe of their vitality and their strong sense of purpose. I was proud to see how integrated they were with one another, and I found myself sad to let go of this group. I would miss their generous sharing!

Through my experience both as a teacher and as a parent, I've been lucky to see sharing circles in all OC age groups. Throughout the classrooms, consistencies in the form and content of sharing have taught me about communication both inside and outside the program. The rules of sharing circle seem to extend beyond that situation as a framework of courtesy that becomes more sophisticated as the participants are increasingly able to consider another's point of view.

In fact, I think that the very heart of OC socialization may be found right in the middle of sharing circle. Visitors to the fifth/sixth-grade classroom commonly admire the maturity of social exchanges, the willingness of children to listen courteously and respond thoughtfully. There is so little apparent adult-imposed management that sharing circle and the whole classroom seem to run magically all by themselves!

But at the same time, this "magical" sharing circle is a huge, constant, and reliable source of exasperation for teachers and parents. This circle is where OC philosophical rubber meets the road, where a teacher has a daily opportunity to see students either as learners or as distracters of learning.

Frustration comes when sharing time looks and feels like the children are active members not in an academic community but in a social or play community. This is when the children seem to seize the opportunity to perform rather than inform.

For example, the first-grade sharing circle might find Ryan crashing together two action figures with all the sound effects. While the children fall over with giggles, Ryan seems to become more involved with his own play and less able to hear a guiding adult ask him to choose the next sharer.

The sixth-grade sharing circle might find Carrie raising her hand again today, as she has every day for the past three weeks, to tell about a dream she had last night. Her dream always includes Tom Cruise and Dave, the founder of Wendy's Hamburgers. Some of her classmates will groan and roll their eyes, some will snicker, but they will all listen to hear who among them was also in the "dream."

And Carrie's teacher will allow her to continue, aware that for a class member to be included in Carrie's dream is to be included in the group in a special way, "like a blessing from the Pope."

But scenes from sharing circles such as these push parents and teachers to the infamous OC question: Is my child really learning anything??

There are parents who have actually left the OC as a result of the frustration they feel about the apparent lack of "real" learning objectives during the significant time devoted to sharing circle. Many parents seem to view the tolerance toward children's ownership of their circle, especially their whimsical circles, as a sign that anything goes in the OC, and that time management is so loose that the children dictate the structure (or lack of structure) of the curriculum. As frustrating and tiresome as these "play" circles are for adults, they too have a purpose that I've come to appreciate after some reflective discussions with OC teachers.

When I was a new teacher in the OC, I wanted to manage the children's sharing more than I did as an experienced OC teacher. The benefits of trusting children to handle this activity came as I developed a wider view of the possibilities by observing other classrooms. It was in those other classrooms that I saw children at their own developmental best. When I took a look at each age level, I noticed and appreciated the variations that were possible in sharing circles, as well as the consistencies that actually qualified the exchange as a sharing circle.

The "circle" space itself, where members of the class sit facing each other in a space that allows each person to be in front, is a consistent component of OC classrooms. Each room features its own large rug space without furniture, to allow for this integral feature of OC mornings and afternoons. Even in older grades, where this space takes more physical room because the students are bigger, the need for uncluttered "circle" room isn't compromised.

OC teachers who have found themselves in a traditional or non-OC setting have tried to pull students out of their desks to gather in a floor circle, only to find that it has not worked. There seems to be something happening in the OC at circle time, from kindergarten through sixth grade, that doesn't "just happen" otherwise.

One teacher speculates that kids who routinely sit at desks may listen in a detached way. These students will skim the flow of auditory information to pick out instructions directing them to perform according to expectation. When suddenly moved to a circle, these students apparently lack skills that are important to a communicative exchange, to the give-and-take of what may be interesting as well as important.

As well as being used for sharing, circle time is used several times each day for scheduling and announcements, activity choosing, and problem solving. In some cases, such as open-ended discussions about math, circle is also a good configuration for instruction. The kind of listening and thinking required in circle goes hand in hand with a collaborative learning model where students build on one another's ideas and a student may benefit by contributing.

Time is another limited resource in a regular schoolday, and time is devoted to circle as deliberately as space is. The implications of meeting daily and regularly in circle, especially over several years, are intriguing. Students don't simply learn to listen for directions; they fully expect a meaningful exchange. While children learn to respect others' interests that they don't necessarily share, they also have less patience for someone dominating their time without allowing them to participate. The older students become, and the more ability they have to consider other viewpoints, the more capable they are of stretching their understanding to find a way to relate to the topic at hand. As a result, a sixth-grade student will tolerate a lecture format longer than a fourth- or third-grader. But students who have become accustomed to an exchange of information are also the last ones to become passive, to expect to be entertained or coerced into learning. In circle, each parent, teacher, and student in the program grows to expect that the speaker is saying something important enough to expect listening.

Attention to the face-to-face dynamic of circle enables some key principles that I see as vital to the enigmatic OC philosophy, as well as descriptive of an attitude I might expect to find from an OC graduate: In this kind of circle, no one is allowed to be just a face in the crowd, passive and voiceless. Teachers, as leaders of the circle, will many times stop a discussion long enough to draw someone, whether child or adult, into the circle. The teacher will encourage and help a person to take an equal place beside the others rather than tucked behind or sitting in front of another. Kindergarteners and first-graders may even be coached in the skill of asking students to make room for them to sit in circle ("Excuse me, can you please move over so I can sit here?"). Even if the circle participants have nothing to say, they still have a unique position in the circle, face to face with those who are speaking and leading. Even though some may choose to only follow along at the moment, they still have an equal chance to impact the group because they share an equal position with the others.

Maybe most important is the notion that on the floor, in circle, each participant is a learner and a teacher. Children and adults have parallel expectations of each other. For instance, each raises a hand for a turn to speak, and each will select from among upraised hands for responses to their topic. Parents may learn from students, or teachers from parents; all may learn from anyone who offers information in this mode of communication. Participants eventually learn to speak with consideration of their audience's interests, and as listeners, they learn to tune their ears for important tidbits from sometimes surprising sources.

Throughout the younger grades, this notion of listening and speaking with purpose is taught at circle. In the first/second-grade class, Leslee encouraged the children to differentiate between questions, which are supposed to relate to the topic at hand, and comments, which can shift focus in the direction of the one making the comment but are also supposed to relate to the topic under discussion.

Of course, the kids play with this. When Leslee encouraged "questions only" in order to keep the focus on the sharing student, many students playfully came up with this "question": "Did you know I have one of those too?" Play such as this is part of learning to distinguish between building appropriately on another's contribution and shifting the group's attention elsewhere. Obviously, the children who invent such a tricky question understand the difference quite well.

Sharing circle in Pam's kindergarten classroom. Several children and a co-oper are eager to be called on by the "sharer" for questions and comments.

In any class, as sharing time becomes an anticipated part of the day, children begin to scrutinize all sorts of sharing rules, such as frequency and rotation of sharing turns and duration of sharing time. The students ask to have these issues explicitly designed; the solutions vary, mainly in relation to the students' age. For example, for sharing in kindergarten, I decided that my students would take their turn for sharing only on the days that their parents took their co-oping turns in the room. Although that teacher-imposed limit may seem very simple and straightforward, the children soon learned that there would be entire weeks when they did not have a sharing turn, because parents were "off" every third co-oping week in kindergarten (to avoid flooding the room with 22 adults divided between four mornings). This was a limit for which both parents and children had an easy reference, and it seemed to work fairly well, although parents felt their child's frustration during the "off week."

The oldest OC students are allowed to share as often or for as long as they care to, as long as they can agree between themselves. This level of kid ownership represents many years of learning, with hours and hours of guidance from teachers who doggedly insist that children listen to and inform one another.

An example of this kind of instruction occurred in Donene's third/fourth-grade classroom with the issue of how long sharing turns should take. Donene found that these students tended to take long turns and to include details that seemed only useful in prolonging the turn. After discussing this issue with the children,

Donene found they agreed on the problem, and together they arrived at a solution. Donene agreed to loan her own watch so that the sharer could be timed by someone of her or his choice. After two minutes, the timer would signal "time's up." Donene found that the two-minute limit helped her students prioritize. And the skill of defining main ideas fit into her overall teaching plan in many ways. Frequently, Donene had her students take a few minutes to first write their sharing highlights in journals so they could use writing as a tool to refine their thinking.

In the higher grades, where students are more capable, they are artfully led through these sharing issues by their teacher, Carolyn, who is a master at handing group decision making back to the students. When an issue such as how to handle sharing turns comes up, Carolyn might facilitate their problem solving in this way:

Carolyn (with group sitting on the floor in circle): It looks like it's time for sharing. Last time some of you seemed disappointed that you didn't get a chance to share, and I've also heard some kids mention that sitting for too long is really hard. I'm wondering how you are going to make sure everyone gets a chance this time. Do you think we need to keep in mind how long we've been sitting in one spot?

Student: You could make a hand signal or just wink to us when our time is up.

Carolyn: But I might not be interested in something someone else is very interested in, and cut the sharer off too soon. You want me to make that decision?

Student: Well, maybe if we know how much time we have and then see how many people want to share, we can keep an eye on the clock and sort of know when to stop.

Carolyn: Want to try that? OK, we have about ten minutes until lunch time; how may people want to share?
(Twenty hands go up.)

Carolyn: Uh-oh, what are we going to do now?

Student: Maybe the person who has something really important can share now, and some other people can wait until the end of the day.

Carolyn: What's really important and what isn't, so I can know how I would decide?

Student: Well, say if your hamster died, or if your parents are getting a divorce, or something big like that is important. But if you just want to say what movie you saw last night and what kind of candy you bought, then you might want to wait.

Student: I can wait.

Student: So can I.

Student: I want to share.

Carolyn: OK, who else wants to share something kind of important right now that they don't want to keep for later?

(Five hands go up)

Carolyn: We have about five minutes left, and I'll just call on you starting on this side of the circle, and when you're through the next person can go ahead and start. Will that work?

The students agree that this should work. And invariably, once the students have developed a solution to a problem that they see as truly theirs, their solutions do work, or they are refined further.

Anyone walking into Carolyn's sharing circle midyear could see a group of students from ages 10 to 12 with an almost unbelievable social maturity. Their interaction would appear effortless and problem-free, with minimal adult-imposed structure. This is the payoff, the shining product and answer to the question "Is my child really learning anything?" And for the uninitiated, the building blocks to this kind of learning can be difficult to discern or appreciate.

In order to produce such a socially responsible exchange, OC teachers are microscopically tuned to the developing capabilities of their students. Carolyn knows her older children are capable of much more responsibility than they are initially willing to assume, so she consistently hands their own problems back to them. In her room, questions of frequency, duration, and content of sharing

Fifth/sixth-grade circle with co-opers and Carolyn (at right).

become practice arenas where students can negotiate. Carolyn firmly invests precious classroom minutes in that kind of learning.

I think it is safe to say that every OC teacher has at one time or another had to defend the intentional investment of sharing time against the protests of those who feel the shortage of time. Behind the scenes, the casual observer or the once-a-week co-oper doesn't see a teacher using developmental knowledge to augment children's ability to decide for themselves. Carolyn, for example, will ask her artful questions day after day until the children learn to use the management skills they may not be initially aware they have.

Also behind the scenes, Carolyn will meet individually with students who have obvious trouble with duration, frequency, or content in sharing. Such students may complain that no one listens, or, worse, they may not notice that they have lost their audience somewhere along the line. For example, Suzi may ramble on and on even when her listeners have become squirmy. At this point, Carolyn makes a mental note to find an opportunity to chat later with Suzi about the skill of anticipating an audience's interest or attention span. This particular skill may even become one of Suzi's goals for the term, her progress shared and congratulated by parents and teacher.

Teaching moments, the magical times when a teacher lucks into a situation where curiosity is hot and motivation is high, are indeed a fortunate consistency in sharing circles. Whether the situation involves a child's ability to interact socially or a new and fascinating curriculum area, teachers and parents have a lot to gain from observing what is happening among the students at sharing circle. For this reason, teachers may insist that parents be a part of circle rather than be tempted to scrub the sink, chat, or any other behind-the-scenes work during circle time. It is very common for units of study to be discovered as interest escalates about a topic introduced by a student during sharing circle.

Of course, it doesn't always come about so magically. Leslee recalled one time when a student shared a photo of his brother Jack and a navy submarine and told the class how his brother was traveling around Antarctica. His teacher, Leslee, immediately recognized the potential for rich discussions from this sharing; she imagined learning about boats, geography, polar regions, or ocean currents. After hours of sharing that seemed ordinary—action figures and stuffed animals—Leslee was thrilled to see so many hands shoot up as the student asked for the customary questions and comments. One by one, he selected three from among the waving hands to question him further or add something interesting. And with these questions, Leslee watched her expanded curriculum evaporate into thin air: "Is that your brother with the moustache?" "My dad is named Jack, too." "I like the picture a lot."

I enjoy this story because it reminds me how often I was wrong about student interests. As well as being wrong about what I thought they would like, I was surprised many times to find their interest sustained by topics I thought were not very full of possibility. To begin with, I was not very interested in troll dolls, baseball cards, or skunks. But I saw long periods of teaching evolve around such ordinary sharing topics within my own classrooms. Furthermore, the children taught me so many things about them that I developed an appreciation I hadn't ever anticipated.

In the OC, research projects and reports frequently take the form of sharing as part of a "Share Fair," where students present their topic as an area of expertise for an enthusiastic audience. That audience may well include students and parents from other classrooms who share interest in the topic and have heard that it is being presented. At presentation time, students enlist a helper to hold visual aids and assist them with materials they have organized carefully in advance, sometimes asking the helper to rehearse with them.

After attending another school for a few years, a former OC student, Valerie Magarian, stressed the importance of communication in such reports:

> Doing reports in the OC makes sense. It doesn't just make sense to the people who are reading them, it makes sense to the kid writing them. If you can choose what your topic is, you'll be interested in the report. In fourth grade in the OC, I couldn't decide between two topics I was interested in writing about and presenting—Guatemala and buffaloes. So I did both. It wasn't a hassle; it was fun.
>
> After everyone has written their reports, it's fun to have everybody who wants to, read your report, and you can read theirs. You get to know what

A student answers questions from classmates, co-opers, and the teacher in a "Share Fair" presentation about bats, in the hallway.

A co-oper visits Valerie's Share Fair presentations, as she explains the written report and her posters, clothes, and objects related to Guatemala and buffaloes. (Photo OC archives)

they're interested in when you read about it. If you read an assigned report, it might not be so interesting because if it is not written enthusiastically, then it is hard to learn enthusiastically about it. It makes a difference if someone else reads your report, because you can hear someone else's opinion and answer their questions. It's rewarding to have other people listen to you talk about what you spent a long time on. If the only person who reads your report is the teacher, and maybe your parents, what's the point of writing it?

A co-oper who moved to another state reported that after a year at a traditional school, her children didn't remember that they had done reports in the OC. "They now thought of reports as copying details from an encyclopedia to get as many pages as possible filled with ink for a teacher to grade. I reminded them of OC reports they had loved—Pompeii, Spain, pandas. They immediately remembered and pointed out that at OC they had *chosen* the topic, researched and understood it, and actually communicated it to people who wanted to learn about it by asking questions and offering comments." For OC children, the format of communication was linked to sharing and was very different from the idea of turning out a "report" simply for a grade.

To watch young children assume careful control of every detail of a project suggests to me that the children "own" their learning. The idea of ownership carries with it an ability to control. OC adults, teacher and parents alike, all deal with issues of control as students begin to own their sharing circle. If students seem out of control, well-informed teachers will guide students back to a purpose, rather than stepping in and taking control. This may seem roundabout and pointless to bystanders if they don't understand how critical it is for students to see themselves as responsible.

Allowing students to own their sharing circles can call for utmost patience and understanding, especially during "performance" circles. After experiencing a good deal of frustration with "play" behavior in sharing circle, I began comparing stories with other teachers.

Together, we noticed that each one of our groups had a characteristic game they played at sharing circle. Denise's first-graders always began their comments with a singsong "I like it a lot . . . ," while my kindergartners were busy each day with a game of sharing their parents. In fact, I noticed my students' game becoming more elaborate every day. A child began by "placing" the adult in the middle of the circle—an act that by itself was enough to inspire shrieks and giggles from the kids—then described the parent as an object, telling the other kids where they got "it" ("from my Grandma") and what it is made of. This is where elaboration really kicked in: The list of what it is made of would always begin with "blood and guts," then go on with a new and impressive list of body parts to improve on the last sharing. A typical parent sharing might be "This is my Mom and I got her from my Grandma, and she's made of blood and guts and brains and muscles and tendons and cartilage and tonsils. I'm ready for questions and comments." At the conclusion of questions and comments, the child would "walk the sharing around," presenting the somewhat bewildered parent to each member of the circle by gently pushing the adult from one giggling kindergartner to the next for a closer look, much like a child might present any item after sharing.

I wondered if I needed to just impose a little more adult structure to sharing time so that it would more closely align with my listening-speaking teaching goals. Considering what I saw as pure silliness from my class, a familiar question came to mind: "Are these children really learning anything?" I wondered if maybe I had lost control and had to get the kids back on task.

Maybe more to the point, what task did I want my group to resume? I tried to talk with the kids about the difference between informing and performing. I tried to encourage them to bring in items that fit with our study of science, of animals, of weather, of initial consonants. I did my best to elicit questions that "helped us know more." The children nodded brightly and smiled their understanding and agreement. And the next sharing time, a fresh parent was placed in the middle of the circle, and the game began again as if I had said nothing.

On the surface, play seemed to be the primary task at hand with my kindergartners' sharing. But as an early childhood educator, I appreciate the value of play. What could the children be getting from this specific form of play? Gradually, we teachers began to suspect that these ritual-like performances were filling a need we hadn't seen. We felt that our objectives for sharing were straightforward and reasonable. But without fail, each classroom had a similar group-specific game at sharing time.

Putting our heads together, we began to see that each classroom's game was a sharing ritual that included all members of the class and actually defined them as members of the group. Each student knew the rules, anticipated the punch line, and delighted in taking a turn to perform. And if it was fun for the kids to see their parents confused, it was even more fun to see the teacher at a loss. We began to see child-invented sharing games as one big in-joke, and gradually we began to appreciate the sense of inclusion this game created among our students.

Most important, I think that not interfering with the students' control of their sharing time was a demonstration of trust. This trust, on the part of parents and teachers, was important in empowering the students to own the process of discovery and delight in communicating their learning. It is also important as a tool for sorting through issues and deciding where to focus energy. No matter how confused we teachers were, or how afraid I became that I might have been "losing control," we supported each other with the trust that the children were learning *something*. This assumption allowed us to use our resources to ask more questions, rather than using our energy to manage behavior. With our new insight about inclusion and ownership, teachers were able to also become included, to share the joke and extend it to baffled parents.

But the bigger payoff to this particular form of play is harder to trace: It is a child's sense of ownership that motivates rehearsing a Share Fair, that expects interest on the part of listeners, that compels further investigation in a topic the child will always remember and love. After spending seven OC years sharing, assuming an equal position in the group, I believe an OC student probably sees a slightly different world than a student who has learned to wait for instructions from behind a desk or to copy material from the encyclopedia. I think an OC student is more likely to express a unique point of view, is less likely to see opposing views as threatening, and may instead see opposition as an opportunity to think further and to extend learning. At the same time, OC students see their world as one they have an opportunity to affect, recognizing that they are the only ones who can express their unique points of view or act on them.

The children in my kindergarten room came to me from preschool experiences where they learned to speak, listen, and interact with people for authentic reasons. Although there are important and practical times when students must simply be compliant (such as a fire drill), I believe a student emerges from the OC with a healthy understanding of what it means to be conventional as opposed to compliant. OC students come to understand courtesy as a means to having a meaningful exchange with others, not a heavily imposed management device.

Courtesy, conventionality, consideration, and caring—these are the bonding elements that can lead students to ignore obstacles and distractions in order to enjoy learning from one another, even if the obstacle is the teacher herself, and even if the distraction is as big as the zoo.

Learning to Manage Time

David Magarian, *student, age 12*

One of the most important things I learned at the OC was how to manage my time. I learned this by making my own assignments that I needed to keep up with by myself. In the OC, kids don't have to do their work every day at a certain time. They learn to keep track of their progress toward deadlines that the teachers help them set. For example, when I worked on math, I would have maybe two weeks to turn in the same amount that I do in my new school (in another state) in two weeks. But I didn't have to stay on somebody else's schedule; I chose the time to do it within the two weeks. When I got frustrated with my work or just tired of it, I could take a break, go get a snack, or play a game and then come back to it. After a little bit I always got back into it.

To set deadlines, kids get together with the teacher to make a plan for how much should be done by the end of a certain time. The teachers help plan the schedule, but they're doing it in a suggestive way that still helps kids learn how to manage their own time; it's not just the teacher's decision. If a teacher would plan the schedule, kids wouldn't learn how to manage their own time—they would just do it when they are told. If kids plan to do too much, the teachers suggest doing less, because the deadline needs to be one the kid can meet. When kids set their own deadlines, they feel committed to them because they planned them.

Often a teacher helped me when I had trouble getting started on hard activities by asking what I still needed to do and talking with me about how to get going. Once I got going on the activity, even if a co-oper said, "You've put in your time, you can go on to something else if you'd like," usually I would just keep going on it because by that time I would have gotten into it, like a good book that I don't want to put down. By having the choice of when to start, I learned how to get myself into the activities I didn't like, and I learned that I might like them when I wasn't forced to do them.

David, engrossed in his book at a time he chose.

I could also move ahead if I felt like it, and most kids do that at some point in the year. OC kids don't tease each other if one or the other is ahead, because everybody works at different rates on different subjects. Some work quickly in math; others work quickly in writing or something else. It's not competitive, so people can help each other make progress. The whole class helps each other learn to manage their time so they can work effectively at their own rate.

I learned that in order to meet the deadlines I set (or the ones that the class as a whole set), I would have to plan my time. There might be times where I'd like to do something else, but I learned that I needed to stay on track to meet the deadline. I learned from my mistakes. That's what the teachers and co-opers always said, and they said it enough that it got into my vocabulary too. And I also made plenty of mistakes to learn from!

Helping Children Learn to Make Responsible Choices

Donene Polson, *teacher and parent*

As an OC teacher and parent, I have learned that making responsible choices is an ongoing process. A few years ago, I envisioned myself as "Supermom." I made sure my son was getting his nutritious, low-sugar lunch, and I tried to anticipate anything that could come up by laying out his clothes, lunch, and sports equipment the night before. Or I would pack up my other three kids, ages one to five, and drive 20 minutes across town to bring my son his forgotten books, papers, lunches, or sports equipment. I did this at least twice a week. I was great! I gave myself the "Mother of the Year Award."

Then one day Mark's first-grade OC teacher met me at the classroom door and asked me to consider letting Mark go without lunch the next time he forgot it. She gave me an article to read on teaching kids responsibility. She said that without his sack lunch, he would be forced to find other options; he could charge his lunch in the school cafeteria, or he could ask his friends for help. Could this possibly work? The next time he forgot his lunch, I stayed home and waited, just knowing that he was probably going to starve. However, when he came home he was fine and happy—all of his friends had shared their lunches with him! After that incident, he started putting his own things by the door and getting them ready to go for school. Another day he had to sit on the sidelines at the pool when he forgot his swimming suit. From then on, he remembered to take his own sports equipment.

As I allowed my son to experience the logical consequences of his behavior, he learned to be more responsible. Helping children to make responsible choices in school begins with making sure that choices are available, then allowing children to learn from the logical consequences of their choices, with support from adults in reflecting on the process and results.

Planning to Include Choices

Parents are sometimes concerned about the children's use of time because so many choices are available in the OC. "This looks like too much fun." "Are my children really learning basic skills?" "How do the kids know what they're supposed to do?"

The program—rather than being chaotic—has a structure that ensures choices and works to allow appropriate consequences of children's choices. The routine and schedule provide both variety and regularity, so that children can find activities of interest and learn how to schedule them to complete both the optional ones that they are most attracted to and those that are required. For example, one required activity is attending a book group—they choose which book group and what time to attend but not whether they will attend. Other required activities in the classroom, such as math, problem-solving cards, writing, science, and spelling activities, are offered several times a week; children choose when to accomplish them and help to determine their goals within the activities.

In my class, if a child has not completed all of the "no-choice" activities, he or she may need to work on them during times that other interesting activities are offered. Since the interests of the children are used to build the curriculum and the children are so involved in choosing the focus of study for the month, they usually prefer not to miss classroom activities.

A safe environment that is structured to support making choices is essential to developing the willingness to take risks and accept consequences. When I went

A student erases her name from "Presidents Activities" once she has finished it.

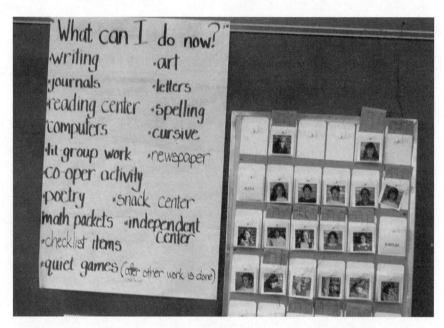

A list for third- and fourth-graders to consult, showing possible activities they can choose whenever they have completed what they were doing, to aid with transitions.

to school, I was always afraid to raise my hand, for fear that I might be wrong. I struggled to find what I thought the teacher wanted for the answer. In a safe environment, kids can take risks and fail without being defeated, can try again and succeed. Providing a variety of activities and allowing choice among them gives children the opportunity to learn how their choices impact their own learning as well as the learning of their classmates.

Assisting Children in Learning Responsibility with Logical Consequences

A problem that we all face today is that there are fewer built-in consequences for children than there used to be. In the agricultural society common in earlier decades, children all had important jobs that contributed to the family. If a child did not bring in the wood, the family was cold. If the cow did not get milked, it would bellow with pain and lose its ability to give the family milk. What are the consequences for children in today's society?

Parents often anticipate their children's needs and provide for the child before the child even feels those needs. Children do not see the direct results of what they do and the consequences that follow.

There are so many parents in OC classrooms that at times, adults are tempted to give students the answers to questions without letting them search for the answers or figure problems out themselves. If this were to happen regularly, adults would keep children from learning the relationship between choices and consequences by never allowing them to make mistakes or by "rescuing" them inappropriately from the consequences of their poor choices. In either case, children miss an opportunity to learn about the relationship between their decisions and the consequences.

During a poetry unit in my class, the children and I learned many lessons on responsible choices. After spending several weeks with mini-lessons on different poetry styles, listening to and reading about many different poets, and writing and "publishing" our own poems, the children's poetry books were on display for parents and students to read and make comments. The majority of the class met the deadline and, when they evaluated themselves, felt great success. But it had also been easy over the weeks to look busy or enjoy friends without putting effort into the project; some children did not finish the work on time. They were not able to enjoy others' interest in their work and the pride of accomplishment experienced by the students who were prepared. This was a built-in logical consequence that helped them learn to take advantage of resources available to them and to make the best use of their time in the future.

As teacher, I also learned from this unit—to hold conferences more frequently with students to support them in managing their time and responsibilities. I found from experience that children need to be given the chance to learn on their own (as my son learned to be responsible for his own lunch). But it is also important to provide support for children so they can learn how to manage their own time— they need opportunities to make responsible choices *and* help in evaluating the results.

Adults can help children learn about the consequences of their choices by helping the children reflect on their experiences and discussing the relationship between their choices and the consequences for themselves as well as others. The idea that solutions to problems must not make problems for others was an important insight I found in Jim Fay's "Love and Logic" tapes. If a child calls Mom at work so she can bring a forgotten assignment to school, Mom may have to make up the missed time at work. This converts the child's problem into the mother's problem. When discussing potential solutions with a child in the classroom, we try to help the child develop a solution that does not make it someone else's problem.

If a child has difficulties in making good choices, and if after several conversations about this issue the child still does not share in the "vision" of making responsible choices—if the child is not participating appropriately in classroom activities or is distracting other children—I call a parent-child-teacher conference. At one conference recently I said to the child, "Can you tell us why we're here today?" He said, "It's because you're writing about responsibility for the OC book. I wouldn't be here if you weren't thinking about it all the time!" We all had a good laugh and then rolled up our sleeves and went to work. We set small goals and made a contract to help divide the day into smaller parts to set this child up for success. After several weeks of checking in with me on his assignments, and with his parents' support, this child was able to make better use of his time and complete the work.

For children to learn to make responsible choices, it is important for them to foresee the possible consequences of their choices. This is assisted by discussion among children and adults about goals, responsibilities, and alternative choices to achieve those goals. As part of the evaluation of each student's learning progress, the children, parents, and teacher look at how well the children make responsible choices in using their time, organizing their work, participating in activities, and contributing to the community of learners.

Problem Solving among Children as Curriculum for Responsibility

When problems arise between students, the logical consequences of problem solving provide opportunities to learn about responsibility and choices. The process is time-intensive but crucial to their learning. It helps children learn that if they work together responsibly to resolve conflicts, their perspective will be understood, and generally they will be able to reach solutions that will help both parties.

When students need help in problem solving, the teacher and students involved find a private space where they agree to listen to each other and be willing to find a solution. Each child speaks, focusing on individual interpretations and feelings about the event, and is not interrupted until all the details of the incident

A teacher (Leslee) helps students in a problem-solving session.

have been given. The teacher restates the problem to the children, and they either agree or redefine the problem. The teacher asks for possible solutions to the problem, and when consensus is reached, the solution is tried and later evaluated to see if it worked or if another solution is needed.

If a problem includes a number of students, such as sometimes occurs in questions of fairness in the use of playground equipment, we bring it to a circle for discussion. We do not use peoples' names or blame or accuse; we discuss what happened and define the problem as concisely as possible. Then we discuss how we will try to resolve the problem. Most problems can be remedied by revisiting the class constitution that the class created at the beginning of the year, which has guidelines that cover just about every potential conflict.

There are usually many opportunities for learning problem solving in kid co-oping activities. For example, Egg Baby City provided constant negotiating and problem-solving experiences. The children learned a great deal about conflict resolution and responsibility in discussing such issues as the fairness of the Egg Baby City Council's rules and the perception that council members were bene-fiting from their political position. The opportunities for children to consider different perspectives on problems is a key aspect of developing problem-solving skills and responsibility.

Making Responsible Choices: A Skill for Life

My son Mark, age 15, reminisced about his experiences in the OC and how he felt they affected his concept of responsibility:

In the OC, each day I would choose activities to participate in. I would mentally map out a schedule for the morning and the afternoon. I think this has been an important skill for junior high and high school. Today I still ask myself how I can make the best use of my time. I map out a mental plan to do my homework and have time for my hobbies and other activities that I enjoy. In America today many people are making millions of dollars by teaching and selling products that help to organize time. In the OC I learned how to do this for free!

I have learned that responsible choices pay off in both the short run and the long run. My dad has always told me, "It is better to learn how to fish than to be given a fish." . . . My dad would help me on my English papers, but as time progressed I needed his help less and less. If my dad did all of the work, I would have never learned how to write English papers. I think there always is a fine line: We need help to some extent, and we need skilled role models to show how things can be done. . . . If my dad didn't help me at all I would have written badly and improved slowly. The concept is a lot like the training wheels placed on bicycles; if the training wheels are never taken off, the kid will never learn to balance and freely ride and experience the joy of riding.

In the OC, students themselves help frame an environment that promotes learning how to make responsible choices in order to facilitate their own learning as well as the functioning of the classroom as a whole. Consequently, when students leave the OC they take with them a foundation for lifelong learning as responsible and contributing members of their broadening community.

PART FOUR

Teachers Learning about Teaching
Children in a Community

What may appear as "wasting time" to an adult can often be a learning experience for a child. I learned an important lesson from two second graders who seemed to spend an inordinate amount of time in the loft making up songs, which concerned me and their parents. I kept thinking "What is the learning here?" And then one day I really listened to their songs. They were singing about the words they had learned in a book we had been reading and about the math concepts we had discussed the day before. They were singing about their friends and their relationships. I finally realized that there was a lot of learning going on. This was the way they were transforming the classroom learning so that it made sense for them. These girls are now in college. (And probably still singing!)

—Leslee Bartlett, OC teacher

As I reflect on the challenges and rewards of being an OC teacher, I realize that each challenge has its own reward. That realization took me by surprise, because I take each challenge so automatically, or as it arises, knowing that there is learning or value in everything that occurs. Sometimes the learning is obvious. Other times I go on a search to find it. But it's always there. Being a constant learner, in itself, is an ongoing challenge. Sometimes, at the end of a long teaching day, as I reflect on my exhaustion, I feel I can't possibly learn one more thing. It's that constant learning that is a challenge and also a reward.

—Carolyn Turkanis, during her nineteenth year teaching in the OC

Teacher, classmates, and co-opers learning from a Share Fair presentation.

Teaching by Learning from Children

Carol Randell, *former OC teacher*

In a learning community, a teacher learns a great deal from students about how to chart the direction of the curriculum. Observing the strategies the students are using and listening to what they are saying provides a way to learn from their thinking, which is essential for a teacher to be able to help students make connections and build on prior knowledge.

Learning from the students is also essential for teachers to build the framework of their own ideas about what is likely to work with a new group of students. Over the years of teaching, I learn from each group of students how to keep their learning moving in a productive direction. I am guided in thinking about how each new group of children is likely to build their concepts and how I can best aid them by my learning from previous students and my reflections on my own previous strategies for trying to help them. All the talking that we do in the classroom helps me learn about the children's ideas and make my next decision about how to help lead the process down a productive path. I get a window into what the children are thinking when they explain things to me and each other, and with what I have learned from previous groups, this knowledge helps me know where they're going and what they need to do next.

An example of building instruction by observing and learning from children's strategies occurred in a second-grade math lesson where the class was trying to determine how many "pogs" (decorative cardboard game pieces) had been purchased by the cafeteria to give away at lunch. We had salvaged from the garbage the 70 punch-out cards that the pogs had come in.

Background knowledge that I brought to the situation (in large part from my learning from previous students) was that our problem could be solved in a variety of ways: simple counting, repeated addition, multiplication, using counting tallies, combining groups, or using a calculator. My goal and sometimes challenge

Carol (by the chalkboard) and the class and co-opers listening to a student's idea during a writing mini-lesson. (Photo by John Schaefer ©)

is to allow the students to try various approaches and determine which works best at their skill level.

I watched three students tackle the problem of figuring out how many pogs the cafeteria had given away by first determining the number of punch-outs per card. I heard John say, "Oh, 24. Gee, I wish there were 25." I could see that John had a good idea. Previously I had seen him notice that four quarters equal a dollar. I thought he perceived 25 as a "friendly" number that would combine easily into groups of 100. I refrained from suggesting this, however, because I thought it would be more valuable if he could figure out the approach on his own.

I watched John start to add "24 + 24 + 24" in his head and quickly lose track of where he was and start to get frustrated. At this point I asked John why he had initially wished that there were 25 on each card. He answered that he knew that four 25s made 100. I told him not to give up on that idea, because it still might help him. Suddenly a light seemed to go on and he said, "Let's *pretend* that each card has 25. It will be easy to put them in piles of 100. At the end we can subtract one for each card!"

The other two boys who had been considering the problem understood the sense of the idea and eagerly started making four-card stacks on the floor. They quickly counted up how many hundreds they had. Then they went back and counted how many cards they had (70) and subtracted that number from their total. They were excited and engaged and had a solution for which they felt great ownership. From this conversation I was able to build future lessons on the idea of rounding to "friendly" numbers, making estimates, and adjusting to get accurate information.

Students need to be discovering but not to be totally on their own in seeking the path. A teacher usually knows where they are heading and can provide direction along the way. Teachers are constantly guiding by knowing the subject matter and providing a framework for the students' efforts.

The teacher is also not alone in finding the path to discover the frameworks that aid students. Teachers' frameworks are guided by learning from students' approaches over the years and from learning from the current students' ongoing efforts. When the teaching situation is truly open-ended, allowing students to make their own discoveries, they sometimes take off in unexpected directions, and the guide gets taken on the journey and learns unexpected things along the way! These realizations become part of the teacher's own learning, to aid in the instruction of tomorrow's students as well as today's.

Risking Saying "I Don't Know"

Joanne Slotnik, Marilyn Johnston,
Leslee Bartlett, Carol Randell, and
Marilyn Osborne, *current and past OC teachers*

To learn, teachers need to be willing to take risks. Although they are classroom leaders, they don't have to know it all. When we had our 20-year reunion of former and current OC teachers, one former OC teacher commented that admitting what she did not know to her teaching colleagues at her new school made her uncomfortable. Others pointed out that even as new OC teachers, saying "I don't know" sometimes felt too risky. With more experience in the OC, however, they gained the confidence necessary to comfortably admit when they were uncertain or lacking knowledge.

We began speculating about the sources of our initial discomfort. One teacher described how her own child's teacher, in another school, felt compelled to maintain the appearance of always knowing exactly what she was doing even when she herself had many questions. She felt the need to demonstrate that her class was in control and that the kids were progressing at the same rate as those in the other classes. Without the support of other teachers, she could not disclose that she had much to learn.

We speculated that a basic tenet of the OC—that learning is a process—encourages people to admit when their understanding is incomplete. No one, including the teachers, is expected to know everything. In a collaborative learning environment, people can say, "I don't know," and then use that acknowledgment—whether with students, parents, or teachers—as the starting point for learning. For example, when a child comes up with a question, a teacher is valued for responding, "Great question. Let's go learn about it. I want to know the answer, too." If the accepted approach is that "we're all learning together," then no one has to carry the burden of always being the expert. This is the heart of collaborative learning.

Functioning as a learning community doesn't just happen. In communicating with parents, OC teachers have to help them see that it's okay for teachers not to know everything. The notion that "I don't know" is a legitimate answer that forms a sound starting point for collaborative learning is a new idea for many parents. Parents often want teachers to "know the answers" and believe that the teacher's job is simply to communicate a body of information—the curriculum—to their children. Gradually, parents learn that it's okay for a teacher to say, "I don't know much about this either, so let's learn together." Eventually, parents see that they, too, can say, "I don't know."

Marilyn, a former OC teacher who is now a university professor, speculated that when a teacher or someone else takes on a new role, they are often expected to immediately know the role and understand all it entails. She reflected on the importance of being able to undertake a new project without knowing all the answers:

> When I started my collaborative project [in the role of professor], I had a huge room of school teachers and administrators who were thinking of joining the project. I got up there and said, "I really wish I could tell you what this project is going to be, so you could tell whether you wanted to be a part of it, but I just haven't got the slightest idea, because we are going to build this project together." They just sat there. I think it sorted a few people out of the project initially, but people kept coming back. Now we're three years into this project and people often say, "Now I know what you meant that first night" or "It took me ages to figure out what you meant by 'I don't know'—you're supposed to know, you're from the university."

The process of collaboration, whether in the classroom or in other settings, requires openness and flexibility so that people can learn from each other.

Several of us who have gone on to other professions have found that having learned to risk saying "I don't know" continues to be important in our other work. Joanne, an attorney, noted that her years teaching in the OC, where teachers were expected to say "I don't know," have helped her argue cases in court.

> There have been times when a judge asked me a question and I had no idea what the answer was. Some of my colleagues will search for an answer and try to fake it, but they're not fooling the judges. The judges know that they don't know. I'd rather just say, "You know, I'm not sure about that. Let me research that, and I'll submit a response by the end of the day." It's easy for me to say that to judges, but most lawyers feel like they have to know everything. . . . My learning as an OC teacher has extended into my later professional life and community work, which is all being done in a collaborative manner.

When risk taking in learning is an inherent goal and the learning environment is supportive, all participants in the community can feel free to say, "I don't know." One of the marks of likely success for new teachers joining a community of learners is comfort with the process of learning, where no one knows it all and everyone learns from everyone else. When we are all learners, each experience becomes an opportunity for learning.

A New Teacher Learning to Share
Responsibility with Children

Jessica Seaman, *teacher*

As a first-year teacher, I sometimes felt that I was learning more than my students. I learned more about teaching and how people learn in my first year of teaching than I had in my five years of college education. Maybe that's because some of my training at two different universities actually conflicted with OC philosophy. My training had taught me that my students really couldn't learn unless *I* was in total control of my classroom, but the more control I used in my classroom, the less my students learned (and the less fun we all had).

I remember giving a lesson that I thought went really well during my student teaching at another school. Later, an experienced teacher told me that I had not been strict enough in enforcing the classroom rules, because some of the students were reaching into their desks or fidgeting with things while I was up in front teaching. So I put into practice the "listening position," an idea I had heard about in my management class. The "listening position" had four rules that every student had to follow while anyone was up in front of the class. First, everyone needed to be sitting flat on their bottom on their chair, with the chair on all four legs and under the desk as far as it would go. Second, the tops of the desks had to be completely clear, leaving no room for distractions. Third, everyone's hands had to remain on the desk at all times. If a student needed an item in his desk (even a pencil or text book), he needed to raise his hand and ask permission. Fourth, all eyes had to be looking forward. A very natural way to learn, don't you think? I am sure it felt more like being in a prison. The consequence for not being in "listening position" was getting your name on the board. As subsequent infractions occurred and checks were added to your name, things started to happen—phone calls to your parents, being removed from class, being taken to the principal's office, and so on. You know, the usual!

After the first couple of days of trying this new technique, I was ready to give up (and so were the students). I was putting five or eight names and checks on the board during every lesson. Think of all the wasted time! But my mentor encouraged me, saying that it would get better with time as the students got more used to the idea, and I must not let up in the beginning stages, so that the children would know that I meant business. Well, it did get better, but not because the children got more used to the rigid "listening position." I just got too tired to keep up this very controlling discipline technique. Looking back, I can't believe that I really tried it. It felt so unnatural, so against the way that children learn (or that adults learn either, for that matter). But I was keeping the children well under my control—just as my supervisors wanted.

A different technique was created by another experienced teacher to ensure a safe and orderly route to one's desk (a worthy goal but carried out in a very unnatural way). It was called the "traffic pattern." To get to any desk in the room, there was a very specific walking path for each student to take. But this was not all. When entering the classroom, a student would need not only to follow the correct traffic pattern to the desk but to follow it with mouth closed and arms folded in a straitjacket position!

Children are full of life and energy; they want to experience and learn and absorb all that is around them. That's why I love being a teacher—I like being surrounded by the kind of contagious energy that children possess. One of the things that drew me to teaching in the OC was the philosophy that being able to move about and discuss things with others enhances children's learning and that children can be trusted to make good choices about their learning when given the opportunity.

Obviously, in this new setting, I couldn't successfully use the management techniques I had been taught, but I still felt I needed to have some degree of "control" in my classroom. I experimented with several ideas and quickly learned that the kids could handle a lot of this responsibility on their own.

I began opening up decisions to my students, such as the kind of behavior that is appropriate for learning in our classroom, how long to make an assignment, how big a reading goal the class should have, where to put up a bulletin board display, how to schedule computer time, how literature groups would be chosen, what kind of food and activities we would have at our holiday celebrations, and what kind of assignments they would have. I was a little nervous at first. I didn't want to be overtaken by 30 or so 9- , 10-, and 11-year-olds, especially in front of their parents. But the kids *always* surprised me.

Most of the children loved challenges and chose appropriate tasks for their level of learning (sometimes with a little coaxing). Occasionally, when a few children had difficulty with this kind of decision making, I only had to open up a discussion in circle, and their peers came up with solutions that would work for them. This sharing of decisions soon became one of my favorite parts of teaching in the OC.

Sharing responsibility with the children helped me solve another problem that was bothering me during my first year. I was beginning to feel overwhelmed trying to impress the children, the parents, and the faculty. It was difficult to balance all of my responsibilities in the OC with my responsibilities at home. Though I was a part-time teacher, my teaching was all-consuming—it was very draining emotionally and physically.

I remembered my mentor at another school, during my student teaching year. The kids loved her, the parents loved her, and other faculty members thought very highly of her. The children took home a lot of great work and fun projects that looked very impressive. For a long time I wondered how she did it. Then it became very clear to me: Her life was consumed by her teaching. Although she had four school-aged children at home, she was at school well before contract time and stayed until the janitor had to kick her out almost every night (and she expected me to do the same). She also took a lot of work home with her and told me that she had turned her entire basement into a teacher workroom. She purchased her own binding machine and copy machine so that she could always work on school projects at home. I could imagine myself in a basement every waking hour, ignoring my family.

Partway through the year, I began having the students help each other a lot more—to help myself stay sane and still feel that I was a good teacher in this learning community. Before they came to me for help, they had to ask three other people first. It could be another student or a co-oper, but they had to ask some-one. The students usually found their answer before coming to me. This not only made my time more focused but also gave the children more opportunities for learning. I wonder how much responsibility and ownership the children felt who were in my mentor's classroom? She was doing a lot of work for them, like publishing their stories, typing their poems, gluing, cutting, and putting books together for them. It really was not the students' work.

As I came to realize the meaning of teaching in a "community of learners," I began having the "community" help out with the daily work. The children edited each other's papers, checked off their work in the record-keeping book, and helped me with curriculum planning. I also started feeling more comfortable sharing my work with the co-opers (most of them were glad to feel needed). In the process, the children and the parents had more ownership of the learning that was taking place.

Communication is the key to making this kind of shared responsibility work. We had discussions in circle about the things that were going well, about areas of confusion, and especially about expectations. What did I expect of the children? What did they expect from me? What did parents expect? And what could chil-dren expect of parents? It takes a lot of communication, but it is worth its weight in gold when the students realize their potential in the classroom.

One of the most important phrases I have learned is "Let it go." I needed to allow the children to make mistakes. Small failures are part of the learning pro-cess for students, teachers, and parents—for the whole community. Before I was comfortable with this issue, I spent a lot of class time (and home time) trying to tidy up certain students' "messes." I was doing extra work that really should have been done by the students. One boy who had a very hard time staying on task was not completing his work, and I felt like I was finishing up his tasks or letting too much slide. I made phone calls, we had conferences (with and without his parents), and I watched him carefully on a daily basis so that I could help keep him on track. His learning was suffering, and I was doing more work because of it.

Instead of trying to fix everything that wasn't up to par, I just needed to let the natural consequences take place. For example, when he didn't turn in the solar system project that he kept putting off, it became homework, and he missed our optional classroom activities until it was completed. Earlier, before I was comfortable with letting it go, I would have spent most of class time helping him finish his project rather than allowing him this responsibility and the resultant learning.

When I see the children making poor choices with their time and energy, I feel bad, but I have become comfortable with letting it go and allowing the more natural consequences and learning to occur. If students turn in less-than-adequate work, I allow them to fix it and make it better. More important, I expect it of them. Making mistakes is an important step in learning.

I learned to relax. At first, I thought that I might be intolerant of all the energy in the classroom—there are always children, parents, and teachers everywhere, doing all sorts of teaching and learning in the halls, outside, under tables, in the loft, and walking around the room. But I am surprised by how comfortable I am with the "busy" noise in and out of the classroom. Since I have created the underlying structure and have learned how to observe the signs of that structure in the classroom, it becomes easy for me to get wrapped up in the excitement as well. In fact, sometimes I don't even notice the noise. My teaching partner walked in one day and asked, "Does it seem a little noisy to you?" It was noisy. But then I listened more closely and I heard children discussing their work. I heard poetry being read. I saw students enjoying helping each other finish tasks. When I relax and listen for the learning that is happening, I am always surprised and pleased.

I also learned how to choose when to deal with or let go of issues in the classroom. No one can deal with all the issues at hand. There has to be a lot of trust that other people—students, co-opers, and other teachers—who are responsible for specific situations can handle them, so everyone doesn't have to use their energy in areas that are not essential to their responsibilities. Rather than trying to *control* the classroom, I learned that I could depend on the classroom community to take care of issues, and I learned how to help foster this shared responsibility.

"The OC community"—a phrase mentioned often by parents, teachers, administrators, and students—was a very hard concept for me to grasp as a new teacher. There were certain words, policies, and procedures that I couldn't understand. It helps to be teachable and be able to admit to children and parents and to myself that I am learning as well. The more I allowed myself to be a learner, the more the community became a part of me.

Although I learned a lot in my first year, I believe I still have a great deal to learn in order to grasp the OC philosophy. The whole idea of the learning community feels like a way of life that just grows over time. In my first year, I was just beginning to sprout!

PART FIVE

Parents Learning Principles of Children's Learning in a Community

As my co-oping activity in my son's classroom, I was doing a social studies focus on the Japanese-American internment camps. My grand finale was to measure (with masking tape on the floor) the actual size of the internment barrack and then to lead a discussion about what life would be like for your *family to live in this limited space for several years. My son grabbed one of the tape rolls and randomly (it appeared to me) started to put masking tape (without measuring—hurumph!) on the floor. I tried to get him to participate in my planned project, but then I decided to go on without him. The rest of the children proceeded with my planned project.*

When we turned around again, it was obvious what my son was doing . . . making an aerial map of the internment camp, complete with guard towers, shared laundry and dining facilities, and fencing all around. The kids joined him and loved sharing it with the other kids in the class as "circle time" formed around it. The direction my son's idea took the project was even more productive than what I had planned, and it ended up informing us all. The lesson I learned is obvious—to be flexible!

—Jean Reagan, co-oper and former Steering Committee co-chair

A co-oper enjoys a story that a child reads to him, speaking through a tube used like a phone.

Becoming a Cooperative Parent
in a Parent Co-operative

Barbara Rogoff, *parent and researcher*

Over the years that I spent as a co-oper for my three children in this parent co-operative school, I gradually came to understand the philosophy and become part of the structure of this learning community. It took a long time for me to grasp the underlying principles—the "common thread" that weaves through the practices of this community. An understanding of the principles gives participants a basis for knowing what to do, but at the same time, it seems that participating is essential for finding the principles.

When I was a new co-oper, my career as a developmental psychologist was largely unrelated to my activities in the classroom. My choice to send my first child to the OC, over a decade ago, was based on the suggestion of a colleague in the psychology department at the University of Utah, who said, "Just think of all the research you can do in the OC!" and talked me into coming to visit his daughter's classroom. At the time, although I liked what I saw for my daughter, I could see no way that I could make use of the OC as a research site—it didn't connect with the way I was studying children's learning.

Over time, though, what I learned from the challenges of seeking this program's principles of learning, in order to participate in it, has transformed my research and scholarly work. It opened my eyes to this way of thinking about learning, which I believe can contribute to advances in developmental and educational research and theory. The program philosophy is apparent in my 1990 book, *Apprenticeship in Thinking*, though at the time I wrote it I did not recognize the depth of its influence in my work.

A key question that perplexed me as I struggled to understand how to participate in a community of learners, as a parent new to the OC, was how adults and children can collaborate in learning. This is a puzzle to many parents as they enter the program; it is also a classic issue in the fields of developmental psychology and education.

Lessons for This New Co-oper

During my daughter's kindergarten year, I spent the required three hours a week in the classroom, helping with instruction. That is, the other parents seemed to be helping with instruction, bringing in science projects and helping with the reading program. I myself had no idea what it meant to help the children learn to read, or even how other parents (the ones with older children in the program) knew they were supposed to do anything. So I watched the other parents and the teacher, and helped children with ongoing math activities or writing when the teacher asked me to. I snooped through the box where the reading records were kept (unaware that this was not considered "snooping" but "being informed"), to see if I could figure out how reading was "taught" and also to see if my daughter was learning to read.

I worried about whether my daughter was learning, not knowing that other new parents had the same worries. I complained to my mother, who had been a teacher in a one-room school, "I just can't tell if she is learning. She isn't doing ditto sheets." My mother laughed and said, "Oh, those are for the parents, not for the children. That's how teachers try to reassure parents that the teachers are doing their job." She asked if Luisa was enjoying kindergarten; since she was, my mother suggested leaving well enough alone.

In our first-grade year, my worries continued, and by then I knew from hallway conversations that other new parents had similar worries. How do the children learn to read when they spend a lot of time doing other activities? Aren't they wasting too much time playing games and making their own choices about how to spend their time? The co-opers' activities seemed at times to be too heavily weighted toward arts and crafts—what about "academic" learning? Some of the children who were more outspoken or badly behaved seemed to get most of the attention in my activities—what about the needs of children who are cooperative and ready to learn?

I tried to figure out how the academic *work* of school could be balanced with the *fun* that this program promoted as essential to learning. The classroom teacher was always supportive and tried to help parents like me understand the contributions to children's learning of play and of making choices—she sent home articles with the weekly parent letter and discussed the issues at classroom meetings and recess.

I fretted about my concerns to a few other parents in the class. One of them reassured me that her older child was doing extremely well and that the children do learn. She prodded me to go beyond complaining and do something about the issues that I saw. I would shrink when she urged me to suggest some ways to improve things or try to improve them myself; I would whine, "But I'm *new* here." She didn't let me off the hook: If I saw something that needed "fixing," she said I should speak up and try to work on it.

My immediate issue was that co-oping itself was so frustrating for me. At first I felt uncomfortable trying to make other people's children do things and had to force myself to try to direct them. But then it seemed like I spent most of my time trying to capture a few wayward children who didn't want to do the activity that I had brought in, to force them to learn my lesson. Even if I managed to get them to the table where I had set up my activity, I still had to spend most of my time trying to get them to cooperate, and meanwhile the group of three or four other children sitting cooperatively trying to do my activity gradually fell apart, as I did.

I couldn't get out of co-oping, because it was required in order for my daughter to be in this parent co-operative program. But after many co-oping days I left very angry with a few children and upset with myself that I had lost my temper and had not been able to "manage" them.[1] The teacher was very supportive but I tried to hide what I considered my failures in the classroom, so she had little idea of my struggles.

To address my frustration, I realized I needed to change something about my attitude, at least. I started by deciding (huffily) that those few uncooperative kids weren't worth my time and that if they didn't want to come to my activity, fine. I'd focus on the large number of cooperative kids and just let the teacher know that so-and-so hadn't made it to my group. (That, it turns out, is what I was supposed to do, not try to solve all the problems myself.) I'd think of participation in my group as a privilege, not an obligation—and the privilege would be earned by cooperation.

Then the mother of one of the boys with whom I had the most difficulty casually told me in class one day, "I hear you're having some trouble getting my son to participate in your activities. I know he can be pretty aggravating. If you go head-on with him, he'll always win; he's really stubborn. But if you approach him in a cooperative way, asking him to join you, he may join in." So it wasn't just the *kids* who needed to be cooperative for the activity to work! It took me some time to figure out how to become cooperative *myself* with the kids.

As I realized that I really needed to change something about how I co-oped, I started talking with my daughter about my dilemma. It was her advice that really helped me turn the corner. I told her that I was really frustrated with co-oping, that it hurt my feelings and made me mad when some kids didn't want to do my activity, and that it seemed wrong that the kids who were ready to learn had to sit and wait while co-opers like me spent all their time on the few uncooperative kids.

Luisa, with seven-year-old wisdom, suggested that I try to make my activity *fun* for the kids, and still be a learning activity at the same time. I admitted, "But I don't know *how* to make it be both fun and a learning activity!" (Fun and learning seemed to me to be opposites, like play and work.) Luisa suggested that, rather than just reading with the children and trying to make them write something about what they were reading, I could have an activity where the kids would make commercials for books like on *Reading Rainbow* on TV. Then it would be fun and they'd be reading and writing. I liked this idea, and Luisa and I set about elaborating it.

I asked the teacher if we could have a *Reading Rainbow* Club and just include the kids who were cooperative, because I thought they were shortchanged. Leslee said yes but that the club should be open to anyone who wanted to join, not exclusive. So the "membership" could vary from week to week; anyone who was interested in really doing the activity could be a member. Luisa and I made a cardboard box into a TV set for the kids to sit in to read their commercials, and I brought along about a dozen of my favorite picture books for the children to choose from for their commercials.

When I described the *Reading Rainbow* Club activity in morning planning circle to recruit my first group of about six kids, there was a lot of interest. When that group of children presented their commercials to the class from inside the cardboard TV at a circle later in the morning, there was even more interest. Astonished, I found over the ensuing weeks that *all* of the children wanted to participate in *Reading Rainbow* Club, and they were all cooperating, even the ones with whom I had previously been having such trouble.

The children were motivated to write a great commercial, especially once they realized that they could only say what they had already written, when they were "on the air" in the TV box in front of their classmates. They generally read several books (which was more than I expected of them) to decide which one to choose for their commercial. They were very task-oriented and helped each other with reading and choosing books.

They needed help to figure out how much to say about the book to interest their classmates in really reading it, without giving away the whole story. This help came from me, from other students in the group as they wrote, and from the other adults and students when the children presented the commercials. An especially effective commercial would elicit comments like "Wow, that sounds like a great book—can I see it when you're done?"; a commercial that was too vague would get comments like "But what kind of a book *is* it?" These comments gave the kids immediate feedback about the effectiveness of their commercials. Over the months that *Reading Rainbow* Club continued, the children's commercials really took form. To cap off the activity, the kids were invited by a local television announcer who had heard about the kids' commercials to present several of them on real TV.

What did I learn from this? I learned that children themselves could be sources of inspiration and ideas about what would be of interest and of value for their learning. I learned that once I treated the children as my allies rather than my adversaries, in a collaborative mode, even the most "difficult" students could cooperate. I learned that my activity was not the only way that children would be engaged—that the parents were cooperating with the teacher, who had responsibility for overseeing the overall scope of the children's activities. I figured out that learning could be fun, particularly when the activity in which the children were engaged was one in which the "curriculum" aspects of the activity were means to an end that made sense and was interesting to the children, not just arbitrarily assigned. And I learned that I, too, could have fun (and learn!) in the activities I led for the children.

It took me a few more years to figure out the importance of several other aspects of the program that had bothered me, especially the central nature of children making choices and leading activities. In the early years of co-oping, I was distressed because I thought that the children wasted a lot of time making

Barbara in third grade, still learning with the students. (Photo by John Schaefer ©)

choices about their activities when they could be concentrating on learning to read or write, using their time efficiently. Part of my concern was probably based on my own need for efficiency, as a full-time working mother of Luisa and younger twins. I had little awareness of the pacing of children's learning.

But part of my concern came from ignorance of the importance of children's learning to manage their own learning and motivation. For adults to cooperate with children to help them learn it is necessary to understand and work with their perspective, experience, and interests. I was used to thinking of children as recipients of adult instruction. Although I was coming to think of children as contributors to their own learning, I somehow thought that children should just quickly make the choices that adults would want them to make! I focused on the "content" of academic instruction rather than the process of learning itself. The idea that people need to *learn* how to manage their time, to see the consequences of their choices and planning, and to manage their motivation were beyond me, despite the efforts of teachers and veteran co-opers to help me understand this.

The children's learning in this area was not apparent to me until we moved out of state for a year when Luisa was in fourth grade: I volunteered in my children's new school and could see the difference in motivation, attitudes toward learning, and planning of time. It became even clearer as Luisa and her classmates left the OC and went to junior high: They reported that compared with the students who had attended other schools, many OC students felt that they were more organized and on top of their schoolwork because they had learned to take responsibility for their work at the OC and also because they were still interested in schoolwork (rather than "burned out," like many of their classmates).

During my early years at the OC, I wondered why the teachers would allow the children to "waste" a whole afternoon in activities that were designed and led by children (in "kid co-oping")—creating plays, doing crafts, looking at rock collections, and so on. I thought that children did not have the expertise to offer much to each other and that the kid co-oping activities were chaotic and a waste of time.

Then, over the years, I noticed how OC kids seemed different from other kids in being able to help each other and in leading groups; the kids attribute these skills (and learning to teach) to kid co-oping and classroom collaboration. OC graduates and their parents report that in junior high, many OC graduates are leaders among their peers in diverse ways: coordinating student groups, leading sports teams, being sought as counselors by other students. Junior high teachers report that OC students stand out in helping the teachers know when something needs to be clarified and in facilitating the functioning of groups in classroom activities.

The opportunity for OC children to be involved in leading and teaching others—and interacting with co-opers whose approaches vary—may facilitate the children's adjustment in different educational settings, such as when they make the transition to junior high. The children's awareness of the process of helping people learn may aid them in discerning the structure of a new educational setting. For example, my three children each spent some of their elementary years in other schools when we lived out of state. Their understanding of educational

A kid co-oper teaching her group to play the Hanukkah dreidel game. (Reprinted with permission from the Deseret News.)

processes has been enhanced by seeing the contrasts with the OC way that they had come to know well. They saw and appreciated the OC way rather than taking it for granted, and they have spent a great deal of time considering what kinds of situations promote learning and foster appropriate social relations in schools.

As a new parent in the OC, I struggled to understand issues that did not make sense to me from the perspective with which I entered the program. Through participation, I began to understand the principles of learning as a community and to understand why the brochures about the program referred to it as "The OC: A Parent *Co-operative*." My thinking about learning transformed from the idea that people learn by receiving knowledge from experts to the idea that people learn by participating actively, along with others who are co-operating in the community.

My transformation connects with classic issues in human development and education that were discussed at the beginning of this book. It also connects with issues faced by other newcomers to the OC, as I learned once my colleagues and I began to do research on the transformations of thinking involved as adults join this community of learners.[2]

Other Newcomers Learning to Cooperate in This Parent Co-operative

Like me, other newcomers sometimes experience "culture shock" as they try to align themselves with the principles and practices of the OC. Their "upbringing" in a model of teaching and learning that relies on adult control of children's learning, widespread in U.S. schools,[3] is inconsistent with the ways of the new setting. At first, they wonder who is in charge, how the classroom is organized, and whether it should be more "structured," with more teacher control. They worry that if adults don't take control, "academic" learning may not occur; they associate learning with being taught in a direct, controlling fashion. They often do not see the teachers' subtle ways of helping children make responsible choices or of monitoring the children's learning over the day.

In response to a survey asking co-opers how they develop an understanding of the program's philosophy, a parent explained what helped her make the transition to knowing what she was doing. Her response highlights the importance of recognizing the difference in principles involved in the OC and in her prior schooling: "I finally let go of a traditional classroom situation and the way I was educated that performs in a completely different manner and attitude."

However, newcomers frequently attribute OC practices to the "permissive" end of the pendulum swing as they move away from adult-controlled structure to the ready alternative—giving children freedom. Some parents argue that children should be left to their own creative process of discovery, not conceiving of the possibility that children can make choices in the presence of guidance. As one co-oper put it, "A problem I see is the constant struggle between the traditional classroom [model] and the child-centered philosophy." Newcomers struggle to understand that the principles of a community of learners embody a distinct and coherent philosophy rather than a compromise between the extremes of the pendulum swing between adult control and child freedom.

Compared with old-timers with several years in the OC, new co-opers more often interact with the children in ways that seem to reflect one side or the other of the pendulum swing, using an approach that either relies on adult control or relinquishes adult involvement to allow for child freedom. Many co-opers seem to make a transition toward a collaborative way of interacting with the children around their second or third year in the program. They reconceptualize the process as one of collaboration, rather than either adults or children being in charge.

Comments on our survey from several experienced co-opers provide a view of the importance of collaboration and mutuality, with adults providing leadership in a collaborative way, not as authority figures. One co-oper noted that with more experience, "it is much easier, less of a power struggle with the kids, more of a negotiated process. I've opened myself to learn from the kids, so now it's a two-way process."

As in my own development as a co-oper, many of the issues for newcomers center on figuring out how to co-operate in a community of learners. They struggle to understand that

- Learning builds on children's and adults' interests with individual choice as well as responsibility.
- Evaluation of student progress occurs during collaborative assistance.
- Collaboration in learning occurs throughout the whole program.

Learning is built on mutual interests with individual choice as well as responsibility. Many newcomers (like me, in the early years) worry about allowing play and fun at the expense of school*work*, which is not supposed to be fun. They do not yet understand how important interest, curiosity, and enjoyment are as resources for learning. A co-oper gave this response to our question requesting advice for new co-opers: "Relax. Listen to the kids. Prepare a *lot*, but you may only use a *little* of what you prepare. Go with what direction the kids are most interested in."

When we asked the children what advice they would give a new co-oper to make a classroom learning activity effective, their first response was usually "Make it fun." When asked what makes an activity fun, children often elaborated, "When we get some choice in how to do things." Sometimes the children added, "The co-oper needs to have fun with it, too," reflecting the perspective that the community's collaborative principles build on mutual interests.

Some parents, coming from traditional schooling ideas about learning, worry because they and the children think the children do not have "homework." OC children regularly extend their school learning at home—reading their literature group book, researching information for a project, finding newspaper articles for a current events discussion, extending a project that was exciting in the classroom, and so on. However, since these activities involve children's ideas and choices rather than being teacher-assigned, the children do not see them as home*work*, even if they spend hours on them. A co-oper, after characterizing the OC philosophy as "teaching children to love learning," commented on her child's adaptation to junior high, "Homework is a new concept for her but one she is intrigued by—not tired of." In the OC, children's interests are such a part of their learning in and out of school that what they need to do is often what they want to do—making assigned homework a novelty.

Evaluation of student progress occurs during collaborative assistance. At first, newcomers have trouble recognizing learning without grades to motivate and tests to examine whether the recipients of instruction have received the information transmitted by experts. The teachers often ask these parents what evidence would convince them that their child is learning, and they respond to the parents' concerns with examples of improvement in children's work, along with observations based on daily collaboration with the children.

Gradually most parents become skilled in seeing the learning in everyday activities, as they collaborate and reflect on learning with the children. One co-oper, whose child had previously attended another school, noted, "I used to say, 'What did you do in school today?' Now I know what's going on and I can say, 'Did you do your rough draft today?' 'Are you finished with your book?' I guess I can keep track of specific things."

Evaluation that aids learning is built on adults having a cooperative role, providing guidance and feedback, rather than controlling children (and later checking to make sure the information was received) or avoiding providing children with the aid of their involvement and feedback to stay out of the children's way as they discover the world.

Collaboration in learning occurs throughout the whole program. Although new co-opers often worry that they need to ensure that each child is receiving their instruction, old-timers see that children balance their involvements in activities with different people. There are multiple opportunities for children to get involved with the subject matter, connecting with different individuals.

As one co-oper advised, in response to our request for suggestions for new co-opers, "Just take it *easy*; hey, if something doesn't work, live and learn. You aren't the only thing or person that these kids see or learn from." Old-timers help the teacher stay abreast of children who may be having difficulties, but otherwise they trust that the teacher is monitoring the bigger picture for each child's learning.

Experienced co-opers come to see collaboration with children as an important resource guiding their classroom efforts. Collaboration with the children provides an important source of continuity from one day to the next and helps adults know what is going on and how they can effectively assist. For example, if children are reading novels in shared-reading groups with different co-opers on successive days, it is not always necessary for each co-oper to be on top of what happened in the book or in the group before the day begins. The children can tell the co-oper what is going on.

The children's reflection on the previous day's reading also provides them with the opportunity to summarize for a nonartificial purpose—the co-oper needs the information (rather than simply testing the children on whether they understand the story). A co-oper who asks the children, "What are we supposed to be doing today?" provides the children with a chance to reflect on the purpose of their activity and how what they did yesterday relates to what they are doing today.

Through my involvement over the years as a co-oper and then as a researcher in this parent co-operative learning community, I have come to see the central feature of the OC philosophy as collaboration with flexible roles and with leadership (provided especially by those who are more experienced but also on occasion by those with less experience). The learning of adult newcomers, as they begin to understand a community of learners, is facilitated in the same ways that the children's school learning is—cooperative assistance with mutual interest in the activities, feedback during collaborative assistance, and collaboration with the group.

For many new members of the community, coming to engage with children in "the OC way" requires a long period of being "legitimate peripheral participants,"[4] provided with some direct instruction but mainly with opportunities to observe, discuss, and participate with more seasoned members of the community. As Leslee Bartlett pointed out earlier in this book, newcomers' development occurs through personally *becoming part of the structure*, in widening fields of participation. A parent in her seventh year replied to our question regarding how her co-oping skills and understanding have changed with experience: "I feel like the OC is now part of who I am."

A co-oper in her third year wrote about what had helped her make the transition to knowing what she was doing: "One thing that helped was being more involved. My first year I felt more like an observer than a participant." She advised new co-opers, "Listen and watch co-opers with more experience." Certain aspects of the community's functioning are difficult for newcomers to see until they have begun to align themselves with the direction of the group, as Pam Bradshaw points out later in this book.

The need to participate in the practices of a community of learners, in order for newcomers to align their thinking with the philosophy, suggests that learning itself is a process where understanding and personal roles transform through participation. My own participation in this community of learners—as a co-oper learning how to *co-operate* with kids and with other adults—gave me the opportunity to change my ideas about learning and how I can assist others in learning. It convinced me that cooperative participation by adults is a key to supporting and transforming children's schooling.

Notes

1. Some people have asked me if it was really as hard for me as what I'm describing here, wondering if this is fictional to make a point or distilled from several parents' experiences. No, this is how it was. Fortunately, I stuck with it—and the experience was so transformative for my thinking and ways of engaging with children that people who know my scholarly writings and my family in recent years may have difficulty believing that I struggled with this before.

2. B. Rogoff, E. Matusov, and C. White, "Models of Teaching and Learning: Participation in a Community of Learners," in *Handbook of Education and Human Development: New Models of Learning, Teaching, and Schooling,* ed. D. Olson and N. Torrance (London: Basil Blackwell, 1996); E. Matusov and B. Rogoff, "Newcomers and Oldtimers: Development of Parent Volunteers in an Innovative Educational Institution" (unpublished ms.).

3. L. Cuban, *How Teachers Taught: Constancy and Change in American Classrooms, 1890–1980* (New York: Longman, 1984); K. P. Bennett and M. D. LeCompte, *The Way Schools Work: A Sociological Analysis of Education* (New York: Longman, 1990); M. Greene, "Philosophy and Teaching," in *Handbook of Research on Teaching,* 3d ed., ed. M. C. Wittrock (New York: Macmillan, 1986).

4. J. Lave and E. Wenger, *Situated Learning: Legitimate Peripheral Participation* (Cambridge: Cambridge University Press, 1991).

Kindergarten, Again

Howard Bartlett, *parent*

Just because I was going back to kindergarten at the age of 42 was no reason to be nervous. After all, I had breezed through kindergarten 37 years earlier, or so my mother assured me with a warm smile as she leaned in the bathroom doorway watching me shave.

"So you're going co-oping," my mother said.

I stopped my razor at the end of its dull and somewhat painful passage up the length of my neck. I replied with a tentative yes.

"What does a co-oper do?" My newly widowed mother had moved out of New England during the summer to help with the raising of our son, Bartie. She was a Yankee down to the depths of her crusty soul, suspicious, sure of what she knew, forever ready to take on the world with a mixture of honesty and determination that left little room for doubt that she would do her best to stick around forever to ensure that her own would have a safe passage through the world.

"Co-opers help out in the classroom," I replied, rinsing my razor under a brief stream of water. I knew that my reply was too short. My mother already should have known. My wife, Leslee, had been teaching in the OC for 10 years. I had written many letters home explaining the philosophy of placing the child at the center of the learning experience.

"Help out? How do you help out?" Mother shifted restlessly in the doorway. I knew her well. She was concerned that this unusual school might not be good enough for her grandson. Questions she already knew the answers to were her own way of being nervous. Like all the first-time parents, she was letting a piece of herself go that morning. A school with no desks, no grades: How could she be sure that her grandson would get the basics? The idea of communication and understanding before competition sounds good. Childhood is a journey, not a race. That sounded good, too. But still...

"We come up with learning centers or activities, or we help students problem solve when there is a dispute. Or we might go through stories children have just written and help them 'book spell' the words they spelled their own way. In this way beginning writers don't have to get into matters of success or failure, right or wrong. They just learn how words are supposed to be spelled when in a book. The program is full of little confidence builders like that."

Mother laughed, "You sound like you're giving a lecture." She paused before she continued, "But what about . . ."

"Oh, Mother. Can't you just let me finish my shave? I have so much to do just to get out of here on time!"

"Well, that's fine. Just fine! There's no reason to get angry with me. I was just wondering, that's all."

Mother left and went into the kitchen, to get Bartie cleaned up, I hoped. I shouldn't have been so short with her. I usually feel protective toward the older people in my life. I gave my face a final rinse and walked into the kitchen. My naked, gently protesting son was being wiped clean with a damp washcloth. I looked at the two of them there at the food-smeared table, a generation separated by the middle spot that I occupied.

"Mom. I'm sorry," I said softly.

My mother looked up, her eyes big with tears that had yet to spill. "Oh, honey. Me too," she said. "It's just that I love this boy so much."

"Me too," I replied.

Walking over to the table, I picked up my damp, squirming, bursting-with-life son. Mother slowly stood. We hugged then, three generations trying to be one.

From where Bartie and I parked on the hill to the east of school we were able to see the playground that swarmed with students waiting for the 8:30 bell. From our vantage point there was no difference between them other than the color of their clothes, hair, or skin. They ran, laughed, and shouted, the patterns that they made an ever-changing mosaic.

"We'll go see Mommy now?" Bartie was looking at me quizzically, wondering why I was waiting so long after having turned off the engine.

"We'll go see Mommy now," I echoed. The top of his head fit perfectly into my cupped hand, and with a gentle pressure I wagged it from side to side.

As soon as we got out of the car, Bartie slipped his hand into mine. It was comforting, this touch of his, so much so that just then I wanted to stop his growth, forever keeping him my five-year-old boy.

We descended the steps to the playground. An old uneasiness came over me. Schools, no matter their grade levels, have always made me feel this way. I remember too well the mad rush for grades, the competition that was taught before communication and understanding, the students who glowed at the head of the class: Ozzie White, Doc Fletcher, mere names now that bring recollections of a kind of envy that had been taught me at the expense of wanting to be just like them.

Down on the playground, Bartie was holding my hand more tightly. Young people rocketed past in pursuit of wayward balls. Shouts and laughter punctuated the sound of hurried sneakers on gravelly concrete. Here and there groups of children were talking. The scene was so right, so complete, given the knowledge that at that moment it was being repeated on every playground across the state.

We threaded our way toward the low-slung building that houses the OC. The heaviness in me refused to lift, despite my assurances to myself that here is a school so unique that it does not even grade. When it comes time to measure progress, a meeting is held with the student, the teacher, and the parents. Each has a chance to comment on how the student is doing, the areas in which progress is being made, areas that need more attention.

It is through the difficult process of letting go that we are able to honor the fact that it should always be the child who is at the center of the learning experience. Learning is about all the feelings, the touching, the talking, the exploration of a world so new that we who have grown to adulthood can barely remember the path we followed to maturity. When we turn around and offer a map to those who are still more dreams than reality, it must be with the utmost care so that we build hope instead of fear, love instead of hate, an understanding that learning is something that can last a lifetime.

I learned how to let go of Bartie during that first year as a kindergarten co-oper. With Thanksgiving close at hand, Bartie and six fellow students were making a miniature Pilgrim village on a flattened-out piece of cardboard that had once been a moving box. My group of seven students and I had walked about the neighborhood and gathered sticks with which to make our cabins, dried grass for their roofs, miniature trees, boulders, gardens, all the fixings for a wonderful Pilgrim village.

After we built our cabins, we decided that the next step was to draw the details of our village on the cardboard. I planned a dirt road down the middle, a stream to be crossed by a wooden bridge, fields turned to fallow for the winter. It was to be a well-planned village, the kind that an overly large wanna-be Pilgrim might design.

To each of my seven students I assigned a task. Easy enough, I thought, hauling out the crayons. In no time at all my village builders were using colors other than the ones I had planned, drawing in areas other than the ones I had designated. Greens and reds and purples were replacing my planned-for browns and tans of late autumn. The bridge that Bartie was supposed to be drawing was off in the middle of what was going to be a field, and it did not look like a bridge at all.

I corrected them many times. "No, use this color. Draw over here."

My charges obeyed for a little while, but as soon as my back was turned, they would wander off into other areas and other colors. Eventually I reached the point where I was about to cry, "No, you're doing it all wrong!"

I controlled myself. Taking a step back, I watched as Bartie drew his bridge. It was a red scribble that suggested that he was more intent on watching the color pour off the end of the crayon than he was concerned with the proper structure and location of a bridge. Red, red on top of red, getting redder all the time. A feast of red. I thought of all the times when the world was nothing more than the two of us crouched on the living room floor with paper and a bunch of crayons. No plans. No designs. No concern with the future. Just a few short years during which I almost drowned in the exquisite pleasure of (just) holding my son while he slept, or reading to him from books whose words and pictures spun incredible dreams out of threads that we, in turn, used to tie the first knots of our love for learning.

Taking a deep breath, I let go. I thought of the parents of my six other village builders, thought how they too were being forced to let go. It is through letting go that we learn about the true nature of our children as inch by inch they slip from our hungry grasp.

Soon I too was crouching on my knees. One by one, I asked the children what they were drawing. With a pen I wrote their responses beneath their creations. That way, when it came time for the parents to take a look at the village, they would know what each drawing was as well as the thoughts that were running through their child's head at the time:

"It's rain. I like it when it rains on Thanksgiving. It makes it cozy."

"If you lay your head down and look at it like this . . . you're lying on your back looking up at the waterfall."

"It's a blueberry bush. As soon as I'm through growing it, I'm going to pick the berries for a pie."

"I wish we could have Thanksgiving every day," Bart responded, looking at me with glowing eyes. Getting down on my knees, I planted a kiss on top of his head, grateful for the lesson he and his fellow artists had taught me.

Parents' Learning about Children's Learning

Leslie Lewis, *parent and Steering Committee co-chair*

Through their experiences in OC classrooms, parents become learners themselves and transform their way of thinking about how children learn and develop. The parents' learning is an important resource for the children's classroom learning, and it also extends the impact of the OC philosophy from classrooms to homes. Because parents and children share in learning at school, the philosophy and practices become part of many families' home life.

Before our family found the OC, I had been volunteering in my daughter's kindergarten in her previous school—cutting, laminating, filing, and trying to stay out of the way. It didn't take long to realize that the teacher (nice though she was) saw a clear distinction between home and school. She tolerated me, but neither of us had a clear idea how I could best help in the classroom. I wasn't interacting with the children at all. Even when the teacher left the classroom for 15 or 20 minutes to deal with behavior problems, she didn't ask me to take charge; the children were on their own. When a friend and I went to observe the OC, I was impressed that the co-opers and the teacher were focused and collaborative and supportive. Soon after this we joined the OC.

I was motivated to help my daughter learn, like most parents in the OC, but I had a lot to learn myself about how I and other adults can help children learn. Initially, the only thing that made the OC more valuable to my family than the neighborhood school was the parental involvement—I could know what was going on in the classroom as well as being acquainted with the children and adults in my child's life. As to other aspects of education at the OC, such as problem solving and building curriculum around children's interests—I knew nothing about them and did not know what to expect.

My children's education has become one of the biggest educational experiences of my life. Some of my most important "lessons" were how children can solve problems and how adults can support this, how teaching can be integrated around children's interests, and how adult flexibility supports children's learning.

Parents Learning about Children's Problem Solving at School

I knew little about how to help children with problem solving until I came to the OC. The whole idea is positive. "We have a problem. Let's solve it. Let's not blame, argue, fight, or forget it. Let's work it out!" It's very basic, and I try to use it with my kids and others, at home as well as at school. Problem solving includes figuring out what to do when there is a glitch in a plan, or an accident, or an interpersonal problem on the playground. I learned that some of the keys to helping children learn to solve problems were to let them try, listen to them, and ask good questions.

At first I was surprised to see that sometimes children can find solutions to problems that adults are stuck on. For example, one of the teachers had come up with a new check-off sheet to help her first/second-graders make wise choices and accomplish all the mandatory activities. The check-off sheet for the first day listed word search, map drawing, magnet independent center, and so on, but oops, the teacher had forgotten to list the activities that co-opers had brought in. While all the co-opers huddled together at one end of the room, discussing how to handle this dilemma for the children, little Sarah took care of it—printed neatly at the bottom of her check-off sheet was "Co-oper Activity [X]." This young child came up with an effective solution, confident that she could take some responsibility not only for accomplishing mandatory activities but also for classroom management procedures!

Watching a teacher helped me learn to support children's problem solving by listening to them. One day in kindergarten, I was on the playground with the children while the teacher, Pam, went to get school lunches. A child had a mishap on the slide and came to me sobbing, arms out, needing a hug. I picked her up and cuddled her as she related the tragic chain of events. Pam returned during the story, and the child reached for her. As the co-oper in charge at the time of the mishap, I felt the misguided need to respond to Pam's questions even though she directed them to the child. Without saying a word to me, Pam continued to listen to the child. I began to see from Pam's gentle lack of attention to me and intent listening to the child that it wasn't really information Pam wanted. Rather, she wanted to give the child the opportunity to relate the story. The process of relating the events is healing for the child. At that time I saw from Pam's modeling what an important role listening can play.

In my new job as a teacher's aide in the neighborhood school that is part of the campus that the OC shares, I do a lot of problem solving with children from both parts of the school when I supervise the playground during the lunch hour. One day there was a problem involving nine children split into about three groups. I just could not get a handle on it. Then an OC teacher happened by. I asked him for help. He got down to eye level with the children and started listening. Then he asked a couple of key questions—"How did you feel when that happened? What would you do differently next time?" It was really clear to me then how important it is for us to help the children discover the solution by asking good questions.

I notice that lots of the older OC children are real pros at problem solving. They state the problem, how they feel about it, and what they see as possible solutions. They're very clear and confident of the procedure because they've been involved in it over and over again and they know that it works. Students who aren't familiar with this procedure often look for adult intervention, resort to physical conflict, or just give up.

By being involved in the process, co-opers figure out that with the chance to contribute ideas to solving problems, OC children learn how to solve problems themselves. Often families learn to use OC ways of solving problems at home and find that they facilitate good communication between parents and children. Some co-opers also find that what they learn in OC problem solving serves them well in other parts of their lives, as Bill Aeschbacher notes:

> After my kids graduated from the OC, I have run into several major hurdles in life. Realizing that I already know most of the skills I need—I think I learned them in circle—has been very reassuring.
>
> The knowledge that mistakes are to be learned from is something I knew, but I became completely convinced of it in the OC. This knowledge saved me from a lot of suffering. I had seen kids have a problem (like with another kid), refuse to learn from it, go out on the playground, and keep having the problem again and again. I had also seen kids face problems, see what the mistake was, figure out how to change it, and be much better off for it. The kids were good role models for me.
>
> The things a person (even a person with one of the big pants sizes) learns about getting along with other people stand him or her in good stead in everyday life. They are also like an insurance policy that pays off when you get into a situation where you really, really need it.

The children's ideas can contribute to more aspects of school than resolving problems: I gradually learned that children's interests and ideas are central to the OC's curriculum.

Learning about Teaching Built around Children's Interests

In the OC's "integrated curriculum," the different school subjects are a natural part of a central theme that is of interest to the children. It wasn't difficult for me to see the learning of math, writing, science, and other subjects when we read and built curriculum around the book *Naya Nuki*, by Ken Thomasma. We "packed" for a trek like the one Naya Nuki took. We figured out how many pounds we'd need to carry to survive and how many days and miles we'd be traveling. We looked at maps and compared Montana and Wyoming, then and now.

But it is sometimes hard for parents to notice learning in the OC because it is embedded so comfortably in activities. I had a hard time seeing the learning in the Egg Babies activity. Although I grew to trust my teachers completely, there were times when I honestly thought they were nuts to allow egg babies in the classroom (they probably didn't know I felt that way). Suddenly, half the children in Denise's first/second-grade class were bringing in raw eggs, painting faces on them, and designing clothing, cribs, cars, and pets for the egg babies.

The initial lesson to be learned was how much time and energy being responsible for a baby requires. The children came up with egg baby day-care centers, movie theaters, and restaurants. There were numerous accidents resulting in injuries and fatalities, so naturally there were egg baby hospitals, funerals, and cemeteries. (White-out fluid makes the perfect egg baby bandage if the wound is not too severe.)

I thought the children would eventually tire of this activity, but it went on throughout the whole year. I felt better about it when Morgan, my daughter, started blowing the eggs out so they weren't so messy. But I still felt it was a waste of time. "Why is Denise allowing this?" I wondered.

Egg babies followed Morgan and her friends into different classrooms over four years. I still wasn't convinced there was any value to it until, in the third year, I heard Denise talking about philosophy at a meeting. She was describing the underlying theme of it all, the things that I couldn't see:

> If children are immersed deeply enough in anything to plan and build hospitals, arrange day care, bake minicasseroles, and do all the writing and reading and conversation that goes along with that, then learning is happening. They write lists; they make written announcements detailing the workings of their government and tax system; they enlist the aid of other children when they need an expert to build a swing set or put a roof on an egg baby home. They translate their real-life experiences with realtors and doctors and others and bring it to Egg Baby City. Learning is happening here.

My daughter and her friends also helped me understand what they had been learning from egg babies, when I asked them in third grade. My daughter said,

> I learned about money, like how to make change—so that's a kind of math. I learned about competition, because we had stores and other people had stores and it was hard to keep up. I learned about budgeting—we had some restaurants and toy stores, and we had to buy supplies with real money. So some of us had fund-raisers. We brought in treats to sell for real money,

and we bought supplies for the egg baby stores with that. Someone had a toy store, and she asked if people would donate old McDonald's toys.

We manufactured egg baby money. My friend Moey and I were the heads of the government. We felt that money needed to be passed around more, and disasters occurred that needed to be paid for, so we thought up taxes. For every $30 of egg baby money that someone earned, he had to pay $1. It worked great.

We learned about how to get a job and keep it. We were very creative because we thought up all different kinds of jobs. There were casinos, toy stores, a subway, bakeries, music stores, car stores, a realtor, and a bank (we all had accounts). Then on the last day of Egg Baby City, we had a big carnival where you spent all your fake money on an all-day pass for food and tickets. All the rides were for egg babies, but the games and food were for humans.

As I gradually saw the learning in the OC's curriculum integrated around children's interests, I also struggled to figure out how to plan and manage the activities I was responsible for in the classroom. This also required seeing how the children's ideas could add to "my" activities.

Parents Learning to Plan with Flexibility

During the years that I've been in the OC, there have been several occasions when a light went on in my head. A lot of those times occurred at highly frustrating moments of co-oping, such as when the children change an activity about which I had a preconceived notion, and the activity turns out nothing like I envisioned it. When we realize it's all right to let the children add their own flavor to an activity, we relax our expectations a little and become more flexible and less frustrated.

For example, once I was in charge of a small group on a field trip to the state fair with the first/second-grade class. I was responsible for six children. As I ushered them around, trying to keep them in a manageable pack, I realized I was losing. One boy kept darting off in different directions. "He's real trouble," I thought. Two and sometimes three of the girls were so immersed in their own playacting about horses and cows and farms that they weren't even aware when I talked to them. I was on the verge of a freak-out!

But I got a grip. I started observing the children instead of herding them. Whenever that boy dashed away, he went a reasonable distance, and when he arrived at his destination, he'd turn and look back to check on my location. The girls, even in their daydreams, never got too far away before one or more of them turned and alerted the others that our course was changing and they needed to backtrack. They wanted to touch everything, see everything.

I let them decide as a group where to go next. They listened intently to explanations about underground water pollution. They asked the attendants the brightest questions about the sheep, the rabbits, the cows, everything. They petted every animal they could reach, and they were oh so gentle. They were enjoying themselves, being responsible for themselves, and behaving like children. What are the rewards for a parent who participates in a trip like this? Unsolicited hand-holding, easy smiles, and cooperation. But the real gravy was the spontaneous hug from the boy I thought was going to give me trouble.

Another lesson about being flexible in my co-oping had to do with cooking activities. When I was new in the program, I had a frustrating day doing butter-milk pancakes in the first/second-grade class. You can't overbeat buttermilk pan-cake batter, or the pancakes get tough. Here were all these kids going crazy at beating the batter, and it drove me nuts. It wasn't a very successful activity for me or for them. I was so uptight about it because there was a proper way for it to be done and they weren't doing it.

Years later, as I was making corn muffins with the children, I became aware of my progress in being flexible. I had been asked at the last minute to fill in for another parent and make corn muffins. Mentally I was unprepared because I had given the activity no thought and did not have a plan, just a recipe and ingre-dients. I just let these first- and second-graders take it. "We're making corn muf-fins," I said. "Here are the ingredients." The only thing I insisted on was that they wash their hands. I was so relaxed. It wasn't a performance for me; I was participating and assisting the participation of others. The children did it all—measuring, stirring, cleaning—and they learned how to do it by doing it. It was a much better experience just because I was relaxed about what they were doing.

At home, too, I'm much more relaxed now—about mud on the floor, about the way the kids do things like make their beds. The kids make a little mess when they fix meals, but they clean it up. I don't expect them to do quite as good a job as I would, but I expect them to do their best job. I've given them the responsibility to take care of things that are manageable for them, and it's helped me as well as them.

By the end of the first year in the OC, I realized that my whole family had been enrolled in Denise's classroom. What happens at home is a part of children's life at school, and what happens at school includes parents and, on many social occasions, the whole family. In the OC, school *is* life, not just a preparation for life. Denise, Pam, Leslee, Carolyn, Donene, and Jessica were not just my child's teachers. They taught me as well. We're a community of learners.

Becoming an Adult Member in a
Community of Learners

Eugene Matusov, *parent*

I thought it would be relatively easy for me, with my six-year background of high school teaching and tutoring of math and physics, to co-op in the OC classroom with my first-grade son. I was both right and wrong. Indeed, my teaching experience and professional knowledge as a graduate student in child psychology helped me design activities suitable for first- and second-grade children. However, in terms of philosophy of teaching and organization of learning activities, my experience with traditional schooling was more harmful than helpful.

My previous experience prepared me for delivering a lesson to a whole class or an individual. I was used to controlling children's talk, which was supposed to be addressed only to me, and my students had learned early on in their schooling that they could talk legitimately only *to the teacher* and only when it was allowed *by the teacher*. The teacher was supposed to be the director, conductor, and main participant in classroom interaction.

In the OC, I was shocked to discover that this traditional format of instruction was actively discouraged by teachers, co-opers, and children. This kind of teaching was not supported by the children in their interactions or by the classroom structure, with its small-group organization, children's choice of groups, and nonsimultaneous rotation of the children from group to group. However, I did not know how to teach any other way.

A First Try: Lesson Plans

At the beginning of the school year I planned an activity that I called Magic Computer. It was designed to teach the reversibility of addition and subtraction as well as reading and computational skills, and it had worked beautifully with first- and second-graders in the past. The activity involved moving a paper strip that carried "computer commands" ("Think of a number. Add five to it. Take two away from it," and so on) through an envelope with a window, to see one command at a time. The commands were designed so that addition and subtraction compensated for each other; therefore, the last message was "You have got your initial number!" The children's job was to discover addition and subtraction combinations that cancel each other out and write them down on the paper strip, line by line. In my past experience, first- and second-graders were fascinated by the "magic" of law-governed math, which returned children to the initial number after it was changed many times.

I talked with the teacher, Pam, about my plan, and she liked the idea. Thus encouraged, I prepared all the envelopes and paper strips for the children (to minimize cut-and-paste activity), along with a few examples of the Magic Computer.

In morning circle, when Pam gave me the floor to speak, I presented my activity: I showed an example of the Magic Computer and demonstrated how it worked. Because of my teaching background, this whole-group presentation worked very well for me—I controlled the conversation and was supported by the teacher, the parents, and the children in doing so. Many children volunteered to come to my activity; I chose five kids for the first group and said that I expected to see the other kids in my activity later in the morning.

I planned to start by explaining the principle of addition-subtraction compensation. Then the children were supposed to create different combinations of addition-subtraction compensation in their Magic Computers. After they had practiced enough, I wanted them to summarize the principle. Then I would be ready for the next group of children to repeat the activity and instruction.

My plan started falling apart during the very first phase of trying to explain addition-subtraction compensation to my group. I did this by demonstrating the addition and subtraction of stones in an opaque jar, but the children were puzzled about how this stone-and-jar business related to the Magic Computer that I had demonstrated in the morning circle. Vivid impatience to start working on the Magic Computer showed in the children's body movements. Spurred on by the children's impatience, I quickly linked the stone example with the principle of the Magic Computer and distributed materials to the children.

The children worked with enthusiasm. Many of them started copying math instructions from the example that I showed them. After they finished making their own "computers," they started playing with them and with each other. Many first-graders were faced with computational problems, and they could not correctly add or subtract. I tried to help them, but I felt myself getting lost in the chaotic, children-controlled communication. During instruction with some children I was often interrupted by other children; I was reactive, and buffeted by the children's demands.

As the activity progressed, I felt more and more irritated. Three main things bothered me. The first was that the children controlled the communication and I could not provide guidance to children who needed it because of parallel demands from other children. The second thing was that the children redefined the activity that I had brought. In my design, they were supposed to work on the principle of addition-subtraction compensation, not on modifying the Magic Computer. The children tried to modify different parts of the "computer" by painting, cutting, and reshaping it, but I had designed this activity for math and not for crayons-and-scissors art. The third problem was that the children were often not focusing on the task that I wanted them to focus on. They spent too much time talking with each other and demonstrating their "computers" instead of working on new compensatory combinations. My interventions to fix all the problems either were ignored by the children or led to disciplinary problems or even mild conflicts with the children.

However, the real disaster was still to come, when there was a transition from one group of children to another. My model of group rotation—one group goes, another group comes—failed from the beginning. New children wanted to join my activity before the initial group had completed it. Some children who had finished the activity (from my perspective) wanted to stay longer, and others left the group "early." After a while, I had some new children, along with children who kept working on their Magic Computers. They were a mixed group in terms of knowledge about the activity, problems they were experiencing, and the kind of help they demanded from me. My explanation of the compensation principle was rushed, often interrupted and fragmented by the children. The disciplinary problems were exacerbated, accompanied by my growing coerciveness. I ended the activity deeply dissatisfied. I thought that the children did not learn much from my activity and did not like the activity or working with me.

I was wrong. During recess, I shared my feelings with the teacher. To my surprise, she was pleased with my activity. She told me that she had observed that the children were really engaged in the activity, felt comfortable, and seemed to learn a lot. I mentioned that I did not complete the lesson because we did not review the principle of addition-subtraction compensation that the children were supposed to learn. "That's okay," responded the teacher. "We can finish up the review session in our circle after recess." In circle, the teacher asked the children from my groups what they did and learned with me and how they liked the activity. To my great surprise, the children demonstrated that they had indeed learned a lot and grasped the principle I tried to teach. Moreover, they liked the activity and asked the teacher and me to establish an independent center where they could keep working on the Magic Computer while I was not in the classroom during the week. Frankly, I was puzzled by the dissonance between the children's and my experience of the activity.

A Second Approach: Relaxing Control

After a few more weeks, I came to the conclusion that I was overcontrolling my interaction with the children. I waited for an opportunity to experiment with relaxing my control. The opportunity came soon, when at the beginning of a morning circle the teacher suddenly was called by the school office. She glanced at the four co-opers in the classroom and asked me to replace her while she was gone. I was panicked, of course, and surprised that the teacher chose me because

I considered (and still consider) other parents to be more skillful than me in leading the children's morning circle. Besides, I suddenly realized that I did not remember the whole structure of morning circle very well. It was supposed to be a discussion of the calendar and what day today is, about children's home and school experiences of the previous day, possible lost teeth, and so on. I did not know how to start or how to proceed. The teacher did it so smoothly and naturally that I never noticed how she actually had done it. The only thing I remembered was to try not to overcontrol the discussion.

I breathed in and said to the children, "You know, kids, I am not a teacher and I forgot what I should ask you about the calendar, about what happened with you yesterday, and about your tooth loss. Can you help me?—can you remind me what questions I should ask you?" I had not expected how successful my move would be. The circle went very smoothly. The children and I felt comfortable communicating with each other. The children easily took responsibility for asking "the teacher's" questions and responding to them. My role was to direct and facilitate the discussion. For example, when a few children tried to talk at the same time, I asked the children about their rules and norms in this situation. So they disciplined themselves. After the teacher was back, she did not take over, but allowed me to finish the circle. I could not convince the teacher and the three other co-opers in the room that this was not my teaching trick but an honest confession to the children of my ignorance of the morning circle structure.

I learned a great deal from this experience. I learned to relax my control and to trust that the children could lead a discussion. I found that they could teach each other. "Aha," I thought, "this is how I can solve the problem of new kids joining my activity group. I'll use the kids who have already been in the group as teachers!"

I started redesigning my activities. First I abandoned my three-step lesson plan: instruction, practice, review. That structure required too much control by me that was not suitable for the OC environment.

Instead, I designed a two-step activity in a such a way that there was a place for me in the activity as a participant, so my instruction was embedded in the activity. Because I presented the activity in the morning circle for the whole class, we could start the activity without other preliminary instruction. I clarified emerging issues while the activity was in progress. Thus, during the activity, my role was as a partner in the activity and as a facilitator and instructor. This format allowed the children to freely interact and help each other.

In the second step, when new children would join the activity, I planned to remove myself from the activity, allowing new children to take my place in the activity as partners and "old" children to take my role in the activity as instructors. When I felt comfortable that the activity worked well enough and could be sustained without me, I left the group. This sustainable activity structure allowed me to both assess the children's learning (if they can teach other children, they have learned themselves) and effectively teach all the children without meaningless reciting and reviewing.

After I left the classroom, the materials were available for the children for a few weeks so they could continue to explore the activity. Basically, I saw my new role as a co-oper who would initiate math-related independent centers with the children. It sounded good and worked well.

However, after a while, I found two big problems in my new approach to co-oping. First, I was bored doing nothing after I left the group to allow new children to come. Second, I noticed that I was still needed by the children, even if the activity could be sustained without my presence. However, it was difficult to re-enter the group after I left it, because the children did not want to be interrupted to explain their progress, problems, and history of decision making to me, and I was impatient and unskilled in participating without full knowledge of what was going on. These two problems pushed me to revise my co-oping strategy again.

A Third Approach: Designing Activities for Mutual Involvement

I realized that I needed to design the activity to secure my participation in all phases of it. This did not mean that I had to be in the group all the time. On the contrary, I had to have an option to leave the group if I saw that the group needed to take full responsibility for the activity. The point was to make my leaving the group a teaching option instead of being a part of a rigid structure like my previous two-step model of co-oping. I also realized that in pursuing the idea of a sustainable activity, I went too far by deliberately excluding myself, as an adult guide, from this process. The adult's role also has to be sustainable in the classroom activity. Realizing that, I started reconstructing my co-oping model to open it up for a sustainable role for myself in the activity.

The activity wasn't designed with "steps" anymore. New children could join the activity anytime. However, my role shifted from being a partner among other partners to being a participant with a special function. In the newest design, it was my job to formulate children's contributions on a common board. This special role was supplemental to the activity, so the activity could continue without me. At the same time, it allowed me easily to enrich, guide, and extend the activity.

An example illustrates this approach. The following year, in the second/third-grade classroom, the parents and the teacher had decided to focus on helping the children memorize the multiplication tables. I prepared sheets of paper, each with a big 10-by-10 square and digits from zero to nine on two perpendicular sides, for the children to fill out with the results of multiplication. In multiplying digits from the two sides and writing the product in the appropriate place in the square, the children also learned the Cartesian system of coordinates.

Of course, it was possible to fill out the Multiplication Square in many different ways, and the children did so, noticing patterns of increment or decrement of the results, using symmetry of the square, exploiting the numbers that were already in the square, and so on. My job was to write down all these strategies, patterns, and approaches on a special classroom board that could be seen by everyone. It was not boring, because I was helping the children to express and extend their ideas. After a while the children shifted from just filling out the square to seeking new strategies and thinking of patterns of the square. When I came back in a week, I found that the list of the children's discoveries had tripled. Some children were working on the task not only at school but also occasionally at home.

The children discovered some very sophisticated patterns. For example, they noticed that each time the digits are sequentially multiplied by 9, the last digit of the result gets decreased by 1 (9, 18, 27, 36, 45, 54, and so on), and each time the digits are sequentially multiplied by 8, the last digit of the result gets decreased by 2 (8, 16, 24, 32, 40, 48, and so on). For 7, there is decrement by 3 (7, 14, 21, 28, 35, 42, and so on). Thus, each time the decrement increases by 1. This pattern goes on until 5, when the decrement suddenly transforms to an increment that gets decreased. This is a rather complicated and nontrivial pattern that the children discovered and I had not known before.

Looking at the list, I noticed that some patterns and strategies were written by the children and some by co-opers or the teacher. I think that the adults' role was more than writing down children's strategies and patterns on the board; it was providing the children necessary help as well. Children knew whom they could ask for help if they got stuck, and adults could supervise and provide help when necessary. The format of guidance was open and flexible. For me, this was a good example of learning where both the activity and the adult's role were sustainable.

In reflecting on the merits of my experience, I think I reached a "better" teaching technique. In addition, the whole exploration process was valuable. What drove me to experiment was a desire to organize teaching and learning in a way that would be comfortable for all the participants, including myself. I came from an environment where teaching-and-learning comfort was associated with re-spectful adult control over the learning activity. Very quickly I found that this kind of organization did not fit the OC environment and participants. So I moved back, being ready to withdraw from the activity, deciding to give all the control of the activity to the children. I swung from the idea of adult-run activity to the idea of children-run activity, like a pendulum. However, what I came to was *more than* finding a middle point between control and withdrawal; it was a third po-sition—mutuality.

This third approach nurtures collaboration between the co-oper and the children in which guidance emerges from collaborative participation, shared in-terests, and mutual respect. Preliminary planning of the activity by the co-oper has a very general outline rather than a detailed character, anticipating children's contribution in planning the activity as well as modifying it. Children's and co-opers' participation in the activity is active in that it includes not only negotia-tion of the children's involvement in the activity but also the co-oper's expecta-tion of such negotiation. Mutual negotiation of responsibility is a type of interaction that, I found, fits the OC. Moreover, I discovered that it fit me as well.

Reflections on Processes of Adult Learning

I have changed since my son and I came to the OC for the first time. The story I presented here reflects only a portion of all the changes that I underwent. It leaves aside my discussions and disputes with other co-opers, my wife, teachers, my parents, and friends about philosophy of teaching and learning. It leaves aside many aspects of my back-and-forth swings from adult-directed to child-centered philosophy and my final abandonment of both. It leaves aside my observations of children, parents, and teachers in the OC, my reading, discussions as a graduate student in developmental psychology at the university, and, finally, changes in my attitudes and beliefs that go far beyond just finding more effective teaching techniques or a comfortable organization of co-oping in an OC environment. The changes have been about a type of interpersonal relations (not only with children) based on respect, mutuality, and trust in other people that I have started valuing more than I did before.

The third model of co-oping that I presented is not the final model by any means. After our second year of being in the OC, my family moved to another state and, hence, another school, so I could not continue my development as an adult member of this community of learners. I am sure that if I stayed longer in the OC community, I would have changed a lot more as an OC co-oper, for two reasons. First, when I left the OC, I did not consider myself to be an experienced co-oper; rather, I had a flavor of the OC way of co-oping. Second, I believe that learning, as life, does not know the limits of perfection.

When an OC teacher, Leslee Bartlett, read a draft of this essay, she asked me, "Could the classroom teacher or other co-opers have saved you some of the agony of this discovery? I'm wondering how much of that process you truly needed to go through to learn it—or if we could have hastened it?" In this question, she points to two important aspects of adult learning and development.

First, her use of the word "agony" to refer to my process of discovering an "OC way" of co-oping highlights the fact that developmental processes for adults to change their fundamental ideas can be uncomfortable. I agree that this problem exists; however, I do not see the solution as one of speeding up the developmental process. Despite the real qualitative changes that adults undergo (as I did in the OC), learning and development are a way of life in the OC community rather than temporal moments in preparation for completion. I think the developmental process of adult learning should be recognized, appreciated, and expected, not hastened.

I offer two metaphors of how to facilitate adult development to make it a welcome and pleasant experience. The first one focuses on handling the discomforts of development, recalling the custom in the United States when children lose their baby teeth. Kids might experience gum bleeding and discomfort, or even pain and the potential psychological trauma of losing a part of the body. U.S. culture has developed a special folklore of a "tooth fairy" that prepares kids for this potentially unpleasant developmental process. The tooth fairy folklore turns the psychological consequences of tooth loss around and welcomes the process (which can bring the opposite problem of kids trying to speed up the process!). Stages in children's development (intellectual as well as dental) receive some support from cultural folklore; however, little such support is available for adult learning. In institutions such as the OC, where adults are expected to change their way of thinking, it may be helpful to develop folklore to provide adults with an appreciation of the developmental process that they undergo.

This leads me to my second metaphor, building on the revision process in writing. Good writing involves revising drafts before a manuscript is ready for publication. Inexperienced writers view writing drafts as a painful but necessary process that can be overcome with experience. They write their first draft as if it is the final draft, using expectations of the final product (derived from reading completed pieces of literature) as a guide for writing the first draft. Of course, they usually fail, because nobody can write a perfect manuscript at the first attempt. A few such failures may kill future attempts and the desire to write. However, a master writing coach can help new writers develop an appreciation of the process of writing drafts. The master sets expectations for draft writing—criteria for a good first draft (perhaps setting down a few ideas), what it takes to shift from first to second drafts (such as beginning to organize the ideas), and so on. In this example, draft writing is not an intermediate, annoying process but a necessary and pleasurable process—indeed, it *is* writing. Similarly, for adults developing their ideas of the learning-and-teaching process, it would be helpful to have greater recognition of the nature and phases of the process so that it can be recognized and even enjoyed.

Combining the two metaphors, I would suggest that in a community of learners—with newcomers struggling to move beyond the model of teaching and learning that they bring with them—folklore could provide a chain of positive constructive expectations for newcomers. The folklore should not fixate on the mismatch between the newcomer's model and the community model but should focus on how to provide a level of comfort in newcomers' participation. OC teachers already provide such support by trying to help newcomers relax about "covering the curriculum" and concentrate on the excitement they share with the children in the classroom. They seek ways for parents' personal excitement to define their area of co-oping, try to limit the number of children in small groups to parents' current level of comfort, and ask children in circle to comment on what they learned from the co-opers' activities, providing catalysts for co-opers' growth and confidence in themselves and the program.

However, newcomers could be further aided by folklore that helps them expect the developmental process. Pendulum swings from adult-run to children-run approaches should be expected, and even encouraged, because through this kind of experimentation with their own teaching, newcomers have an opportunity to experience the "learning moments" that are the quintessence of the OC educational philosophy. Supported by folklore, newcomers could look for emerging problems as learning opportunities rather than stiffen with the pain of educational failures that are inevitable in the process of learning.

Children Learning from Adults Who Are Learning

Some parents in the OC (especially new ones) wonder if the children's education would be better if only experienced co-opers with sophisticated OC collaborative teaching skills were in the classroom. Although on first glance this idea looks attractive, I would argue that it would be counterproductive for children's learning.

Whether they understand principles of learning in a community or not, all co-opers have numerous strengths: They are experienced parents, they are interested in and care for the children, they are generally interested in the activities they design, and they bring skills and resources into the classroom. These strengths make it possible for the children to learn firsthand from caring adults who are active and interested participants in many activities.

New co-opers usually are kind and generally effective in more traditional ways of teaching and are a resource to the children, though they may not yet epitomize the OC collaborative philosophy. They may have difficulty recognizing the great teaching and learning moments in their activities, but they nonetheless provide children with many successful learning opportunities—as with my Magic Computer, which I, as a new co-oper, considered a failure but the children and the teacher viewed as a successful math lesson.

Furthermore, parents' learning how to teach in a collaborative way magnifies the teachers' and the whole school's efforts to educate children. Many parents report that their participation in the classroom makes them more respectful and collaborative within their families. When faced with problems like children not helping with chores, they share the problems with the children rather than attempt to just fix the problem or coerce the children with rewards and punishments. Participation in their children's learning processes in the OC community becomes a cultural "incubator" and "amplifier" of family development for OC families. It also enhances the connection between school and home, as families and teachers understand each other better.

Children also learn about the learning process itself by having opportunities to observe and participate in how adults learn to handle situations when their way of doing things does not fit the situation. The adults' struggles to transform their teaching give the children a chance to learn how adults recognize their problems, ask for and use help from other people, and experiment to improve. The children have the experience of helping others learn, which aids them in learning about teaching and leadership. In this way, parents' learning and development contribute to the process of children's learning as well as to the creation of the social fabric of a community of learners.

PART SIX

Teachers Learning about
Parent Learning in a Community

Initially during my first year of teaching, I tried to make the parents happy by allowing them to choose what they wanted to do—"Just bring in some kind of activity, whatever you want." By the winter holidays, I figured out that this was not making parents happy or working for the classroom. They wanted more specific guidance in their area of focus. I needed to work on finding the time to think about the day with them, discussing and listening to what went on in each group—how it went for the children, frustrations they may have had, things that went really well. It took me quite a few months to stop feeling so defensive whenever the parents asked me questions. But they were learning too. They wanted to feel part of the classroom, and questioning me and my techniques helped them do that. I wish I had felt more open with the parents during my first year—more willing to give and take and discuss and learn. I could not teach in a community of learners without the parents, and I learned that they needed my guidance too.

—Jessica Seaman, after her first year as an OC teacher

A teacher, Denise, conferring with a co-oper, Eugene.

Qualifying to Help
People Learn
Becoming a Beginner

Pamela Bradshaw, *teacher*

When I taught kindergarten at the OC, I would finish the first parent letter of the year with a quote by Rainer Maria Rilke: "If the angel deigns to come, it will be because you have convinced him, not by tears, but by your humble resolve to be always beginning: to be a beginner."

In kindergarten there were many families completely new to the OC, and the first parent letter found people at various stages of comfort with the whole system. The quote was certainly comforting to me as I approached a new group. It helped me to remember that no matter what I felt my qualifications were, a humble resolve to be always a beginner, along with a deep breath, cleared an emotional path that allowed me to venture into the unknown.

The "unknown," in fact, is the catch. To examine qualifications for parents' success in teaching in the OC, I need to indicate the task that the qualifications are for. The expected tasks that parents perform within the OC can be described, such as bringing in activities, inviting children into groups, and supporting responsibility and decision making. But the tasks that are unanticipated are much harder to classify or define. These include problematic moments when a parent might desperately want a "how to" list of instructions. But "how to's"—and qualifications such as college degrees—might fail someone who is limited to any such well-worn tools. In fact, a difficult situation might be much better met by someone who is willing to shrug her shoulders and just be a beginner.

Something powerful happens for me when I realize I am handling something I've never seen before, something for which I am neither prepared nor qualified, when none of my tricks work. As soon as I acknowledge my "beginner" status, then I open the door for my own learning. The OC was surely a community that supported my learning by providing me with many opportunities to fall flat on my qualified face—to get up, shrug my shoulders, and admit to myself that I needed to think again, to be a beginner.

The following event was key in helping me to reframe my own dilemma, as a teacher, of how to look at parents' qualifications to fit into the classroom. It turned out to be a matter of matching parent inclinations with opportunities in the classroom, rather than matching expertise with carefully defined tasks.

I ran into a fellow teacher at a school district meeting. I was only loosely acquainted with her—I knew she had worked with the OC in its early days, but I did not realize that she had left the program discouraged. I was soon to discover that she had devoted some time to deciding that the OC was doomed.

"How's that parent co-op going?" she asked.

I began to tell her how pleased I was, for the most part, with my classroom. I explained how after winter break the parents and I were going to make use of the district Drug and Alcohol Kit, which came packed with lesson plans, puppets, storybooks, and games. I happily babbled on. "The kit will give us all a little break from lesson planning, as well as really give that district kit a chance to be well used!" I stood back and waited for her to admire my sharp thinking.

"Those parents have no business even touching those drug and alcohol lessons," she told me. "Are you forgetting you went through a week of training to learn those lessons?" My colleague was so apparently disgusted that I wanted to hide. It was true that there was a week-long training seminar, with our substitutes paid by state funds, to orient teachers in the scope and sequence of the state-mandated drug and alcohol curriculum. As I looked at her pointed finger in front of me, I remembered that she and I had actually attended the same training session. She shook her head and gave me a look that seemed to weigh my foolishness. "Those parents aren't qualified to do what you are supposed to do," she concluded.

Not qualified? To do what I'm supposed to do? Her comment left me feeling as though she had caught me trying to break my contract with the district, with the state, and with common sense. I didn't feel like the parents in the room compromised "good teaching," although there were times I was frustrated while trying to move instruction along in a complicated classroom. Was I really making a terrible mistake with the drug and alcohol unit? I began to reflect on what I considered parents qualified to do and what I myself was qualified to decide.

I thought back to the week-long drug and alcohol training seminar. The state had invested significantly in teacher education to ensure that the kits were actually being used and that the basics to substance abuse prevention were indeed being taught. A portion of the training was devoted to updating teachers' knowledge about specific drugs, but even that was done with the understanding that information continued to change, that teachers needed to remain aware of new situations presented to "at-risk" children.

I didn't have to take a competency test upon completing the week of training. Nor did I have to promise to teach any or all of the lessons with which I had become familiar.

My critical colleague must have seen her new knowledge and ability as constituting her expertise after our week of training. The same week of training satisfied my questions about the value of the curriculum, and I anticipated using the lessons that were prepared for me. To my way of thinking, my new understanding and willingness (contrasted to knowledge and ability) constituted my expertise and qualified me not only to use the kit but also to guide its use by others in my classroom.

So rather than try to impart a week's worth of knowledge and ability when I met with the parents of my kindergartners, I brought my understanding of the rationale and my willingness to see the curriculum used in my classroom. Before the meeting started, I opened the kit and displayed the puppets along with the children's books and some of the interesting hands-on materials. Beside this, I placed the big lesson-plan binder that held detailed step-by-step instructions for teaching the lessons, as well as the glossary and reference to substances. At the scheduled time in the agenda, I explained about the drug and alcohol curriculum, my week of training, and how I felt the curriculum could benefit our children. I invited parents to take a closer look at the material and to even choose a particular lesson if they wanted to think ahead to January.

The discussion that followed showed me clearly which parents were qualified to teach the lessons and which were not. A few parents, upon hearing the words "drug and alcohol," remembered their own drug and alcohol education. Memories of scare tactics, of misinformation, of distrust and issue-clouding raised their concern. They had many questions, more than I could adequately answer in the time allowed, and at the end of the meeting it was clear to me that it wouldn't make sense to have them use the kit. Their understanding and willingness was low, to say the least.

But other parents listened to my explanation of the rationale behind the lessons and seemed to like the decision-making exercises, the poison-control information, the self-esteem lessons, and the lessons developing a vocabulary to describe emotions. They were willing and eager to look more closely at the kit and use it.

Both groups of parents had a classroom experience that fit their qualifications. Even the parents unwilling to handle the Drug and Alcohol Kit were still able to contribute to instructional momentum because the classroom was always heading in more than one direction. That is, as well as a current topic of study, there were usually one or more concurrent or parallel topics, such as the sea, inventions, phonics, or number concepts.

Parents new to the program frequently want to know how to behave in the classroom, how to fit with what they perceive to be the mysterious "OC way." It can be particularly frustrating when a new parent begins to get an idea of the possibilities and then has a miserable experience when giving it a go. This is when I would hear most often about lack of qualifications. The terrible feeling of "not getting it" becomes more acute after having a difficult experience. Parents cry out for instruction, for "no-fail" activities, for hope.

Now, after my reframing of how to look at the issue of qualifications, I can see at least one clear example of how my efforts to provide parents with "how to" instruction fell flat. In fact, I learned that I couldn't just hand parents "how to's," as much as I wanted to. Parents have to be willing to move with a certain amount of trust in a common direction—to align themselves with where the classroom is going.

A fine example of a big "how to" failure happened one snowy evening when I met with a group of parents at a parent's home. This was a meeting sponsored by the reading/writing committee, which met about once a month with a teacher to share lessons and to review reading strategies that helped students. At this point in the OC, teachers were utilizing some reading and writing strategies that seemed foreign and unwieldy to parents.

In the area of spelling, for instance, teachers were asking co-opers to encourage student's writing efforts by allowing phonetic spelling for first drafts rather than strictly requiring only the "correct" spelling. This practice was raising eyebrows among parents who were afraid that their children were being allowed to get away with sloppy work. Teachers asked the parents to go along on good faith, to trust that the teachers had the training that qualified them to make this sort of pedagogical decision. But to many parents, this new way not only seemed to contradict their own schooling experience but also looked frighteningly inadequate. What if their children never learned to spell correctly and used unconventional spellings for the rest of their lives?

In the classroom, teachers tried to give brief bits of explanation at odd moments to questioning, sometimes confrontational parents. The reading/writing committee was formed in response to a need felt by parents who wanted greater access to a teacher for extended discussion and "how to" help. At the first of the year I had happily agreed to serve as the teacher on the reading/writing committee.

After a few meetings and a lot of discussion within the committee, many of the parents agreed that it would be a good idea to have me actually model a reading session with children where I could demonstrate some ways to support and enhance children's reading strategies. We planned an evening meeting where parents would bring a child or two for a demonstration lesson. I also offered to bring a handout that would list important ideas, so that parents could see a correlation between what I did with the children, the theoretical basis for those teacher behaviors, and how parents might use the understanding in their co-oping. Someone suggested that it might be useful to tape this meeting for interested parents in the future.

On the evening we had agreed to meet, I walked into the living room of the hostess to see a parent stringing electrical cords across the carpet. Big lights were perched on stands, a huge television-type video camera was pointed at a chair, and a clip-on microphone lay on the coffee table for me. I was stunned. A parent explained to me that they had taken advantage of a father who worked at a local TV station to tape our meeting. The equipment in the living room could light and record me as well as any press conference. As children and more parents arrived and saw the equipment, they began to buzz with anticipation. The whole scene looked very important and grand and was a much bigger production than the quiet evening of discussion I had imagined when copying my one-page handout. The more excited the parents and children became, the more I wanted to stay in the other room.

I remember dragging a comb through my hair and saying something weak, like "This is too much," to a parent who knew about the video equipment. She suggested that I put on some lipstick and held a white card next to my face to check the light meter. I decided I better just forge ahead, and I passed out my handouts to the group of gathered parents. I nervously borrowed some lipstick from a smiling mom, then called the children to the carpet in front of my lighted chair, clipped on the microphone, and began to read the story I had brought for them.

With the children around me I relaxed a bit, let myself forget being in the spotlight for a while, and engaged them in the kind of discussion that I hoped would illustrate the topics on my handout. The children listened and commented, questioned beautifully, and enjoyed the reading. We had a story time that went so perfectly that by the time we were through with that portion of the "show," I was feeling pretty confident. Okay, I thought, if they want a recording of what it means to teach in an interactive way, I'll give 'em what they came for. Without so much as a break, I launched merrily onward, explaining each of the handout points.

I was on a roll. And while I might have been vaguely aware that I had been talking for a long time, I didn't know how to stop. It seemed that with the lights on me, the parents were somewhat content to sit back and take it all in. No one asked questions, and I didn't solicit them. There was no discussion, just a performance from me that seemed to be straightforward and, I was thinking, probably very useful. (Everything you always wanted to know about reading instruction but were afraid to ask . . .)

As for the parents who were ready to pull their children out of the OC because of this obscure, strange teaching model that had the children spelling everything wrong, they just didn't seem to exist during my hour-and-a-half monologue. I took the silence from the living room chairs to mean that insight and acceptance ruled. Finally, the camera operator signaled that the tape had run out and that I should stop until he could load a blank video. As far as I was concerned, my explanations were transferring nicely into "how to's" that would provide these parents with all the co-oping activities they might need for the rest of the year. The bright lights stayed on me, but some of the parents quietly rose and began to move a bit after sitting quietly for so long. Too quietly.

One parent had been sitting backward on his chair. He took a moment to pick up the handout I had given him, and, clearing his throat, he gestured with it toward me. The room was still quiet as he spoke.

"Why do we even care about all this gobbledygook," he asked with an angry edge to his voice. The quiet room now became silent. It felt as though everyone who had been courteously listening to my long and ever-so-involved performance now held their breath.

"Well really," he continued, "I can't see one bit of difference any of this stuff makes. Why can't I just go into the classroom and see my daughter learning to read the same way I learned to read?"

With dawning horror I realized that this good-hearted dad had understood absolutely nothing I had said. He had been watching the "Pam Show" for an hour and a half, only becoming more confused, more at a loss than he was to begin with, and now had a good amount of anger attached to the ideas of interactive instruction. He began to wave the handout at me. "You want us to come in and do everything different, you want us to learn what it took you four college years to learn . . . ," he began.

The room erupted in conversation. Several parents gathered around the angry dad, some to agree, some to calm him down. I think someone tried to explain to him some items on the handout, but he was upset and would remain so. Some parents came to me as I put on my coat and picked up my bag, but all I wanted to do was leave. I felt I had given it my best and failed worse than miserably.

Later, I would look back on this episode with less humiliation, but more as an illustration of futility. It is futile, I have concluded for myself, to offer a recipe-book type of instruction to assist in a situation where one must actually make decisions among human beings. Recipes, or "how to" guides, are useful only when one is manipulating objects that clearly cannot act or think for themselves. The same set of instructions would be treacherous if a parent came equipped with only that tool into a situation chock-full of surprises and variables. In the OC, children are not seen as items to be manipulated, managed, or controlled. Rather, they are approached as willing learners who may be excited, guided, and mentored. Instead of offering parents a script or outlined process, it may be much more useful to draw parents into a process of their own where they learn to interact with students in a way that appreciates a student's learning potential.

In order to appreciate the learning potential in a child, it may be counterproductive for a parent to look for only a closed set of behaviors to show learning. In other words, a parent might best be qualified for an OC environment by cultivating a willingness to be surprised, an expectation to be delighted, or a certainty to see learning in many different forms. A parent "qualified" with tight expertise, with narrow expectations of student performance and behavior, could actually be hobbled by such a qualification.

The example above was probably my worst case of missing an opportunity with parents despite my best effort. Many parents later told me they did benefit from the demonstration lesson. A few even expressed appreciation and let me know I hadn't completely left them behind as I had the frustrated dad.

I believe that these parents were able to view my demonstration lesson as analogous to their own experiences, or as a way to help them decide what action to take in a reading lesson to further the children's engagement. That poor father—I had lost him before I began because he had no experience analogous to the situation I created. I lost him as soon as I assumed that everyone agreed children would best be engaged in a story.

In short, my lack of interaction with him in the demonstration was the very opposite of what I was encouraging parents to do with children. A classic case of not practicing what I preached!

But the whole learning experience does serve to illustrate a quality that seems essential for any adult's OC success. That quality is not a cultivated ability to teach, nor is it any particular expertise in a given subject matter. That quality is

A co-oper participating with the children in his group in a geometry activity involving rulers and protractors.

the ability to sense and to align oneself in the direction a learning activity is taking.

The capability of such alignment, for parents, teachers, and students, seems to follow a glimpse of the big instructional picture. The parents in my room who used the state kit simply wanted to, and their willingness became the perfect, undeniable qualification. That qualification alone enabled them to think on their feet, to keep a clear sense of purpose while interacting with kindergartners who could tip over a science experiment or eat the result before anyone noticed.

As the teacher and coordinator of my classroom, I tried to survey a parent's abilities and willingness. If a parent didn't already have an idea about what he would like to do in the classroom, then I could make suggestions about what he might enjoy doing. Some parents quickly picked up the pieces of the OC puzzle and began comfortably contributing, while others labored long and hard and still didn't see that they were doing a "good job."

Parents launching into involvement with the OC are at first confronted with a lot that has nothing to do with the program. They seem to first recollect their own education and any leftover resentments or problems they had with it. They have a sense that the OC is different, and even if they chose to have their child attend the program because it is different, they still have to reconcile the differences as beneficial. A mother of one of my students, an enthusiastic supporter of the program, missed having desks in the classroom. The issue of trying to convince me to place desks in the classroom became central for her; in fact, it became a focal point for any dissatisfaction she felt. She never did reconcile this dissatisfaction and ended up leaving the program.

In addition, many parents have to deal with their identity as contributing adults. Parents need a way to assess their facilitation skills more than their teaching skills. They need to be willing to be a learner like everyone else, but they also need an alternate measure of their success. The teacher's job becomes one of giving parents enough pieces of the OC puzzle that they can act freely with a sense that they are furthering instruction rather than trying to access a list of rules to use in a given situation. Parent stories of "happy accidents" when their plans were actually augmented by an unexpected event are common and gratifying. The feeling of alignment, of working together in a shared direction, becomes the measure of success that a parent—or anyone—needs in order to continue making an effort.

When I think of a parent who became aligned with the whole classroom's direction, I remember Mallory's dad, Bill, who left his law office for the morning to co-op in kindergarten. Knowing that many parents face a challenge in adapting their workplace identity to what is needed in the classroom, I wanted Bill to have a way to meet the children individually on his initial visit. Bill didn't have a particular idea in mind, so I suggested that he take a stack of paintings the children had done the day before and pin each painting to the bulletin board with the child's name, asking for any comments the child might have about her work.

Another parent might have been dissatisfied with this task and may have asked to do something that he considered more important, such as playing a letter-identification game or doing an arithmetic activity. But Bill relaxed into the task; he settled into spending the morning with the children and seemed to enjoy getting to know them. At the end of the morning, the children's paintings were displayed with their names and some comments that each child had offered to Bill. I noticed that Bill had written the exact words each child had said, precisely as the child had said them, and I realized he must have resisted the urge to correct the children's grammar or vocabulary.

This ability to appreciate the children as they were, rather than feel obligated to manipulate them to fulfill an idea of "teaching" them something, at once established a connection with the children and let me know that Bill was aligned with the classroom. In spite of being an expert at his office, he wasn't afraid to be a beginner in this kindergarten room. At the end of the morning, Bill had many ideas about what he might bring in next, which told me that he was not only willing but excited to rejoin us.

But more than anything, after helping Mallory collect her papers, Bill stood by the door to leave, and I noticed him do something that convinced me of his qualifications for the OC. Seeing oneself as a learner, especially among five-year-olds, can be disquieting and uncomfortable; frustration can certainly be expected. But as Bill turned to scan the room before leaving from his first day of kindergarten co-oping, the smile on his face seemed to convey a certain ease, a satisfaction in being a beginner.

A New Teacher Learning to Share Responsibility with Parents

Karen Steele, *teacher*

When I enrolled my son in the OC, the aspect that most excited me was the opportunity for my husband and me to be involved in his educational life; we had a view of education that incorporated the family as an integral part of the learning experience. When a job opened up for a kindergarten teacher in the OC the next year, I was eager to apply. I espoused the philosophy of the OC and saw teaching in the OC as a way to try new things that I had not been able to in my eight years as a special education teacher. I knew that I would love teaching in a program with this degree of parental involvement. My experience as a parent in the OC made me feel that I had a good grasp of the logistics of including parents and how they would work in my classroom.

I had not realized how much my training as a teacher in a traditionally organized classroom would affect my ability to truly integrate a different philosophy of teaching and to work with parents in my classroom on such a regular basis. The expectation of how my classroom should run stemmed from my traditional training, which led me to believe that the teacher should be completely in control of what happens in the classroom.

I began my new teaching position with a mixture of enthusiasm and trepidation. I would have the parents of my students there watching my every move! As I began to learn how to adapt to this scary thought, it became clear to me that I had not anticipated the amount of adult interaction that would occur on a daily basis. The suggestions, encouragement, decisions, criticism, complaints, and praises that are a natural part of teaching suddenly occurred on a scale that I had never experienced before. As the kindergarten teacher, I found it especially hard because many of the parents were new to the OC as well as new to kindergarten. They were learning how to be effective in the classroom as well as feeling anxious about how their young children were getting along in their first school experience.

Sometimes I felt as if I had a class of 52 students—the 26 children in my class plus their co-oping parents. The hardest part of the day was when the dismissal bell rang, because I had as many parents as children needing to ask me something or talk to me about a particular project or concern or idea they had in mind. Of course all of these things are important, and I felt I needed to be there to address them. But their importance did not diminish the exhaustion I felt at times.

As a new teacher in the OC, I sometimes experienced my situation as a power struggle with parents. The strong feeling of involvement that many parents in the OC have when it comes to their children's education contributed to my struggle. It was one of the aspects of the OC approach that drew me to the program as a parent, but it was a challenge for me as a teacher.

Very soon I began to identify the struggle within myself and started to figure out where I, as the teacher, fit into the OC community. In the second week of school, I came home to find a hand-delivered letter from a parent offering "suggestions" for running my morning circle. My first reaction was "How can this person have the nerve to tell me how to teach! I have been conducting circle time like this for years!" I was not prepared for receiving such suggestions from parents, since I had never had parents critiquing my teaching before on such a personal level. I was not sure how to respond, or even if I had the right to respond.

Now, a few years later, I can see that new teachers go through the same sort of process that new parents go through when they enter the OC community. I needed to move beyond the approach that I had learned before—"the teacher in control of all situations in the classroom at all times"—to become able to share responsibility for the classroom with parents. The attitudes "I know best because I am the teacher" and, conversely, "I know best because I am the parent" are both counterproductive in building relationships for working together. A couple of parents in my classroom spent many hours helping me sort through the situation and come to a different perspective.

Earlier in this book, Eugene Matusov suggested that a community of learners could develop some "folklore" to help parents as they go through expected phases in their learning process. Folklore—such as the tooth fairy myth—can turn a potentially uncomfortable process into a pleasurable one or even an essential rite of passage. Developing some folklore for adult learning in learning communities could provide new teachers, as well as parents, with a very helpful tool. My traditional educational training and past practical teaching experience within a different kind of schooling did not provide me with such tools for my own development.

As I have reflected on the power struggle that seemed to occur during my first year of teaching in the OC, I realized that it was connected with my inexperience teaching in a parent co-operative. As I became more confident in what I was doing, I was also able to let go of the feeling that I needed to be in control. I was able to see myself working with parents in a partnership, sharing responsibility with them. An essential part of the folklore may be the need for patience and understanding.

Experience seems to be necessary for teachers to learn to work effectively with parents. As I watch the more experienced teachers, I see that they too sometimes struggle with their roles vis-à-vis the parents, but they have developed strategies for working in harmony with parents. They have the ability to retain their professional dignity while helping parents feel that their suggestions and concerns are valid and worthwhile to the classroom. One teacher told me how much easier it is for her now to discuss curriculum and techniques with parents, thanks to her experience. For instance, when parents question her about a technique, she feels comfortable talking about it because she has seen generations of children learn this way. The confidence she feels about her teaching techniques is then extended to the parents.

Another experienced teacher told me that she looks at potential "confrontations" with parents as a chance for growth, both for herself and for the parent. When teachers can trust themselves, as well as their belief in the OC philosophy, they can look at these experiences as opportunities—learning moments—for themselves and the parents.

From the experience of teaching in the OC, I am learning which approaches work well and which do not work so well. I am learning how to respond more constructively to "constructive criticism," accepting that parents and I can disagree and even have a heated discussion about something and still enjoy each other as friends and colleagues. I am finding that I can learn—along with the children—from the wonderful teaching moments that happen because the parents are in the classroom. From learning to share responsibility with parents, I have learned about curriculum topics as well as about children and the process of learning, both others' learning and my own.

A Teacher Learning about Adult Learning

Denise Nelson Mavor, *teacher*

The approach of autumn puts me into a reflective mode, thinking about co-opers and their learning in their prior year in my classroom. One seems to be more relaxed about herself, her abilities, and her daughter's. Another has really had great success with "I-messages" to handle problem solving in tense moments. I remember when a third didn't really like a particular child; now look at them sitting together! I wish that I could have helped a fourth to understand my suggestions about how parents can be effective in the classroom. I inevitably end up with this final question: "How might I do things differently this year?"

As a welcome breeze came through the west windows, blowing tenured milk-weed seeds off the science shelf and into the classroom, I scanned the familiar circle of six-, seven-, and eight-year-olds and co-opers. I felt a warm smile growing on my face as my eyes lingered on Briand's mother—I've been observing the confidence and patience Cindy has developed. She was sitting in circle, attentive to the children who had sighted the ghostly umbrella seeds suspended in air. The children had paused to inspect, capture, swat, and hail their arrival—loud enough to draw the entire class's attention. "Cool!" "Don't hit 'em, you guys," cautioned Keith. "They're mine, remember? I brought them when school started." "I caught one, Keith! Here, you can have it back," Sarah said, modeling behavior for other classmates to follow. Circle was lively as the children caught the floating seeds and put them away. The last one landed on Cindy's head. "There's one in your hair, Mommy, I'll get it." Briand excitedly picked it from her mother's hair and returned it to the science shelf. Cindy smiled through it all, having made progress in relaxing and enjoying the kids.

The Co-oping Commitment Develops into
Conscious Co-oping

In August, when the teachers meet with the parent group to plan co-oping responsibilities, some parents who feel capable of teaching in a basic skills area, or at least feel adventurous, sign on to help teach one of those subjects. Other parents choose to assist the teacher by teaching or supervising an activity designed by the teacher or begun by another parent. This "back-up" co-oping role is sought after by some new and seasoned co-opers, as it requires little or no preparation, and due to the lack of ownership for developing the activity, failures are not as traumatic.

Co-opers who choose to help teach in a particular curriculum area are expected to be cognizant of their objectives; develop a lesson plan with the concepts and

Denise, at the chalkboard schedule, orients co-opers to the activities for the day.
(Photo OC archives)

skills children need to learn at their particular phase of development; gather materials; motivate, guide, and check for understanding; and help each child put closure on the experience. All the while they need to respect differences in learning styles and rates and individual skills without losing sight of the goals. Except for the lesson design, the same is expected of co-opers who choose to assist teachers or work on activities initiated by other co-opers, and all co-opers are expected to engage in small-group management, active listening, and promotion of higher-level thinking skills.

In the beginning, co-opers almost always have great concerns about how to co-op effectively. Here are questions that co-opers frequently ask teachers:

- How do I prepare activities for different ages and intellects? I think I expect too much of the little kids but don't know how to tone it down. I'm having a hard time keeping the interest of such a wide age range.
- How do I make my expectations clear for behavior and learning objectives?
- It's difficult to hold kids' attention, handle discipline, and try to teach a concept. The kids are so hyper—what do I do when this isn't working for me? It's too noisy. One child's attention span is so short. I can't keep him at my activity. What should I do?
- What do I do when a child tells me, "No, I don't have to!" or ignores me when I make a direct request?
- How do I guide the children positively when I feel so controlling?
- Where do I fit into the scope of the OC curriculum? I want the big picture. I want help planning a block of six weeks or so. I feel unorganized. Where does the co-oper's responsibility end and the teacher's begin?

In the process of discussing these questions with the teacher, other co-opers, and the children themselves, and reflecting on what they observe and try in the classroom, co-opers become increasingly conscious of the process of aiding children in learning.

Since I was a co-oper for my two oldest children for two years before I began to teach in the OC, I have some recollection of how challenging co-oping was for me in the beginning. I was scared and merely put in my three hours each week and went through the motions to keep kids in my activity. I didn't know how to present my activity, get kids to listen and do what I expected, and keep them from escaping. I thought that the kids sensed that parents like me often weren't a step ahead of them and took advantage of this situation. I didn't know whether the children got the key concept or how I could have extended the learning for kids who were ready for more. As a new co-oper, I was never sure if my decisions or my suggestions fit the OC way of doing things.

I had very supportive teachers, but I always felt like I was imposing or like they didn't have enough time to answer questions such as "What is going on here? Should I be doing this, or should I be doing something else entirely?" I wished that someone, the teacher or a "seasoned" co-oper, could just sit down with me and tell me step-by-step what to do, and why I should do it.

Because I'm a perfectionist, I wanted to be a "clone" of the classroom teacher—her style, her knowledge, the "secret" understanding of how the classroom works, how the kids learn, and "the OC way" with regard to making choices and being responsible. But there comes a time when most of us laugh at ourselves—at our need to perform and do it right. Eventually, we really join the OC community of learners. We grow through our interactions with children, teachers, friends, and ourselves. After years of experience and occasional frustration, many co-opers become "master co-opers." They become conscious of the processes of learning and their co-oping strategies become unconscious.

Supporting a Co-oper's Learning Experiences in My Classroom

Now, as a teacher, I am learning how to help new co-opers make their transitions to conscious co-oping. Now that Briand's mother, Cindy, has three years of classroom co-oping experience and is evolving into a master co-oper, I asked her to reflect on her co-oping skills, frustrations, and successes and the wisdom gained in apprenticeship—as well as the guidance or training she still desires. She described her first-year struggle with the issue of managing activities (which resembled my own issues as a new co-oper) and pointed out the guiding role of small conversations between co-opers and teachers during ongoing activities.

> My first year in the classroom, I was as anxious about co-oping as I was about my only child starting kindergarten. . . . It became clear, as I knew that it would, how important it is to me that I have control and have things go the way I'd planned. I felt scared, frustrated, and inadequate as my need for control heightened with each co-oping experience. I just didn't know any other way for a while, until one day during a disastrous co-oping activity, I asked the teacher for help.
>
> I had a large group of children making puppets for a fairy tale. Kids were fighting over parts, who was going to play what, who was going to narrate, and none of my demands helped. . . . They probably made it worse. I went to the classroom teacher in tears. Her suggestion allowed me to "open it up." I went back to my group of chaotic kids and did just that. I let them be free to explore the puppets and make their own puppet shows. That's all it took.
>
> I am always amazed at how teachers, with just a few words of advice— whether it's how to talk to balky kids or those with short attention spans or how to help with redirecting a faltering activity—seem to know just what to do. I really hate to bother the teacher, even though she doesn't seem to mind. But I had to that time, and I still do.

I've learned a lot while co-oping over the past three years. I've always embraced the philosophy of the OC. But I have gained more confidence and patience. I'm now more able to "let go." It's less of a power struggle with the kids, and I better understand expectations of the kids and age appropriateness of my activities.

Cindy reflected on how she has developed as a co-oper: She can now work supportively with the children, rather than focusing on controlling them. Some aid came from my efforts to help co-opers learn how to support the children's writing process—through discussions in the classroom and at recess, and at a meeting in which co-opers worked with a small group of kids, actively listening to them and asking them to reflect on their writing strategies and their topic, to support revision. Cindy later reflected:

> I used to work so hard to get the kids to write that I exhausted myself in the process. I have let go of my need to be liked by every kid and to be so in control of everyone and everything. Instead I go into the experience with a positive attitude and focus on supporting these children for who they are. My priority became "What do these children need; how can I support these children in their writing process?" Not rush them through their process, but support them.

Cindy's growing awareness expanded from fighting to get it right in a somewhat undirected manner to an enlightened dimension of co-oping and teaching where the parents' and teacher's focus is the learning itself rather than the performance aspect of teaching.

Through the experiential nature of education during co-oping and discussing the experience with other co-opers and the teacher, Cindy has learned that her listening helps writers believe in what they have to say. Rather than taking control, as we all did in the beginning—speaking first, rushing in with evaluations, directions, and suggestions—Cindy now listens. Rather than perpetuating the children's dependence on her topics and ideas, she lets the children explore and dream. Rather than coaxing and pleading with the children to write and neglecting to listen to what is important to the writer, she simply asks, "How's it coming?" Her assistance is open, to tap the writer's creative energies. She has learned that our goal is to teach the children to be self-determined, competent, responsible writers and critics, and she has learned how to make that happen.

I asked Cindy, "If you could better understand a particular aspect of co-oping, what would it be?" She responded:

> I would like to find positive ways to support children in finding their goals, meeting them, and evaluating the process . . . positive guidance rather than locking horns so that when I get "I don't have to" or "I'm done" (whether they are or not), I don't respond with the same indignation my parents or teachers would have with me—not that I'd have dared to [refuse], but these kids do, some of them. I don't want to shut them down, but it pushes my

buttons. I have to remember that I am the adult and I've watched you teachers skillfully respond, listen, and redirect.

I'd also like to know how to plan a motivating learning experience for a wide age range of kids and know that my objectives fit the big picture. When I speak of motivating, I'm thinking of the kind of activity that kids don't try to escape from or act out. I want to know how to keep them interested, focused, and acting appropriately.

Still Learning How to Support Co-opers' Learning Process

Every year my cycle of reflections on what I do and how I might do things differently causes me to take some new actions in an attempt to create informational, experience-based, process-oriented experiences for parents in a supportive format. It takes so long to become a master co-oper—can this process be abbreviated?

The process of assisting co-opers in their own development is an ongoing goal of OC teachers, because the co-opers' skills are a key support for the children's learning in the classroom and throughout their lives. Assisting the co-opers to learn involves discussing current problems as they occur, as well as offering special workshops and casual opportunities to watch the teacher and other co-opers handle challenging situations.

I had always felt that the answer to the program's co-oper training efforts was to have teachers do the training. In other words, teachers should teach co-opers how to teach. Teachers should be released from their classrooms several times during the year to mentor parents within the co-oping setting or to hold workshops on teaching strategies, discipline issues, curriculum development, learning styles, and communication. Although the OC traditionally holds an annual workshop on co-oping issues, run by the Philosophy Committee, this didn't seem like enough to me. With the support of teachers' more focused mentoring, I felt that parents would be more confident in the classroom and more productive in their co-oping.

One year, I focused my energies more systematically on this issue and learned an important lesson about co-oper learning—and my own role. I developed a series of three "parent training" workshops spread over one year, each with a different theme, given three times to make it easy for all co-opers to attend.

I wanted to deliver my knowledge to the co-opers. During the first round of three workshops, called "How Kids Learn," I spent most of the two or three hours delivering information. It was basically a lecture format—"Let me *tell* you what I know"—dominated by teacher-talk. Many co-opers were frustrated rather than informed by the session. I did not succeed in helping them understand the philosophy in a new way or come to new realizations regarding the dilemmas that puzzled them.

I felt a real sense of enlightenment when I designed the second round of workshops to be much more interactive than the first, changing my role from lecturer to facilitator. For the theme of these workshops, "Building Relationships with Kids and Solving Co-oping Dilemmas," I asked co-opers who felt comfortable and confident in the classroom to sit with less experienced co-opers to discuss difficult co-oping situations generated by the co-opers themselves. I presented the idea of proactive involvement and requested that they focus their discussions and problem-solving energies on issues and problems that they could influence.

As I walked about the room, it was abuzz with learning and support—co-opers helping co-opers with classroom issues. For example, a new co-oper expressed her frustration about getting one child to write, and two parents with more experience insightfully pointed out that this wasn't so much a writing issue as a power struggle: The child was saying, "You're not going to make me write." The other co-opers and I gave the new co-oper some techniques to try, but most important, we gave her permission to back off and to get to know the child and work together with him—an approach that she found extremely helpful.

In the concluding round of co-oper workshops, called "Listening and Communication," the enlightenment I attained in the second round carried over. I asked parents to help one another with perplexing or frustrating co-oping situations. While listening to two seasoned co-opers help a new co-oper with han-

Two co-opers consult with each other behind the teacher, on a class field trip. (Photo OC archives)

dling a power struggle, I realized they had probably learned how to resolve this matter from their many years of reflective appraisal of their own co-oping practices. Because they don't have the same authority that teachers do, co-opers develop their own techniques that work for them as they lead the activities they sponsor and encourage students to participate.

So now I've come full circle, and my big "Aha!" is that parents need to teach parents, and they do. Teachers can teach theory, curriculum development, and application of how kids learn. But co-opers also need to talk to other co-opers from their own points of view, which can involve differing approaches than the teacher's. (Indeed, this is why we try to balance the classrooms with newcomers and seasoned co-opers each year.)

The teachers have a role to play in the co-opers' conversations, too. At the workshops, I contributed my thoughts in the co-opers' discussions, and it was my job as a teacher to encourage and organize the opportunities for co-opers' reflections. Some of the information that I attempted to "transmit" in the first round of workshops turned out to be helpful when interlaced as support through the second and third rounds of workshops. But I have come to realize that just as children need involvement not only with teachers but also with other children in order to learn, parents need involvement not only with teachers but also with their peers in the context of co-oping and reflecting on their co-oping activities and experiences.

I learned that as a teacher, I have things to learn from the co-opers, as I do from the children. In a community of learners, we all participate as valued partners in finding solutions together, knowing that each of us has an important role to play.

PART SEVEN

Communities Learning Together, Creating Learning Communities

One idea throughout this book is the impact of this program on all who have been a part of it—why is that? Why will I (and most of the authors) always value my role in the OC and see my time spent with them as one of the most growth producing educational episodes of my life?

—An anonymous former OC teacher's note on the last page of an early draft of this book that we circulated for questions and comments.

A teacher and co-opers discussing an idea. (Photo OC archives)

Teachers Learning Together in Forming a Learning Community

Marcy Clokey-Till, *former teacher*
Theresa Cryns, *former teacher*
Marilyn Johnston, *former teacher*

The three of us, teachers from the early years of the OC, have yet to find professional situations where both the challenges and the support are as strong as in the OC.[1] (Marcy went on to start her own business boarding and training horses; Theresa is now principal of a private school; Marilyn became a university professor.) Perhaps the combination of challenges and support was the key to why this was such a powerful context for our growth and development—and for the development of this learning community.

We trace a significant strand of our intellectual growth and development to our participation in the early years of the OC (and, before it, the Thoreau School). Its influence has followed us into our subsequent personal and professional lives, permeating the crevices of our minds and feelings in ways that we have only recently come to appreciate. Our recollections of being teachers in the OC are filled with sharp images and memorable experiences; it was a time of challenge, exhilaration, and exhaustion. We have likely romanticized some of these memories, yet the pains are also vivid. What is most evident is that it was a time of immeasurable learning, for us as individuals as well as for the development of the program as a whole.

Many aspects of our participation in the OC prompted this learning. The inherent ambiguity of our loosely defined roles and the changing nature of the program created a challenging environment for us as teachers. Our roles and responsibilities as teachers were ill-defined, collaborative decision making was an unfamiliar way to make educational decisions, and the curriculum was open-ended and required the integration of student and parent interests. As a consequence, we developed a strong, mutual support system, which in turn encouraged the risk taking that nurtured our further development as teachers. The intense support and challenges are the basis of the initial and continuing development of the curriculum and philosophical principles of this community.

Former OC teachers (Marcy, Marilyn, and Theresa) learning together as they write their contribution to this book at the authors' workshop we held.

Fluid Roles and Responsibilities

Our roles and responsibilities as teachers in this developing community of learners were fluid and nontraditional. Responsibilities were rarely written down—instead, they developed as we worked to implement the emerging philosophy of the program. As teachers, we thought about ourselves as the hub of a wheel. The spokes, representing our responsibilities, went out in many directions and eventually fit together to make a complete whole. Our image of connectedness and wholeness, however, often felt like more an ideal than a reality. Our daily lives often felt more like a wheel with no outer rim and with tangled spokes that led in too many directions.

As new needs emerged, we often had to create roles and responsibilities on the spot. An example is provided by Marilyn:

> We did not have an office, secretary, or principal until we became a public school program. Before that, responsibilities associated with these tradi-tional roles were shared. For example, the school telephone was in my third-to sixth-grade classroom, and as a group we decided how to share the responsibility for answering the phone and taking messages. John, a small-for-his-age, thoughtful fourth-grader, was in charge of answering the phone

one day. In the midst of a phone call, he came running over to a small group of us sitting on the floor discussing a book. "Who's our principal?" he asked with urgency in his voice. "The man on the phone wants to talk to the principal." I didn't have a ready response and did not want to interrupt the flow of our group conversation, so I said, "Tell him you're the principal today and try to answer his questions." He returned to the phone, had a rather extended conversation, and went back to his classwork with a grin of satisfaction.

Sometimes responsibilities developed spontaneously as the need arose, as with John's telephone call; other times responsibilities were discussed at length. Some teachers and parents took on long-term responsibilities where they had particular abilities and interests, but other roles were passed around. John was "the principal" that day because we needed one, but most of the time the traditional responsibilities of a principal were shared. We often traded responsibilities among students, teachers, and parents, in order to help develop skills as well as a sense of ownership.

We teachers were committed to working with parents and children, but there were some distinct responsibilities that we alone carried. We felt a particular responsibility for all the children's learning as well as the successful continuation of the program. Parents naturally were more focused on their own children and did not always take the program as a whole into account. We also felt responsible for educating new parents about the school's philosophy and for helping them to work as effective co-opers in the classrooms.

As teachers, we felt a shared sense of ownership, knowing that the program's success or failure lay squarely on our shoulders. We knew each other's strengths and weaknesses and depended on different teachers' abilities in different areas. But we also often did things that were not in our areas of strength because there were so many demands on everyone.

Collaborative Decision Making

Decision making took place in many different ways and places and among various groups of adults and children. The question "Who will be affected by this decision?" determined who would be involved. Is this a parent-child decision, a classroom decision, a faculty decision, a whole-program decision? Things were negotiated and renegotiated because there weren't clear rules for decision making; there was only a general commitment to democratic principles and collaborative procedures.

It was often hard to know who should decide and when something had been finally decided. A disagreement about a decision could be raised by anyone, and the matter would then have to be taken up by some group somewhere for further discussion. The topic of "who decides what" was much discussed, including with the children.

Initially, most decisions were made by the whole group. The 22 parents who created the Thoreau School worked together to build the curriculum, find a building, gather equipment, and hire a teacher. As our size increased, it was not possible for the whole group to make all the decisions. Eventually, as teachers, we identified some areas of responsibility that were within our realm. We became more comfortable with making these decisions and then checking them out with our students and parents. Other decisions needed to start with the students and parents in order to incorporate their ideas and interests. Deciding who was to make what decisions remained a delicate issue that required an ongoing willingness to rediscuss issues if people who were not involved in the decision felt left out of the process.

For example, there was the recurring issue of parents who could not co-op during regular school hours. Sometimes a family desperately wanted their child in the program but could not get off work during the day. They would offer to do other things at home, such as administrative tasks or curriculum preparation. In other cases, a family had been in the program for some time and then their situation changed—because of a divorce or an illness, for example. As new situations emerged, decisions had to be made. Should the situation be handled by the teacher and parents of their classroom, or was this a matter that needed to go to the whole group? More generally, if we have a commitment to classroom co-oping, should we make exceptions, and if so, for what reasons?

The ambiguities of decisions like these entailed endless conversations. In addition, there were routine decisions that had to be made. As teachers, we had conversations at recess and lunch, after school, on the phone, at evening meetings, on camping trips and retreats, and in the car to and from school. The conversations included questions, disagreements, plans for experimentation, and even bewilderment, as we created ways of making decisions and accomplishing our goals; our learning was immense as a result.

Shared Ownership

The collaborative way in which decisions and philosophy were constructed was the key to our sense of shared ownership. As teachers we had to decide how the classrooms and curriculum were going to be designed, taking the interests of everyone involved into account. This was far more extensive than the typical range of teacher decision making, which is limited to the confines of the classroom.

We had a sense of responsibility that is hard to achieve in settings where public responsibility increases with one's ranking in an administrative hierarchy. Typically, teachers are at the bottom of the hierarchy. School administrators make the important decisions; they take the heat but also the praise, while teachers carry out the mandates of curriculum designers and are evaluated by experts who know little about the teachers' individual goals, circumstances, or students. With the opportunity to make decisions came a strong feeling of commitment.

While we felt a particular kind of responsibility as teachers, we also shared this charge with the parents and children. We couldn't have carried out this project on our own. We needed to build a consensus within the larger group, nurture parents' continuing trust in the program's worth, and learn enough from what we were doing to keep the program developing in productive directions. We had to work together in ways that produced fruitful outcomes.

A strong sense of ownership meant that teachers and parents could question things that would have been outside their purview in typical educational settings. For example, an ongoing debate began the first year as we questioned whether having recess fit our philosophy. If the children were in a highly social environment all the time, did 10-minute recesses serve our purposes? Recesses in traditional classrooms are given so that children have a chance to exercise and talk with friends, because they don't get to do these things in the classroom. Our children, however, were moving around and talking with peers all the time. We initially built recess into the schedule because we had not thought to do otherwise. But we began to see that recess often interrupted the flow of the social interactions and learning in the classroom. Many children did not like recess anyway; they were busy and did not want to be interrupted. Other children liked the fresh air and sports activities. We tried many variations and gave children choices. Each time we tried something different, we talked about the results and implications.

It often seemed that there were no "right" answers—the decisions were inherently open-ended. Sometimes we decided on something and it worked well, but then with another group of children or a different classroom it was not successful. For example, one year the usual approaches to helping children plan their day were just not working. So we decided to create a Starting Group— children who could not productively get started with their day came to this group to get help with planning. Some children were required to start their day with the Starting Group because it was clear that we needed to create more structure for them if they were to succeed in using their time well. We came to understand the need for both careful planning and continual flexibility in order to meet changing individual and group needs.

We came to realize that many aspects of school, like recess or planning time, could be handled in a variety of ways. The process of reaching decisions became as important as the results. It was in the process that ideas got developed, beliefs became informed, and ownership was jointly constructed. Even if the outcome of the decision making failed, the process was usually constructive because it built our sense of community and commitment.

Mutual Support and Sharing

Support and sharing were critical to our success as teachers in the OC. Marcy reflects on her expectation of collaboration with parents and other teachers:

> I did my student teaching and beginning teaching in the OC, so I always had parents as well as other teachers in my classroom. I developed as a teacher thinking that it was normal to have other people watching me, not necessarily criticizing but offering ideas, suggestions, and collaborating. It

wasn't until I went back to graduate school and started listening to teachers in other schools that I learned that it was exactly the opposite for them. When someone came into their classrooms, they felt scrutinized and criticized. That was very surprising to me.

Traditionally, teaching is done behind closed doors out of the sight of parents and other adults. But in this program, everything was public—our teaching, our thinking, our stamina, our beliefs. The risks of this exposure were lessened by the socially constructed nature of our learning together and by the ways we thought things through together before or while they were happening. Theresa recalls her surprise when she learned that teachers in other schools often work in isolation: "I'll never forget when some professors from the university came to visit the OC. One of them, in comparing us to traditional schools, said, 'Most teachers close their doors and think they're the only ones doing a good job.' My mouth dropped open. I thought, 'They what?' In my mind, teaching was about learning from others."

The parents were watching it all. If a parent was critical of something, if a lesson did not work, if things fell apart, or if it was hard to figure out what to do with a difficult child, there were always others to help figure it out.

Teaching in the OC *is* about learning from others. Learning came as we worked with parents and with each other. It was this social nature of our learning that pushed us far beyond what was individually possible. It was hard to tell where an idea had originated. Even if one person initiated an idea, it was often developed further in conversation with others. The interactive nature of this process created shared understandings as we helped each other examine and reconstruct some of the implicit assumptions we held as individuals.

Faculty support was essential to problem solving and to our willingness to continually test our professional efforts in front of everyone. Our Friday teacher planning meetings, especially in the early years, were where we did a lot of sharing and problem solving about our teaching. Over food, we would talk about how things were going—the ideas that were working or not working, or a problem with an individual child. Sometimes there were tears; always there was laughter. When we needed help with something, everyone pitched in to analyze the situation and offer suggestions.

None of us have since found a professional setting where this kind of trust and consistent support are so persistently present. If the program had been less demanding or our goal less complex and novel, if we had less sense of ownership over the decisions and the program's success, maybe there would have been less sharing and support—and less learning.

An Emerging Curriculum and a Developing Philosophy

As the teacher group together struggled with issues, debated points of view, and developed shared purposes, the practical realities and the emerging philosophy were inextricably mixed. Neither the curriculum nor the philosophy were handed to us as mandates; we had to decide for ourselves.

Curriculum development was the focus of much debate and planning. At first, we had few curricular guidelines because the program began as a small private school where state requirements were very broad. Even as the program became the OC and moved into the public school system, where we had to accommodate to the school district guidelines, we were committed to shaping the curriculum in ways that encouraged student and parent ownership and involvement. None of us knew precisely how to put this principle into practice. So, again, we had to make it up—try something, look at the results, measure it against our philosophical tenets and objectives, and then fix what didn't work.

The decision-making process about curriculum was inherently open-ended; each year we made revisions to build on current interests and resources. Curriculum got developed through emergent interests in the classroom; successful activities had openness as well as structure. Fruitful activities were extended in successive years, and as teachers, we rethought the curriculum with each child, considering what was needed to develop each child's best work.

We thought about curriculum development in its broadest sense—it included everything the children were doing and learning—what they learned from the content, from the structure, and from other persons in the learning environment. The discussion around curriculum development nurtured our intellectual growth as teachers. If we hadn't had the support of each other, this kind of program and curricular development work would have been much harder, maybe impossible.

Over time an evolving set of arguments provided a foundation for explaining what we were doing. These philosophical principles guided our conversations in many contexts—in our monthly parent meetings, with the steering committee, in the philosophy committee, and later with school district administrators.

The need to discuss and explain what we were doing contributed to the development of our philosophy. We talked a lot to parents who were thinking about joining the program, parents who were puzzled by things in the classrooms, and parents who didn't agree with something we were doing as teachers. We continually had to justify what we were doing. Sometimes we had ready answers because we had talked about the issue in depth in other contexts. Other times we had to construct reasons on the spot, and then we would talk about the issue later in the teacher group to refine our thinking. Many times we had to admit ignorance and figure things out together with the parents, developing principles together.

During one controversy, the teachers realized how thoroughly we shared perspectives as a result of discussion. In preparation for a meeting with a group of parents, some of whom had been lobbying in favor of setting up homogeneous skill groups for reading and math, we had discussed the issue thoroughly in the teacher group. We had a productive, but rather heated, discussion of the issues in the classroom meeting. Our primary argument was that permanent skill groups were antithetical to our philosophical commitment to integrated curriculum and multiage grouping. After the meeting, the two teachers who shared this classroom realized that they had so thoroughly discussed these issues between themselves that they were, in fact, finishing each other's sentences.

Of course, many issues were not so clear, and in addition, some decisions are perpetually unfinished. But some matters were clearer, and over time these issues provided teachers with a stronger foundation from which to build their instructional plans and work with parents. Continuing discussions are key to the development of the principles that guide everyday classroom activities.

The Downside

This all may sound too good to be true. However, teaching in the OC had its disadvantages—especially stress and time shortage. This experience continually felt challenging, and when things in one's personal life were at a weak point, it was overwhelming. Because we knew each other so well, our personal lives were mingled with our professional lives. Support and care carried over to all parts of our lives, not just work, but this could feel threatening as well. There was no place to hide, no way to look stronger than you were because others knew you too well. In addition, knowing each other well meant that we had to deal with each other as whole persons, and it took time to deal with these many aspects of our lives. We had to pay attention to our feelings and disagreements, different personalities, and contrasting styles of working. We had to talk about our feelings as well as our ideas.

We were spending a lot of time together, especially in the early years. Marcy, who was single and didn't have kids at the time, felt okay about being at school from 7 A.M. to 7 P.M. She was really focused and learning a lot; it just felt okay. However, there was attrition of teachers who believed the sacrifice to their personal lives and families was too great. Work often encompassed all aspects of our lives. Our children attended the school, our husbands co-oped, and we went out socially together, often talking shop on the way. The advantage was that it integrated our lives; the disadvantage was that work became our lives. Marilyn's husband once joked about adding on bedrooms for the steady stream of OC people who were continually in the house. Sometimes it felt like the effort and sacrifice were worthwhile for professional and personal growth. At other times it just felt all-consuming and overwhelming.

One reason it felt overwhelming was our high expectations. We needed to know the children well, but equally important, we needed to know the parents. They were in the classroom every week, so the learning environment had to be responsive to both children and parents. Some parents were resourceful and independent; others needed careful nurturing to be successful co-opers. Some parents new to the program needed help to learn how to work with children in ways that supported the philosophy. For example, one parent came into her first co-oping morning with a bag of M&Ms to reward children who finished the task she was doing at her table. Her center was very popular, but we had to talk later about how rewarding children detracted from the internal motivation we were trying to build.

Parents also had a great deal of access to teachers—they complained, argued for their children's needs, gossiped, and called us at home in the evenings. We wanted to connect home and school, so things that went on at home were relevant to how children would deal with school. Sometimes distraught parents would call in the evenings to ask for help with their child. Even if it was not directly school-related, it probably had implications for what the child would be like the next day in school. These connections helped us to be more sensitive teachers, but it also meant that our time was not our own.

In Retrospect

Now, years later and miles apart, our OC experience has stayed with us. What we became in the OC has followed us into other parts of our lives. Marcy put it this way:

> My OC experiences helped to shape the person I am. It has influenced all my relationships: the way I interact with my partner, my children, my colleagues, my community, and even my horses. At meetings, I start by asking a question rather than voicing my opinion or my concerns: "Could you explain how or why you came to that decision so that all of us can understand?" The OC gave me the perspective of being able to step outside a situation, examine what's going on, and ask myself, "How can I influence this conversation so that we can learn?"

The OC helped us trust the process of explanation, examination, and justification, and how these can lead to learning. We learned that if we conscientiously engage others in this process, together we can make informed, sensitive, and fruitful decisions. As Marilyn notes:

> I learned more about myself, my limits and potential, and my core educational beliefs in this setting than from any other context in which I have worked. I continually find that what I now do as a university professor in teacher education is directly tied to the values and skills I developed in this shared experience. I continue to gravitate toward experiences that support similar collaborative relations. I look for places where I can learn, for experiences that push me to take risks within a supportive environment. I have come to recognize, however, how rare these contexts are—how seldom we are in relations where there is sufficient trust to allow for conflict, differences of opinion, and risk taking in ways that lead to personal growth.

The bonds, both personal and professional, that we established in the OC have endured. Why, years later, do we still have a vested interest in the OC? Why do we remain concerned with its history, welfare, and future? Why does the experience of teaching in the OC remain a vital influence in our lives? As Theresa explains it, "After years apart, I can still sit down with other OC teachers and talk about issues as if we had just been at school the day before. When we do get together, we can start up our conversations in an instant. In these conversations, I know that nothing I think about or worry about in education will be considered foolishness."

Teaching in the OC nurtured our growth and development. This legacy of learning has influenced how we have gone about our subsequent professional lives, always trying to re-create a social context with the same kinds of conversations, challenges, and support for continual learning. We remain connected to this community of learners whose development we contributed to as it contributed to ours. Indeed, the challenges and supports of shared decision making in a flexible structure that were central to our learning are key to the continuing development and vitality of this community, for its subsequent generations of teachers and families.

Note

1. Several years ago, when 12 current and former teachers had a reunion, the influence of the OC (and the Thoreau School) on our subsequent professional lives was a pervasive theme of conversation, particularly for those of us who had been away from it for some time. Stimulated by hours of talking about our experiences, three of us decided to write about what we learned from being OC teachers. The conversations and experiences of our other colleagues in the program contributed immensely to what we write here.

Decision Making in a
Learning Community

Carol Lubomudrov, *former OC principal*

As a principal, I know that it is never easy to bring together a diverse group of people of different ages, backgrounds, and philosophies to make decisions, even about the most mundane issues. When parents, teachers, and administrators join together to make decisions about the education of their children, it takes commitment, patience, flexibility, perseverance, and a basic belief in the strength of collaborative decision making for the learning community to function smoothly. This basic belief in the strength of collaborative decision making forms the essence of the OC as a learning community.

Before becoming principal of Washington Elementary School, which houses both the OC program and the traditional school for neighborhood children, I had taught for 13 years and been an administrator for 8 years in a variety of settings. I viewed myself as a believer in and practitioner of collaborative decision making. I had a fair amount of experience working with diverse groups, including students, parents, and boards of trustees.

Never, however, had I encountered a group of parents and teachers who had a stronger sense of "community" or deeper implicit beliefs as to how their program should function. This may sound as if decision making in the OC was rigid—which was not the case. It was only that over the program's 13 years, many of its beliefs and processes had become so intuitive that as a newcomer I sometimes had a difficult time understanding how decisions were made and who the ultimate authority was.

I was principal of the OC for four years and never discovered "the ultimate authority." During that time, I did discover that common understandings regarding the importance and value of dialogue, communication, and participation served as threads that formed the fabric of the program. Here I discuss some issues that arose regarding decision making and how they were handled by the community. Notice that I did not say "how they were resolved," since one of the things I learned while working with the OC is that often simply processing or dialoguing about the particular issues brought about closure. I conclude with a discussion of the trade-offs between efficient decision making and the process of learning that we encountered continually as we struggled to make sure that decisions were democratic.

Who's In Charge Here?

When I first became part of the OC, I was given a binder full of information concerning the program (the *OC User's Manual*). During the first 13 years of the program, a detailed organizational structure had developed, complete with an impressive array of job descriptions. As a newcomer to the program, I eagerly searched through the binder for a description of the principal's role. There were descriptions of functions for parents, for students, and for faculty, but no guidelines for the role of the principal. In addition, I was to find out that no matter how extensive and explicit the list of job descriptions, most of the decisions seemed to emanate from unwritten understandings and processes that were frequently referred to by faculty and parents who had been members of the program for some time as "the OC way."

Issues about procedures seemed to arise continually. Even though the OC has a Steering Committee composed of a chair, a vice chair, representatives from each classroom, committee heads, and faculty, participants still were unclear regarding such questions as: Are committees empowered to make decisions? Does the Steering Committee need to approve the decision? Does the entire school community need to approve the decision? And what is the role of the school district, which has ultimate authority over any decisions that are made?

"Who's in charge here?" is a question asked frequently by new parents and faculty, and there does seem to be a need for someone who will take charge in a crisis. This position may fall to the principal, who is responsible to the district for the smooth running of the program. The need for an ultimate authority in a community of learners sometimes raises issues of how frequently the principal should step in and make that final decision and when the responsibility of solving the problem should be made jointly.

An example of this dilemma occurred when an article was sent out in the newsletter produced by the Steering Committee chairs (who are parents) that was seen as inappropriate by one of the teachers. The teacher decided not to send the letter home. The parents felt that they had a right to send out anything they deemed necessary in order to foster communication and information, while the teacher asked whether material sent from the school should be read first by the principal to assure its appropriateness. This basic question of who should have the final say is a recurring one within the OC and is not easily resolved.

My main role became one of facilitator and participant, helping the community focus on the big issues. It was important for me (as for the other members of the community) to trust the people and the process. Administrators are often pushed into narrow roles and narrow decisions when some individual or group wants the principal to step in and resolve an issue. Often people expect the principal to serve as watchdog—to check the contents of the newsletter published by the parents, to make sure that faculty members don't leave early, and so on. I try to resist the pushes to serve as watchdog. My role is to facilitate the whole process by trusting and supporting the parent and faculty committees that have the responsibility to make particular decisions, and to help them and the program as a whole learn through the discussions where they wrestle with the big questions.

My first undertaking as principal was to try to find out how to best support the students, parents, and faculty by seeking answers to the following questions: How were decisions made? Who needed to be consulted or involved in each decision? Who would help implement decisions once they were made? And, finally, who within the program was responsible for the final decision? One might assume that the answer to this last question was obvious—me. But I found that making decisions in a community of learners was much more complex, and it was not always clear who was responsible for the final decision.

An example of the confusion about who or what group constituted the final authority occurred in a committee decision that generated a great deal of discussion. Each spring, a parent-teacher committee determines the grade-level combinations for the following school year. Each year's class configurations may differ depending on the numbers of children in the different age groups, how many girls and boys there are in each group, which children need to be separated, and so on. One year there may be multiage classrooms of first/second, third/fourth,

Principal Carol Lubomudrov (seated) consulting with teacher Karen Steele.

fourth/fifth, fifth/sixth; the next year there may be first, first/second/third, fourth/
fifth, and fifth/sixth. For this particular year, the committee (consisting of all the
teachers, a parent representative from each classroom, and a member of the reg-
istrar committee) felt they had reached a consensus and a final configuration.
What was unclear was who finalized their recommendation.

After much discussion, it was decided that committee recommendations are,
in fact, the final decision because there was a wide representation from all of the
faculty and classrooms. Furthermore, it was hard to determine who else might
need to approve. In other words, the final decision was made by asking the
question, "If not us [the committee], then who?" Trust in one another, in the
process, and in the faculty and representatives was essential to finally reaching
consensus.

The Importance of Dialogue

As I became more familiar with the OC, I saw that the most important aspect of
the decision-making process was the dialogue that occurred among the many
participants. I was to discover that it served at least three major purposes.

First, it set the tone and formed the core of the philosophy for the entire
program. The norm for problem solving in the program was through dialogue
in which various points of view were expressed and diverse opinions offered.
Implicit was the belief that everyone should have the opportunity to have input,
that everyone's opinion should be considered. This was accomplished through
meetings and dialogues.

Second, these dialogues served the function of passing on an understanding of
the OC culture and norms. By listening and participating in discussions, most
new members of the community eventually come to understand and shape what
is understood as "the OC way."

Third, an obvious purpose of dialogue was that it generated solutions. The
solutions not only solved the more immediate problems but also acted as guidelines for shaping future activities and processes. For example, one discussion
focused on whether to admit a particular child with special needs into the program; it was unclear whether the OC would serve as the best placement for the
child. A general discussion of the nature of the OC program ensued, and many
questions were raised: What happens to a child who cannot participate in many
activities of the OC, such as field trips and the sports program? If a child cannot
participate in over 50 percent of the program's activities, is this the best placement
for him? How do we educate all the parents who are teaching small groups as to
the special needs of a child without violating confidentiality? Thus, the function
of these dialogues was not only to make a decision regarding this individual child
but to establish a policy about admitting and educating special needs students
through discussions clarifying the philosophy of the program.

Another example of how dialoguing worked to bring about closure to a potentially volatile issue occurred in the context of one of the minicourses taught
by parents, open to small groups of children across classrooms. There are over a

hundred parents teaching minicourses or offering small-group instruction in the OC each week; I was frequently unaware of the courses and activities that were being offered. As her minicourse, one parent decided to offer a class in astrology that included the use of tarot cards. My first clue that there was a problem came when I learned that another OC parent strenuously objected to astrology being offered in the program. The teacher had approved the session, feeling that the minicourse was appropriate to offer as an optional learning opportunity and that if parents objected to having their child in the minicourse, they could simply not enroll them.

As other members of the community became involved in this question, many other issues were generated by faculty, students, and parents with differing points of view. Should parents be allowed to teach any minicourse they wanted? Could other parents block offerings? Was the teacher the ultimate authority of what was taught in her classroom? Should the district be consulted, and if so, who in the district office was in charge of minicourse approval? How much do we trust our children to make their own learning decisions? Would a decision not to allow this course limit other children's freedom of choice?

Parents and faculty engaged in a great deal of discussion as to how the OC should resolve the issue. In the end, the steering body, parents, and faculty decided that rather than risk a full-blown crisis that might be divisive, hurt the children, and involve central district authorities, the minicourse would not be offered. Fortunately, the final decision was reached through consensus by the members of the OC who were closest to the problem rather than by myself or the district. The dialogues served to enlighten everyone as to the complexity of the issues and provided an outlet where differing points of view were expressed. Members felt that they had an opportunity to deliberate and to be heard. Instead of members taking adversarial roles, the resolution was based on what everyone agreed was in the best interest of the students, parents, and program. In order to engage in the dialogues that form the heart of a learning community, open communication and active participation are essential.

Open Communication

To make informed decisions, a group must cultivate a high level of communication. Keeping all members of the OC learning community apprised of community activity and norms takes a great deal of time and is achieved through multiple means. In addition to the parent letters, in which teachers focus on what is happening in the classroom each week, and the "Updates" sent out by the Steering Committee with a calendar of upcoming events and announcements, articles are occasionally sent out that address current education issues and offer the rationale behind the philosophy of the program. There are also regular classroom, curriculum, committee, and philosophy meetings where parents and teachers come together, as well as faculty meetings. I met with various groups as often as possible to give input and to help facilitate solutions to issues.

A teacher and co-opers consulting together during recess. (Photo OC archives)

Informal conversations are also central to the communication network. In "hall talk" before and after school and during recess, parents, teachers, and students share information, form ideas, and connect with each other. Information and conversations continue on the telephone into the wee hours of the night. Many innovative ideas have been generated by these after-hours sessions.

Of course, word-of-mouth communication can also lead to rumors or embellishments, and as in any closely knit group, a "grapevine" can develop. There are times when the buzz in the halls is not directed toward producing solutions. I suspect that this type of "communication" occurs in all settings but may be more noticeable or vocal in a setting where active daily participation by adults is the norm. Hopefully, cool-headed informal leaders intervene before there is a full-blown crisis. One way the OC has handled the rumor mill is by appointing a parent in each classroom to act as a facilitator to handle issues as they arise. Issues can be brought to the parent who is acting as mediator by the teacher or by any of the parents in the classroom. This person tries to work with the individuals involved to gather the facts and work toward a resolution of the issue, to facilitate open communication.

Participation in Decision Making

Commitment to how the program is run and how major decisions are made involves all members of the OC; joint decisions are made at all levels. Participation varies, however, and involvement often depends on an individual's interest and commitment.

Decision making at the classroom level. Parents' weekly classroom time is the most familiar decision-making level for the parents, as they work together with the teachers to provide the best educational experience possible for the students, jointly planning and implementing curriculum. Parents can relate to the classroom level of decision making because they know the teacher, the students, and the other parents, and the decisions that are made directly affect their children and themselves. The teachers need well-developed organizational skills (along with trust and understanding) to keep all of this energy directed and focused on the learning of the students.

Shared decision making at the classroom level is often challenging for new teachers. It frequently takes several years for newcomers to understand what the process is, the necessity of patience and compromise, and the payoff of belonging to a community of learners; only then do they become able to model how decisions are made. New teachers usually do not have a great deal of training or experience in collaborative educational settings, and it takes time to learn to trust parental participation as an integral part of the educational process.

Shared faculty leadership. A tremendous amount of energy is expended by the teachers who choose to become part of this dynamic educational environment. They dedicate a great deal of time to conversing with each other and with parents and to developing structures that will maintain rewarding and coherent educational experiences for the students. They meet at least weekly as a group and have innumerable daily discussions about all aspects of the job. OC teachers comment that a large part of their commitment to this program stems from the enormous support of their colleagues.

Faculty decisions are made by consensus; the responsibility for coordination has followed several forms. For several years, the teachers experimented with designating one faculty member as the lead teacher. This individual made sure that the program was coordinated, the facilities were in good order, and the principal was kept informed.

One year the faculty decided to share the responsibility for coordinating the group and serving as a liaison with the parent body and with the principal. One teacher took a turn as "lead teacher" for seven weeks, and then the responsibility was turned over to another teacher. Sharing the responsibilities of leadership has several benefits: Everyone experiences the sometimes conflictual responsibility of administering the program; faculty members learn that they need to take multiple perspectives; and being in a position of responsibility for the entire program often gives teachers a better understanding of what it means to be a team member and encourages them to adopt a more global view of the program rather than focusing solely on their own classrooms. The downsides were that it was hard to get a handle on the job in just seven weeks, and follow-through on major projects was sometimes disjointed. So the teachers continue to experiment with the structure for responsibility for faculty coordination.

Programwide decision making. Parents, teaching faculty, and administration are jointly responsible for the decisions that guide the program. These decisions range from all-program curricular activities to program policies to restructuring of the program. Faculty members and parents serve on all the major committees that meet to assure coordination and progress.

Many times, meetings become a forum for exploring ideas and beliefs. Involvement in discussions helps to increase understanding of the complexities of situations. For example, in ad hoc committees of parents actively involved in hiring recommendations, each person has notions of what characteristics the committee should look for in hiring new teachers. Every time a faculty opening occurs, hours are spent discussing exactly what type of teacher would best meet the needs of the program: Should we seek someone with strong managerial skills, or someone who has experience working with parents, or someone versed in innovative education, or an experienced teacher? Everyone learns from this process, and it is much easier to reach consensus on the final decision when time has been spent discussing these issues before the interview process.

One of the strengths of the OC is that we are always seeking ways of improving the program. When problems arise that cannot be handled by the current structure, new solutions are pursued. The group readjusts its course and begins exploring ways to solve the existing problem. For example, for many years the program had functioned with a biweekly faculty meeting attended by parent representatives from the Steering Committee, and monthly Steering Committee meetings led by parents and also attended by a representative from the faculty. This model worked until there was a turnover of faculty members and new faculty were unclear as to which was the ultimate decision-making body. After much dialogue, it was decided that all faculty members would become regular members of the Steering Committee, which would make policy and procedural decisions for the program. Thus, the structure of the OC governance adjusted to become more inclusive, with increased participation and broader representation.

The Trade-Off between Efficiency and Learning in Decision Making

Involvement as a teacher or a parent in the OC requires a tremendous commitment of time and energy in the classroom, planning, meetings, informal conversations, and all the other sorts of participation. The program continually tries to find ways to simplify the co-oping responsibilities and to simplify the teachers' responsibilities and lives. But simplification has never been easy nor completely successful.

When a large number of people work together, and most of them expect to have some level of input, issues arise that push the program to establish more formal structures of decision making. But the idea of control being vested in one person or even one group is contrary to the philosophy of the OC. Even in efforts to streamline the decision-making process—something we worked on throughout my four years as principal—the program continues to be committed to making sure that all members' points of view are heard and considered. When a program has over 120 families plus teachers, there are bound to be issues that raise questions about the efficiency of a participatory democracy.

Often decisions take a long time and no immediate consensus is reached. An example comes from an issue that arose at a steering meeting regarding whether or not the program should pay parents for activities based on their professional expertise. A parent who was a professional choreographer had proposed to organize the students into a dance program and to be paid for it. Ethically, should some parents be paid and others not, since parents were already required to serve in the program? How does one distinguish between a math professor who is helping small groups of students with math and a professional choreographer? Is one more "professional" than another? If the program decides to pay for these services, who is going to foot the bill—only those children involved in the dance program, or all parents? What if, for religious reasons, some parents don't want their child participating? Who makes the final decision, and how? Does the steering body decide? Do the teachers decide? What if one teacher decides that they do not have time for their students to participate in this activity? Does the entire community need to be involved in this decision?

Not all of the issues raised by this discussion could be dealt with at one meeting. Since the Steering Committee only met monthly, it took several months just to get a decision as to whether or not the parent could be paid to sponsor the dance performance. Several larger issues, such as the policy for future requests of this nature, were tabled for future discussion until they could eventually be resolved.

It is difficult to create momentum and move toward a common vision when everyone wants to be involved in the decision-making process. Often when we are in such a hurry to get to a solution, we neglect to value the time we spend together thinking things through. The OC has often been able to deal with immediate issues by setting in place formal structures that often take the form of job descriptions for the responsibilities of the different roles. It is more difficult, however, to examine the total picture to revamp some of the major procedures and historical patterns.

New solutions to issues of decision-making efficiency also have to recognize that discussions are central to adults' learning about educational issues and governance of a community dedicated to children's learning. In such a setting, sometimes the most efficient solution for the long term requires time-consuming involvement in the short term, so that those who share responsibility will have a common understanding of the principles according to which they proceed throughout daily decisions in the classroom and behind the scenes.

I hope the OC will continue to struggle with these issues, because they are the essence of what it means to be part of a learning community. The fact that a group of parents, students, teachers, and administrators can come together on an ongoing basis to discuss basic educational issues is unique and remarkable. Even though glitches are inevitable, we can hope that as we try to work through which issues need to be addressed and which ones are just going to exist because of the nature of the program, the process itself will continue to be valued.

Those who have been a part of the OC community for a long time have developed a sense of belonging and a dedication to collaborative decision making. The diverse group of parents, teachers, and administrators have worked together to foster respect, openness, trust, and equity through shared responsibility. In my writing here, I have sometimes used the term "we." Even though I am no longer the principal of the OC, I will never lose the feeling of belonging to this group of people dedicated to providing their children with the very best educational experience.

Some conflict is inherent in any group. In the case of the OC, such conflict produces growth among the group as a whole and makes the OC a seasoned learning community. It has been able to learn from mistakes, incorporate multiple points of view, and develop a process that values the contributions of all its members. Dialogues, communication, and participation serve as the threads that strengthen the OC and make it a truly unique program in the field of education.

OC Teachers Take Their Learning
to Other Schools

Judy Smith, *former OC teacher*
Mimi Wilson, *former OC teacher*

In 1977, when the OC program was brand-new, and for a number of years thereafter, we shared the excitement and the work, both as parents and as teachers. We are now living in different states, working in very different kinds of schools. Judy is a high school principal in a large public high school in Washington State. Mimi is a fourth-grade teacher in an independent school in South Carolina that is associated with a major school-restructuring initiative (the Coalition of Essential Schools).

In our efforts to contribute to reform in our classrooms and schools, we find that we are returning, about 20 years later, to the basic philosophy that directed our OC experience. In many ways, what we learned in the OC, both in terms of instructional practices and in terms of change processes, is giving us the confidence we need to proceed in our new settings. Personal experiences and the general principles of the OC—along with increasingly compelling research about how children learn that questions the way schools are traditionally organized and how we think about curriculum and instruction—have helped us organize and promote new programs on both sides of the country.

The changes we are working on are not simple ones. We are looking at ways to integrate across disciplines, combining English, physics, and history into an integrated block. Instead of chopping school days into isolated blocks of time, we are exploring ways of lengthening these blocks of time and trying more flexible schedules. We are looking at designing work for children that covers fewer things in greater depth, through more focused inquiry. Believing that children will learn better if they can make connections, we seek ways to challenge students not just to memorize material but to apply it as well. We are working to make it possible for individual students to carry out research and to present their work before a critical audience.

These changes have the potential to challenge the sacrosanct purpose of most schools: to prepare students for the next level and to get them into colleges. The trick is to integrate that important purpose with the overarching purpose of preparing all students for a meaningful, employable life.

Restructuring Schools around Student Learning

There is a big difference between improving schools and restructuring schools. School improvement applies new knowledge and ideas to existing programs. It is a tinkering process. School restructuring, on the other hand, is a process in which entirely new systems and conditions are created. The OC and its predecessor, the Thoreau School, could be called restructured programs in the true sense. As these programs explored how children learned, they created entirely new structures and organizations to facilitate that process.

A major paradigm shift at the center of school reform recognizes that we must organize our schools around students' learning. That means taking a serious look at what the students who come to us need and want, and then designing structures and strategies that maximize the possibility that these things will happen. This concept was at the very heart of early OC deliberations. Hours were spent detailing student needs, followed by even more hours of creative planning and curriculum development. Our work was driven not by textbooks and tradition but by clear and meaningful goals for our students. Because we had clear outcomes and standards, students usually had a clear idea—before they started—of where they wanted to end up, of what they would be expected to do at the end.

In our own work in other schools today, getting others to focus primarily on students—their work and their needs—is a surprisingly difficult task! Curriculum has often been defined by what "should" be learned, regardless of student needs. The focus has been on what the teacher does rather than what the student learns. Instruction is a far more complex task than marching through a textbook step by step. The challenge is to get teachers to focus on what they expect their students to know and be able to do at the end of a unit of study, then to design the steps that will help all students to get there.

In the OC, we seemed to know almost intuitively that we couldn't *make* students learn. The best we could do was to create the conditions and design the activities that would most likely lead to the kind of learning we had in mind. We focused on the qualities of the learning experience that would lead to student commitment, participation, and learning.

To do this, we developed learning activities that encouraged social interaction and interdependence in classrooms that included children of different ages with a wide variety of abilities and interests. Students took turns being leaders and followers, teachers and learners, and, in the process, learned to respect and build on everyone's unique contributions. Today's buzzword for such practice is "co-operative learning." Insights that were inspired by the OC experience taught us the importance of such practices—which extends beyond the social benefits of valuing co-operative skills. In today's (and tomorrow's) world of work, the ability to work well with others is a primary qualification for most employment and, as such, should direct the strategies we use in our restructured schools.

At the OC, we also created learning structures and strategies that empowered students to make their own choices. Most of the time students could choose when to be involved in an activity or independent center and, once there, which of several ways to perform a task or demonstrate proficiency. Usually students could choose a strategy that complemented their learning style and helped them be successful. Sharing a favorite book could take the shape of a written report, a play, a song, an art project, even a dance. Often, students were allowed time to explore their own interests and design their own projects and research topics. Independence was encouraged and fostered. Students were expected to think things through, not simply memorize or accumulate facts. In our current schools, teachers are being encouraged to dramatically broaden the kinds of tasks they give students and the ways their students can choose to demonstrate skill and understanding.

National efforts to restructure schooling struggle with the fact that the ways that student performance is to be demonstrated have a powerful role in instructional choices within classrooms. Hence, to restructure schools around student learning requires rethinking the ways that we observe and evaluate learning. In the OC, we developed evaluation systems that combined quick feedback, self- and peer assessment, and affirmation of performance without the adverse consequences students may experience with initial failure. Students were given accurate feedback on their performance, shown where to improve, encouraged to make changes or to figure out what they still needed to know, and then encouraged to try again—sometimes many times. When something was accomplished, we celebrated that accomplishment regardless of the stumbling that might have occurred in getting there and of the time it took. Students were encouraged to reflect on their work and the work of their classmates. Regular sharing of work occurred; fellow students usually commented on the strong points and made suggestions for improvement.

An expanded definition of student performance focuses teachers' attention on students first, and then on their teaching role as one of helping their students achieve the desired results. Proficiency can be demonstrated in many more ways than by simply answering the questions at the end of a chapter or by performing on a simple paper-and-pencil test. Portfolios, seminars, and exhibitions are examples of new forms of teaching and new ways of learning in which evaluation serves the improvement of student learning. Performance and evaluation systems that tell the story of a child's learning, that take into account effort and individual progress, and that concentrate on the evaluation of what a student is able to do (without penalties for making mistakes while learning new material) are more meaningful and accurate reporting practices.

Taking time to consider how we want children to demonstrate what they know is a very simple yet powerful planning tool for both teaching and learning. It has the potential to effectively drive the restructuring process in schools; at the very least, it helps schools and people who work there be intentional about what they are doing!

What is most important for students to know? In the OC, as we created learning activities for students, we started by defining what the outcomes should be; then we created a road map to be sure that we would get there. By involving students and parents in this discussion, we established its significance and, for the most part, cultivated broad support.

In addition, we believed that *all* students should reach the outcomes, and we recognized that some students needed more time or more support than others. We did not expect that every student would get there at a particular time or at a particular age, though we did expect that they would all get there eventually. We created systems that would recognize and build on this fact. In our multiage classrooms, we often could not tell who was in which grade. Our groupings were very flexible. While we recognized that individual students had different strengths in different areas, we also recognized that different students could perform the same basic task at different levels of intensity and to different degrees.

One of the major obstacles for us in schools today is to change the old paradigm—where amount of time was the constant and student performance was the variable—to a system where student performance is the constant and time is the variable. In our schools today, we are struggling to change systems that are based on time (the seven-period day, the forty-minute math period, or the Carnegie unit as a measure of high school credit, for example) into systems that have more flexible, continuous periods of time and that focus on student performance. We seek structures that allow a fully integrated curriculum, longer uninterrupted blocks of time, and less emphasis on age-grouping of students.

This concept stretches our imagination, for indeed, the old system is efficient, if nothing else. Adapting time to respond to individual student academic needs in an efficient way is one of the biggest challenges we face as we work to reform our current schools. Being clear about required outcomes for all students and serious about providing support is necessary. Breaking down age-grouping barriers helps in this task. Calling on all available resources—parents, the outside community, fellow students, and volunteers—is key.

Courage and Conviction

Abandoning familiar practices and activities is as difficult as creating new curriculum and learning new instructional strategies. This issue is critical to the success of state and national reform and standards initiatives, which are prescribing what all students should be able to know and do. For example, in Washington state, local districts are developing strategies and programs particular to their population that will ensure that benchmarks are met and, as a student progresses through school, "essential learnings" are achieved. In the school district where Judy works, teachers are seriously reviewing what they do in light of these new priorities, with a painful and time-consuming process of comparing what is happening in classrooms with what should be happening. In Mimi's "essential school" in South Carolina, major effort is being made to change teachers' ways of understanding and describing student achievement, with an emphasis on fostering student understanding as "thinkers, doers, problem solvers, and community con-tributors." As teacher attitudes change, so does the curriculum.

As much as the OC has inspired and informed us about teaching and learning strategies as we work to change our schools, even more it has given us the courage to be willing to risk and to ask others to risk. Schools, as we have known them for the last 50 years, are deeply embedded in our culture. The process of changing them is fraught with conflicts and resistance. It can take a very long time and be extremely difficult. While understanding and managing the process of change, involving others, and building consensus are all critical, having the confidence that all the work and time will be worthwhile is incredibly helpful. In a very fundamental way, we find that our efforts at the OC have given us the faith that thoughtful change will result in better schools and programs.

Especially when it comes to areas where change must be based more on an-ecdotal evidence than on empirical data, we can tell OC stories, relate experiences, and talk about the program's success and promise. As our colleagues have con-sidered relying less on texts and more on projects and activities, we have told them the story of the OC decision to do away with texts and ability-based reading groups. It made sense, but it was scary. Why risk groupings that had apparently worked for years to try an independent, individualized program that let children choose what they wanted to read? As we watched our OC students progress very well in an independent reading program (and do well on standardized tests) and enjoy what they were doing in the process, we learned not only to trust this new way of doing things, but to be so confident that we could advocate for such change in debates and discussions as well.

We can also draw on our OC experiences that brought teachers, parents, and, often, students together to talk openly (and continuously) about what was work-ing and what was not—and, at all times, what was best for the kids. By sharing the process of change in the OC with our new school communities, we can encourage their patience and participation and renew our personal sense that the hard work and endless discussions will be worth it.

The issue of the huge amounts of time and energy it takes to talk about students and their needs, to plan thoughtfully, to learn new ways of doing things, and to work as teams and design integrated instruction cannot be underestimated. It is a major stumbling block to change. Simply stated, it is easier to continue doing what has always been done. Once again, we can reflect on our OC expe-riences as we work with teachers in the midst of changing and trying new things. While we understand the extra effort, we also appreciate the exhilaration and excitement that makes the effort worthwhile. The trailblazer teachers in our new schools experience the conflicting emotions of exhaustion, on one hand, and passion for what is happening, on the other. The trick to maintaining momentum seems to be to support teachers as much as possible, to encourage them contin-ually, and to acknowledge them publicly. Their needs are no different from what ours were when we struggled with the same issues in the OC.

Fellow educators may be wary of efforts to expand the ways curricular objec-tives can be achieved, to emphasize cooperation rather than competition, to bring community members into the classroom, to group children in ways that are not

Mimi and Judy (from left) discussing philosophy with other teachers (Leslee and Karen and others).

necessarily defined by age or skill, to encourage risk taking and taking responsibility. But we find that we bring a level of confidence in the potential of these
experiments based on experience begun in the basement of churches and continued when the OC became a public school option. When concerned parents and
teachers in our current schools greet a potential change with the comment, "We
tried this in the seventies and it didn't work," we can say with assurance: "But it
did work. Most educators just didn't stay with it long enough to learn from what
was going on and refine what could happen. But we know a group that did!"

In the OC, we continually learned from our successes and our failures, and
from reflecting on them and discussing them. We constantly returned to the
central mission of schools and the goals of our program and examined what we
were doing in the light of these. This process serves us well in different school
systems. We continually learn from our new experiences. And, through the process of reexamination and justification, we are prepared to explain the changes
we are making in our new schools in consistent, thoughtful, and intuitive ways.

Being empowered to do what we thought would work best in the OC was a
heady experience. This is the same spirit that we can see in our colleagues in
other schools who have taken up the challenge twenty years later. It's not that
one should transport the OC program directly to another setting. It's that the
people in the OC program asked good questions, and had the courage to risk
and create new systems—all in the best interest of students and their learning
progress. And that's what we need to do for all children in all schools.

Never-Ending Learning

Carolyn Goodman Turkanis, *teacher*
Leslee Bartlett, *teacher*
Barbara Rogoff, *researcher*

In the OC, teachers, parents, and administrators continually try to articulate the overarching principles of learning as a community that guide our everyday practices and underlie natural variations across individuals and classrooms. The principles are enacted in varying ways in the specific practices across classrooms, as variations on the theme that makes up the common thread of the philosophy.

The everyday practices that support the philosophy vary according to teacher style and experience, classroom grade levels, and the unique interests and needs of members of the classroom community. For example, some years different teachers experiment with the schedules in their classrooms, arranging all literacy activities in one time block or encouraging varying types of activities within any time block. But such variations in everyday practices are still built around the philosophical principle of purposeful learning activities, as all classrooms support literacy learning with classic and current children's literature that is of interest in their class. The specific types of activities vary across the grade levels to adapt to the interests and growing skills of the students.

Teachers and parents continually examine how everyday practices in the different classrooms fit with the OC philosophy. The common principles that tie our classes together not only provide coherence to the way we do things but also underlie many of the issues with which we continue to struggle in philosophical discussions. That is natural, since a community of learners is a work in progress. The common philosophy has developed from and is understood by working together and having innumerable discussions about the way we do things.

The variations in practices still must remain true to the core principles in order for the school to remain a coherent community of learners. On occasion, differences in interpretation of the philosophy by particular individuals have been great enough to raise concern. At such times, the teachers observe and reflect to come to consensus on how to support the learning of the people involved. With this process, people usually come to understand and embrace the philosophy; sometimes they realize that another learning situation would be more appropriate for them. Discussions about the philosophy are key to the learning of all members of the community and keep the philosophy alive.

In concluding this book, we revisit and reflect on the central principle of learning as a community: creating *instruction that builds on children's interests in a collaborative way, where learning activities are planned by children as well as adults, and adults learn from their own involvement as they help children learn.* Emanating from this principle are other principled features of learning as a community:

- Purposeful learning with a clear goal, building on the children's interests, needs, and prior understanding
- Assessing progress while aiding learning
- Taking responsibility and making choices
- Making decisions and learning as a community

After discussing these principled and connected features of learning as a school community, we end the book by discussing some issues about which we as a community continue to puzzle, which comprise continuing learning challenges for us and for efforts to enhance education nationwide. They form an agenda for our community's (and our nation's) continuing learning: how to support the learning of adults that is necessary to improve children's learning environments, how to balance the time and energy needed for collaborative learning and decision making with needs for efficiency, how to learn from conflicting views, how to adapt to changing needs (such as the changing cultural backgrounds of generations of schoolchildren and their parents), and how to work for improvement of schools at a deep level that respects and builds on the differing approaches and needs of diverse individuals and communities.

Purposeful, Interested Learning

If children are interested in what they are learning and can see the reasons for the learning activity and how it is connected to their lives, they are more likely to thrive in the learning environment—and, indeed, become lifelong learners. In the picture on the next page, the children eagerly attend to spelling, learn new vocabulary, and practice using a dictionary as they enjoy a game of Scrabble, with a co-oper's help.

A great example of a purposeful learning activity is how Denise's class worked on measurement in the math curriculum. The students were designing a habitat for animals, for which they had written and received a small grant. As they designed and built birdhouses for the habitat, the measurement process was part of an activity in which kids could see the purpose of measuring. Measurement served a goal that made sense and was of interest to them. That is quite different from

A spelling/vocabulary/dictionary lesson embedded in a game of Scrabble, with a co-oper's help.

doing textbook exercises on measurement where there is no clear purpose, just going through the motions of measurement.

In an activity with a meaningful purpose, interest, and value, children want to participate; providing incentives that are not inherent to the activity itself may deflect learning. When we celebrate our accomplishments, the celebration isn't used as an incentive for each child to finish the work or do it well; it is not contingent on individual performance. For example, on completion of the class newspaper we may have a publisher's party, where the student editors provide cucumber sandwiches and toast everyone in the class with sparkling apple juice, and all the students read and autograph each other's articles. Everybody celebrates the learning that occurred.

For newcomers to the OC, it is often difficult to see how learning can be motivated without incentives. For example, one new co-oper innocently said to the class, in introducing her activity, "When you come to my table for my activity, I have a little treat for you." A group of boys complained, "You are bribing us! I am not going to go to your activity just because you're going to give me candy!" The co-oper was shocked. Of course, the teacher needed to work with the boys to help them figure out how to raise their objection more appropriately. They were very righteous, saying, "She was going to give us candy if we went to her activity, and that was a bribe. Didn't she know that we need to go to the activity just for learning?" (They probably wouldn't have chosen to go anyway, however.) The teacher said, "I'm really proud of you for seeing it in that light. Why do you think she might have done that?" They talked about how the co-oper was new at this and really wanted them to come and enjoy her activity but was afraid that kids might not come. They talked about how to approach someone in a different manner: "How could you talk to a person so that they could really hear what you were saying and not be hurt by it?" The boys later apologized to the co-oper, and the teacher told her, "I'm sorry that happened the way it did, but I have to tell you I'm glad they have picked up the idea of going to activities because they're going to learn something, not because somebody's going to give them something. That is a deep philosophical aspect of our program."

The children's involvement in developing decisions is an important part of their motivation. If they, together with the teacher, decide that they want to publish a newspaper, they are involved in a way that would not occur if the teacher made the decisions alone. Even when adults bring an activity to the classroom, the scope can be wide enough that the kids have a great deal of choice in developing it. If the children are involved in decisions about writing a newspaper or about what will be good to include in it, they are likely to be motivated and responsible to the group as well as to themselves in carrying out the project.

In purposeful learning activities, the children engage mentally and often physically in the learning activity. We try to find ways for children to be involved in activities with their hands and bodies as well as their minds, but more important than the hands' engagement is the mind's engagement. Sometimes "minds-on" learning is based on discussion, manipulating ideas rather than objects. The teacher and others sometimes give presentations and lessons—but not as lectures out of the context of purposeful activity. There is plenty of talk and analysis and explanation in preparation for, carrying out, and reflecting on classroom activities. For example, in a whole-class math lesson, the teacher might help the children share their strategies for a problem and might reflect on his own strategies. It wouldn't be just the teacher reciting how the problem must be done; rather, it would be interactive questioning and discussing: "What do you think?" "Did anyone do it a different way?" "How are we going to resolve the difference?"

When activities have an authentic purpose, they naturally include learning throughout the curriculum and often contribute to development of the whole child's social, emotional, physical, and cognitive growth. For example, when Denise's first-, second-, and third-graders turned an unused portion of the school grounds into a natural habitat for local birds, their learning occurred across the curriculum as they wrote grants, designed a small model of the habitat, interacted with guest speakers and took field trips, studied the birds and the habitat they needed, planted trees, and worked with school administrators to follow school and district guidelines. In their thoughtful and joyful learning experience, they engaged in literacy, science, mathematical, and social studies curriculum in an integrated way that was motivated by their own interest and purposes in the project.

A co-oper evaluating children's math understanding in order to help them solve mathematical puzzles.

Assessing Progress while Aiding Learning

Assessment can be an ongoing part of helping children in the classroom, in conversations and observation of children's efforts; it does not necessarily require separate testing. If a child misses three subtraction problems on a math test, all one learns is that she couldn't do the problems—one doesn't know why. However, if one engages in a discussion as a child is working on a subtraction problem, it will quickly become clear whether she needs clarification of place value, regrouping, organization on the paper, or basic facts, or whether she should just take time to be more careful. Helping a child articulate the strategies for solving a problem not only allows the teacher to diagnose the child's understanding but also provides learning for the child that goes beyond the math concepts.

Leslee gives an example of how a teacher can evaluate the children's understanding while working with them:

> Making a "hundreds chart" with the class allows a lot of on-the-spot evaluation. Recently I placed a large number chart with a hundred empty squares on the blackboard and asked the second- and third-graders to estimate the number of squares in the chart. They all agreed there were 100. I then wrote in a few of the numbers to get us started, setting up a pattern where 0 would be the first number on the chart—but without writing the 0 on the chart.

As the kids took turns placing the rest of the numbers on the chart, it became clear which ones had a good grasp of place value and, as we neared completion, which ones truly understood the concept of number. Quite early on, someone had put 100 in the last square, since there were obviously 100 squares, but as we began to see the patterns evolving, most kids realized that 99 would be the last number.

A wonderful discussion followed, with a few kids convinced that 100 had to be the last number since there were 100 squares. The rest argued that since 0 was the first number, 99 would be the last. It was suggested that we take the 0 off, since "it's not as important as 100," which prompted a math journal question—"Why do we have zero?" We discussed the answers, which ranged from "Because God made it" to "Zero is important, it is a number and it holds the place of the ones and the tens in the number 100, and if we didn't have zero we wouldn't have 100."

I could tell how well the kids understood the concepts of number and place value and zero throughout that discussion. My involvement in the discussion let me evaluate the kids' understanding and push it a little further. I'm interested in knowing whether the children really understand a concept, not just whether they have memorized an answer.

Focusing on the children's learning is the key to teachers' and parents' moving beyond the view that teaching consists of providing and testing information—a remnant of the early 1900s efforts to make school instruction methods resemble an efficient mass production factory. To coordinate information about the children's progress, co-opers make notes for the teacher about the learning objectives of their activity, the children who participated, and if a particular child got really interested or had special difficulty with it. In worrisome or impressive (or amusing) cases, co-opers sometimes also talk with the teacher about their observations of a child's understanding in their activity.

In addition to evaluating children's progress in reading, writing, and math, adults and children evaluate children's progress in learning how to manage their time and to become involved in activities for the sake of learning. For adults to evaluate a child's progress in learning to make responsible choices, children need opportunities to make choices, and teachers need opportunities to observe how the kids handle choices. Then teachers can, at one and the same time, help the children learn and evaluate their progress, while assisting them in becoming self-directed learners.

Taking Responsibility and Making Choices

Providing opportunities for children to make decisions and to evaluate the consequences that result from those decisions is central to principles of learning as a community. Because this is a lifelong process, we value the times when children make what may be seen as inappropriate or poor choices—it is part of the process of learning to think through ways of handling challenges and see the results of what they try. Through dialogue about their choice and the consequences that result, both the child and the teacher gain insight into this important aspect of learning. Of course, it can be difficult for adults to watch a child make a poor choice. One of the challenges for the adults in the community is to allow children to make choices and trust that they will learn from the experience.

A way to help the children learn about making responsible choices is to assist them in considering the consequences. If the consequences fit closely with the activity in question, the connection is clear to the children and helps them learn to be more responsible.

The consequences of appropriate choices are often built into success in the activity. For example, children who are well prepared for a presentation arouse the interest and respect of the group for the topic in which the student has become expert. For activities such as cleanup, which may hold little intrinsic interest, experienced teachers emphasize that the children's next project will be easier if they have room to work or that they need to put one set of materials away to be able to begin the next (interesting) activity. A teacher may say, "Once we get the classroom cleaned up, then we'll have time for reading a book together. Then we can find our things again and we won't be as likely to lose the pieces of what we've been working on." One of the teachers pointed out, "When they leave stuff out, the tables are messy and they have no place to work and no place to put their things. So it's really to their own advantage." This requires that the children be interested in the activities, of course.

To figure out consequences of inappropriate choices, there is sometimes a need to develop a consequence that is not built in but should be closely connected. The goal is learning, not punishment. If children are involved in determining the logical consequences of poor choices, it helps them make the connections in order to make better choices the next time. Often they need help making the consequences fit with the problem at hand and not being too harsh on themselves. Here is an example from Carolyn:

> During a sports afternoon at the roller skating rink, four sixth-graders continued to skate after the last skate was announced. That confused the other kids, who thought they could go back out on the rink and skate. When I finally got the attention of these four kids and got them off the rink, I asked, "Tell me about what's going on—I'm confused about why you continued to skate after you were asked to leave the rink," and they agreed that they weren't responsible about getting off the rink. I said, "You guys think about it and come up with a reasonable consequence and tell me what you decide." I let them think about it for a while. One of them finally came up to me and said, "You just tell us," and I said, "Well, I have my own ideas about it, but at the moment I'm more interested in your ideas."
>
> Their solution startled me: "We think we should all miss sports next week." I said, "Whoa! That seems kind of extreme, just because you skated around the rink a couple of extra loops. I can go with that, but it seems way too harsh." So one of the boys said, "Because we all went around the rink a couple of extra loops, maybe we should miss a couple of songs." I

replied, "Now that sounds like a real connection—you're saying you would just not skate while the other kids skated for two songs." So a logical consequence was something that made sense to everybody—it was really connected to what had happened.

Short, to the point, connected to the problem . . . Logical consequences usually mean that the consequences follow quickly, to heighten the learning. In this case, when the children didn't get off the rink at the end of the day, it seemed logical to have the learning at the very next sports day and to make sure that the kids understood the connection. The next week at the skating rink the four boys took the responsibility to sit on the bench during the first two songs. I approached them and said, "I appreciate your remembering our decision from last week and your willingness to cooperate." To be sure that the kids understood the connection, I asked, "Now, why are we doing this?" and one of the kids said, "Well, you know, last week I didn't get off the rink and went around twice."

Making Decisions and Learning as a Community

Learning through collaboration is central to principles of learning as a community. All members of a learning community have valuable interests, ideas, and opinions; the differences between individuals' interests and approaches can be a resource to others and can enhance opportunities for learning. Research suggests that engaging in shared thinking and decision making with others is an important contributor to learning.[1]

In the OC, children collaborate all day long, in designing activities as well as in doing them. They engage in dialogue with their classmates and the adults in the room as part of their learning experience. They figure out their roles and group dynamics. They help each other because it's enjoyable to work together, and they collaborate because sharing information and ideas becomes ingrained and expected.

Collaboration itself is a skill that seems to be learned through involvement in shared thinking. This is supported by observations that OC children more often worked together by building on each other's ideas in academic tasks than did children from a neighboring traditional school that had less emphasis on collaboration.[2]

For most of the adults in the OC, collaboration in the community is a powerful learning experience as well. Adults, with the children and the other adults in this community, develop in their ideas of what learning involves and in how respect for varying interests and perspectives can be an important tool for their own growth as well as that of the children. A great deal of the learning for adults comes from grappling with varying ideas and classroom practices, as we all seek to grasp the common thread of the principles-in-action.

The whole program is inevitably involved in a continual process of renewal and change within continuity of the general philosophy, as new generations come

A child showing her first/second/third-grade classmates, the teacher, and co-opers how to play a geometry game that she has prepared for a classroom independent center.

to play the roles of newcomers and old-timers in the community, becoming part of the structure. A learning attitude is necessary—an openness or even a readiness to continue to change, to learn from the smallest child or the newest co-oper.

The teachers report that their reason for remaining involved with this high-commitment program is that they continue to learn. In fact, as Pam Bradshaw pointed out, one indicator of alignment with the philosophy of a community of learners in a school seems to be regarding oneself as a continual learner.

Learning Challenges for the Community and the Nation

Learning, for the community, includes not only revisiting the classic principles of our philosophy with each new generation of members but also struggling with issues that may be built into the endeavor of learning as a community. The issues that we face are pressing concerns for education nationwide:

- How a community can help new adult members understand and use the philosophy
- Trade-offs between efficiency and the time and energy needed for collaborative learning and decision making

- How to use conflicting views and change as learning opportunities
- How to adapt principles of learning-as-a-community in diverse communities

How Can a Community Help Adult Members Understand and Use the Philosophy?

We continually search for ways to help new members understand the philosophy and use the practices of the OC comfortably. A great deal of assistance is already available for new co-opers. For example, experienced teachers and co-opers support parents through ongoing dialogue about the philosophy, informally in the classroom as well as in workshops and monthly parent meetings, and the New Families Committee prepares written materials and has meetings specifically for new families.

Although people often ask for written materials to help them learn the OC philosophy and practices, they seldom seem to find the written materials very helpful, even when they do read them. There are many written materials available in the Parent Resource Library—books on educational resources, curriculum, and philosophy, idea-books on activities, and some materials written by members of the program, such as the *Users' Manual*, a thick notebook providing explanations about the program and its philosophy.

We hope that the book you are reading is useful to people interested in understanding the principles of learning in a community, though it cannot substitute for participating in everyday activities and conversations where principles are put in practice. We have learned over the years that it is important for adults, like children, to develop understanding through participation in ongoing activities and guided exploration of the ideas.

In OC classrooms, teachers purposely model principles-in-action for co-opers, and co-opers report that watching other peoples' approaches to working with children was extremely important in their development. Teachers help co-opers evaluate their own learning as well as the learning experiences they provide for children by asking them how their activity went and how they might change it the next time. An example of the on-the-job guidance that goes on constantly in the classroom is given by one of the teachers:

One morning during recess, when kids were outdoors and co-opers were chatting in the classroom, a co-oper began to express extreme frustration. She had worked with two small groups on planting and growing herbs, and the activity had not gone well. I said, "Slow down for a minute, explain to me what was going on. What have you learned from the kids, and what do you want to change? What wasn't working?"

She complained that the kids weren't listening. They arrived at the Grow Lab table and immediately began looking through seed packets and selecting containers to fill with soil, rather than listening to the short presentation she had planned for giving them some new information before they would begin to plant. I asked, "Did the kids know that you wanted them to do that? What makes today different from any other day?" She reflected that usually her activity just starts by the children exploring the materials provided.

I asked her if she had explained to the kids that this particular lesson would have a different format; she wasn't sure that she had. I asked her how she might begin her third group of the day. She smiled and replied, "Well, I'll begin by explaining that our lesson will start differently than usual and that after a brief presentation, they'll have a chance to do lots of planting!" Her third group went much more smoothly. She shared her expectations with the kids and was eager for suggestions and support.

When a co-oper's activity doesn't go as well as planned, learning opportunities arise for the children as well as for the co-oper. Often the children play a role in improving the activities, by making suggestions and learning not only about how the subject matter can be approached but also about the processes of teaching and of learning from mistakes. Many co-opers report that the children were an important source of their own development in understanding their curriculum area and how people learn. The children's participation in reflecting on adults' as well as their own learning may partially account for the frequent observation that OC graduates are skillful in managing their own learning and in working with teachers and their classmates when they enter junior high school.

When it comes to adults' learning, time is always an issue—both finding the time for people to discuss what they are observing and doing in the classroom and allowing the time for people's understanding to grow. It takes time for people to rethink the principles by which they function. Since we always have new people joining the program, we often find ourselves revisiting earlier issues, as most newcomers have attended schools that functioned according to different principles and need time and discussion to reexamine their ideas. Continuing to discuss issues is an important way for newcomers as well as longtime community members to explore and continue to learn about the ideas essential to our philosophy.

One of the biggest challenges in a community of learners is to support new teacher learning. The challenge starts before we even hire a new teacher, because it's so difficult to explain all the responsibilities of a teacher in a community of learners such as ours. Even though parent involvement is becoming a goal in public education, there is no training available for working with parents as intensively as we do in this learning community, where parents are viewed as partners in creating and providing quality educational experiences for children. Experienced teachers who have had success in a traditional setting report that teaching in the OC is like starting over. Being able to view themselves as learners (and getting that permission from the parents, who need to trust that their children will be learning while the teacher is learning) is a big part of new teacher learning.

An earnest discussion among a teacher and co-opers. (Photo OC archives)

New teachers do have a colleague who serves as a mentor—helping plan class-room activities and organize the co-oping schedule, making regular classroom observations, attending the new teacher's parent meetings, and being available for debriefing and evaluation sessions. However, the environment is so multifaceted that it can be hard for new teachers to even articulate what they need.

It has become clear that teachers need the opportunity to work together and to discuss issues and ideas in order to develop a common understanding of the philosophy, just as the co-opers learn from involvement in the ongoing principles-in-action. This is more difficult to arrange for teachers, who have little time to spend in other teachers' classrooms or to meet together—an issue that educators face throughout the United States.

Trade-offs: Community Decision Making with Wide Participation, or Efficiency?

Collaborative decision making is very important in a community of learners, but it leads to a continual need to examine how decisions are made and what forms of leadership are appropriate. Discussion is essential for learning and to ensure wide participation in the program, but at times community members express frustration at the extent to which committees and classrooms need to revisit decisions and procedures that have already been devised. A co-oper in his third year complained, "I find it frustrating at meetings how 'the wheel always needs to be reinvented.' I like the creativity and flexibility in the classroom, but I think by now certain things should be established after all these years."

However, just as each child needs to participate in the *process* of learning to read and do arithmetic and solve problems, each new generation of adult participants needs to participate in the *process* of learning to help children learn in a community of learners. New co-opers, like the children, cannot simply be handed the information; nor do they just discover the principles on their own. One co-oper pointed out that "reinventing the wheel" occurs "as each parent figures out what to teach and how to teach it." Through participation with others in ongoing activities, adults begin to see and become part of the dynamic structure of practice.

We have learned that each generation of parents and teachers needs to be part of the process in order to understand how to contribute to it. In addition, the principles of learning as a community are not a fixed recipe for action but a philosophy that the community continues to consider. Creative innovations are necessary for any institution to continue its viability, as circumstances and membership continually change. A co-oper referred to this need for change: "The OC is a wonderful alternative but it should not be afraid to evolve. Parents as a group should constantly evaluate the OC."

The continual need to consider the philosophy and to help newcomers become a part of the system provides the program with the sort of challenge to learn that, if taken seriously, contributes to both renewal and evolution of its philosophical base. As the community continues the process of collaboration with new generations and changing circumstances, the community as a whole learns.

An anonymous reviewer of a draft of this book commented on the importance of "reinventing the wheel" for the OC as an educational institution:

> From the perspective of the efficient running of the program, "reinventing" is wasteful of time and resources. This is the perspective of the industrial enterprise, where "progress" is linear. Each new, more complex model simply replaces what preceded. But from the perspective of participants' learning, "reinventing" tools and practices (i.e., appropriating and transforming them) is an essential aspect of the learning process, and providing time and opportunity for each individual to go through this process is (should be) the raison d'être of an educational institution.

Nonetheless, we repeatedly work toward simplifying the decision-making process so that we do not spend inordinate energy on each decision. When Carol Lubomudrov was principal, she prompted us to create a shared governance document to formalize our understandings about who makes which decisions and how.

We often consider whether there are ways to simplify the work. The adults' involvement in the program is intense and time-consuming. The teachers generally look on their professions as a calling rather than just a job. But sometimes the responsibilities are exhausting and the program looks for ways to simplify the teachers' responsibilities, by experimenting with the committee structure or classroom roles.

A recurring question is whether parent participation could be reduced, since it requires major time commitments from parents as well as effort from teachers. The time-consuming nature of the program has become more of an issue over the years, as families have changed, with more mothers employed outside the home and more children having single parents. Many OC parents work full-time or are single parents but have been able to arrange work schedules to support the co-oping commitment. We constantly consider possibilities for reducing co-oping requirements, especially for families with several children in the program.

However, parent participation is crucial in our community—it is the backbone of our parent co-operative program. The program was designed by parents and teachers who were committed to parental involvement. It is important for the children's learning, bringing a wealth of activities and resources to the classroom as well as giving the children a clear message of caring and commitment to learning. The parents' involvement allows them to develop the understanding needed to support the children's learning in the classroom. It also extends the OC curriculum and philosophy into the homes, where many parents use the collaborative approach they learned in the OC. (Some parents report that the OC collaborative principles become especially important at home later, as their children enter adolescence and deal with the issues of junior high and high school.)

One of the reasons that our program has survived these decades is that parents are so involved. A challenge for the survival of innovative schools is for parents as well as teachers to understand and value the new ways of teaching and learning to which the school is committed, which often contrast with the ways that these adults were themselves schooled. Being actively involved in the classroom and in the school provides powerful opportunities for parents to come to understand and support the philosophy. Drastic solutions to simplify the work for either teachers or parents could diminish the quality of the educational experience in our setting, so we are very careful about exploring the possibilities.

In commenting on an early draft of this book, our editor at Oxford University Press, Joan Bossert, observed that the teachers often ask about the relationship of their work in this community of learners to their private lives. Involvement in the community involves an enormous commitment. "Early on, [one of the authors] asked if someone had to be part of the community to be part of the OC, and I think the answer has to be a resounding Yes! They are one and the same. . . . How much are teachers, parents, and the community willing to give on behalf of these children? It is an important question for any educator and our society at large."

How Can a Community See Conflict and Change as Opportunities for Learning?

Commitment to collaborative decision making requires ways of handling inevitable differences in opinion. A great deal of conflict can be averted by respectful conversation and problem solving.

Distinguishing roles also helps prevent conflicts, because it helps people to clarify their intent and avoid misunderstandings. Our former principal, Carol Lubomudrov, provided us with the image of distinguishing which "hat" a person is wearing at a particular time to distinguish our roles in everyday communication within the program. A teacher might, within the space of an hour, talk with another teacher as a colleague, as a friend, as a member of a committee, and as a parent—more than half of the teachers writing in this book also had children in the OC while they were OC teachers. At different times another person might wear a co-oper hat, a parent hat, or a committee chair hat. The distinction between "parents" and "co-opers" is subtle but extremely important (although we often use the terms interchangeably). Co-opers are expected to be team teachers, part of the learning environment, looking at the group as a whole and taking on shared responsibilities, not just focusing on their own children—as they might in their parent role. Sometimes when things get confusing, people ask each other, "What hat are you wearing?" to clarify the communication and decision-making process.

Nonetheless, in a community in which people are invested, there will always be disagreements and conflicts. The question is how to handle them constructively. In the classroom, we spend a lot of time working on problem solving with kids, but sometimes adults have a harder time implementing problem solving among themselves. Naturally, since the adults in the program come from different ethnic, regional, and religious backgrounds with varying ideas of how to handle conflict, they have much less in common than the kids, who work together every day on problem solving and community building.

We struggle with how to manage the disagreements so that we can learn from them and not get muddled by them. If the conflicts are misunderstandings, it is essential to communicate in order to get beyond them. If they arise from a difference of opinion, discussion can be extremely useful, allowing people to articulate and explore the different ideas and possible solutions. We try to use differing ideas as a resource for growth and explore them with mutual commitment rather than avoiding them (to be "nice") or creating divisiveness. To do so requires recognition that conflict is healthy and valuable, as long as respect is maintained.

The issue is not just about feeling safe with each other but about realizing the value and learning that come from addressing conflictual situations rather than avoiding them (or just gossiping about them). We encourage each other to address issues directly with the people involved, as they identify an issue. When direct conversation is too difficult, we use our committee trained to help people dialogue and listen to resolve issues. Conflicts and their resolutions provide constant opportunities for learning and growth, but sometimes the learning is not easy.

Several teachers (including Carolyn and Marcy) engage in a lively and productive discussion, trying to articulate a principle underlying OC curriculum development for this book.

In a program to which people develop such a commitment, there is a natural temptation to protect the program and to resist change or new ideas. This resistance includes concerns about having to revisit earlier decisions, but it also involves a basic clinging to something that works. A new idea can be very challenging or even frightening, because people may worry that any change will disrupt something precious. However, if the program doesn't continue to change, that would also disrupt something precious. While a community of learners maintains continuity, it simultaneously transforms and adapts to new circumstances. We have come to understand that change is the vehicle through which individuals and the program itself thrive and grow.

We try to remain open-minded and consider new ideas to see whether they can be incorporated into our underlying philosophy. Sometimes they can and sometimes they can't—changes should never be made at the expense of the core philosophy. The teachers play a key role in discussing how changes might or might not fit with the philosophy, but the process involves all the adults in the program. Thinking about changes requires considering the program not just for one's own child but for a big population of children, many of whom are not yet born.

Adapting Principles of Learning-as-a-community in Diverse Communities

A change that affects our program, and the nation as a whole, is the demographic shift in the population. The population of Salt Lake City at the time that this program began was overwhelmingly of European American background. In recent years this has begun to change dramatically, with larger proportions of inhabitants from Latino, Asian, Pacific Island, Eastern European, and many other backgrounds.

Although our experience leads us to have confidence in our philosophy for our usual population, the experience of others suggests that the same principles aid in the education of children of quite different backgrounds, including those who have historically had greater difficulties in school. Programs with similar principles have proven extremely effective for bringing native Hawaiian children's school performance to national standards or better; promoting learning of English, Spanish, and academic subjects in bilingual classrooms; and fostering literacy and science learning in inner-city schools structured as communities of learners.[3] There are also important parallels with the principles employed in Japanese elementary schools.[4] Most of these programs do not have heavy parental involvement in the classroom, but some are built on extensive collaboration between parents and teachers, such as in James Comer's programs in inner-city African American neighborhoods.[5]

Important aspects of the principles of learning in a community that are likely to support effectiveness in many different settings include a respect for the resources for learning that are brought to the community by all individuals; an emphasis on collaboration among children, parents, and teachers in the community of learners; the priority given to learning activities that have purpose and interest for the participants; and the explicit attention given to problem solving and communication as learning goals.

Of course, the specifics of how the principles are used must vary from one community to another (for example, in how the collaboration between children and adults is structured, and in the particular roles of parents and teachers). But we think these principles of learning as a community provide the basis for flexible adaptation in varying circumstances and with learners of differing backgrounds, interests, and needs.

We are often asked, when speaking about the OC to others, whether we think that the OC way is "the best way." Just as we feel committed to respecting the different ways that individuals within our program learn, we feel it is equally important to have a variety of educational options available from which families may choose. The learning experiences provided by our program should not be the only way that schools function. On this issue, we can learn from the variety of options offered in higher education. At the college or university level, options abound in approaches to education, and those who choose one or another generally are committed to the form they choose but respect the idea that other forms work for other people.

One practice that we are frequently asked about is whether we see the parent involvement that is required in this program as necessary for good schooling. Although our community requires parents to participate in classroom instruction, and this is essential to our program, many communities would or could not include this practice and could still hold philosophical tenets consistent with ours. A community of learners could be structured in many different ways.

Several of our teachers have left the OC for other positions where there is not so much parental involvement in the classroom; they report that they are able to carry on many aspects of their ways of teaching, with some necessary adjustments. For example, Carol Randell, who taught in the OC for seven years, reports:

> I transferred to a more traditional setting but still hold many of the same beliefs about teaching and creating a community of learners. I continue to teach by building on students' understanding in my present setting but have had to readjust the structure of the classroom, since I now work without the help of regular parent volunteers. This means that I have not been able to offer as many choices of activities and of when to complete them. The way the day was structured with parent co-opers in the OC allowed the children more choices as to what they would do and when they would do it. Even when some activities were earmarked as required, just providing the time choice seemed to greatly alter the attitude of the participants. The students were more willing when they came on their own terms and took more responsibility for completing the work. Having the students divided among several adults also provided the teacher with more opportunities for individual and small-group interactions. This aided in assessing a child's strengths, weaknesses, learning style, and interests. This still occurs in a traditional setting but not with the same degree of regularity.

Former OC teachers who are in schools without extensive parent participation in the classroom also look for ways to help the parents understand what goes on in the classroom. Ideally, they report, parents become involved in a dialogue over shared events in a classroom setting. Marilyn Osborne, a former OC teacher, described how her present school invites the parents of a few grade levels to school to get involved with some of the ideas in their children's classwork. For example, the parent groups do reading activities and get familiar with the books and methods that are used, or work at the math centers, where they can see the ideas the children are working on and understand the children's projects. During this time, the teachers browse around and are available to talk to individuals or small groups of parents. The teachers make a bulletin board of the *parents'* work so the children can see what their parents did at school. The parents' involvement shows the children that they care about what happens at school, and their understanding— gained through participation—helps them help their children. Involvement also helps the parents understand and trust what the teachers are doing.

Parents and teachers in many schools are working to develop ways to communicate between home and school, whether the parents are volunteering in the classroom or playing other roles to support their children's schooling. The experience at the OC points to the importance of some form of engagement between parents and teachers—which could take many different forms, depending on the structure of the school and the interests and constraints of the parent group.

Although practices will vary from one community of learners to another, we think the principles of learning we have focused on are effective in a general sense. We see advantages in an approach that involves collaboration in a community of learners, one where adults provide leadership and support of children's learning and children engage with adults in activities of interest that they have helped to shape. But there are many ways that a community of learners could be arranged, fitting the different circumstances, values, and interests of the participants. Indeed, our principles emphasize adaptation of practices for different people in varying circumstances.

Consistent with our commitment to creating curriculum with children is our conviction that individual communities need to be involved in creating the programs that serve them. Just as there are many ways for children to examine and learn the Big Ideas of the curriculum, there are many ways for communities to develop learning environments that put into practice the basic principles we have tried to articulate in this book. Many of the practices could differ from one community of learners to another, while the principles are held in common.

It is essential for the participants to choose to be involved in such an endeavor and to take part in the development and adaptation of the ideas used in their community. It would be a mistake for anybody to try to implement our philosophy by copying it; packaged curriculum and packaged models don't work well, because people need to be part of the process. This book is meant to be an inspiration, not a manual. It may serve as a starting point or as support for people who are interested in exploring the creation of their own community of learners. It has given us an opportunity to reflect on and articulate our own understanding of learning—and we hope it provides impetus for others to do the same.

Notes

1. For example, N. M. Glachan and P. H. Light, "Peer Interaction and Learning," in *Social Cognition: Studies of the Development of Understanding*, ed. G. E. Butterworth and P. H. Light (Brighton, England: Harvester Press, 1982); B. Rogoff, "Cognition as a Collaborative Process," in *Cognition, Perception, and Language*, ed. D. Kuhn and R. S. Siegler, vol. 2 of *Handbook of Child Psychology*, 5th ed., ed. W. Damon (New York: Wiley, 1998), 679–744.

2. E. Matusov, N. Bell, and B. Rogoff, "Schooling as Cultural Process: Children's Participation in Different Forms of Collaboration and Guidance," forthcoming, in *Advances in Child Development and Behavior* (vol. 29), ed. R. Kail and H. W. Reese. (San Diego: Academic Press).

3. A. L. Brown, D. Ash, M. Rutherford, K. Nakagawa, A. Gordon, and J. C. Campione, "Distributed Expertise in the Classroom," in *Distributed Cognitions: Psychological and Educational Considerations*, ed. G. Salomon (New York: Cambridge University Press, 1993), 188–228; L. C. Moll and K. F. Whitmore, "Vygotsky in Classroom Practice: Moving from Individual Transmission to Social Transaction," in *Contexts for Learning: Sociocultural Dynamics in Children's Development*, ed. E. A. Forman, N. Minick, and C. A. Stone (New York: Oxford University Press, 1993); R. G. Tharp and R. Gallimore, *Rousing Minds to Life: Teaching and Learning in Social Context* (New York: Cambridge University Press, 1988).

4. G. Hatano and K. Inagaki, "Sharing Cognition through Collective Comprehension Activity," in *Perspectives on Socially Shared Cognition*, ed. L. B. Resnick, J. M. Levine, and S. D. Teasley (Washington: American Psychological Association, 1991), 331–48.

5. J. P. Comer, *School Power* (New York: Free Press, 1980).

Index